DECADES

JOY DIVISION
+NEW ORDER

This edition first published in 2021 by
Palazzo Editions Ltd
15 Church Road
London, SW13 9HE
www.palazzoeditions.com

Text copyright © 2021 John Aizlewood
Design and layout copyright © 2021 Palazzo Editions Ltd

All rights reserved. No part of this publication may be reproduced in any form or by any means — electronic, mechanical, photocopying, recording, or otherwise — or stored in any retrieval system of any nature without prior written permission from the copyright holders. John Aizlewood has asserted his moral right to be identified as the author of this work in accordance with the Copyright, Designs and Patents Act of 1988.
Every effort has been made to trace and acknowledge the copyright holders. If any unintentional omission has occurred, we would be pleased to add an appropriate acknowledgment in any future edition of the book.
A CIP catalogue record for this book is available from the British Library.
ISBN 978-1-786751-16-4
Bound and printed in China
10 9 8 7 6 5 4 3 2 1

Designed by Adelle Mahoney for Palazzo Editions

DECADES

JOY DIVISION
+NEW ORDER

CONTENTS

Introduction 6

DIRTY OLD TOWN 12
THE WARSAW PACT 20
DARKNESS ON THE EDGE OF LUTON TOWN 32
PLEASURES UNKNOWN 46
THE END 62
THE BEGINNING 82
MONDAY MONDAY 100
HELLO MAINSTREAM 110
24-HOUR PARTY PEOPLE 130
Y VIVA ESPAÑA 146
SINGLE LIVES 158
JOYLESS DIVISION 166
ONE LAST PUSH 184
HOOK, SLUNG 202
EVERYBODY'S HAPPY NOWADAYS 210

An Afterword 236
Acknowledgements, Sources + Picture Credits 240

INTRODUCTION

Manchester is one of England's great cities, a swaggering northern powerhouse of commerce and culture. Scratch beneath the glossy surface, though, and the poverty is as relatively grinding as it was in the Victorian era, albeit given a very 21st-century twist by the drugs and the pistol-packing gangs. Predictably, perhaps, as in the Victorian era when cotton was king and the cotton barons ruled with arbitrary sway, there is both money to be made and good times to be had. The transport is good, the nightlife is vibrant, the soccer is world-class and there's even a gay village down Canal Street way.

It wasn't like this in the mid-to-late-'70s. Some British cities were still getting over World War II. Manchester hadn't recovered from World War I, the final death knell to the cotton industry which had transformed the backwater into one of the world's most wealthy cities –and, concomitantly, one of the most poverty stricken – during the Industrial Revolution. They had called it Cottonopolis.

The place was dirty, grimy and so run-down that areas such as Salford resembled moonscapes. Salford had a cathedral, so technically it was a city in its own right, but it was part of central Manchester. Culturally, even the punk revolution passed Manchester by, unless you count the ramshackle Slaughter & The Dogs, whose finest moment, "Cranked Up Really High" was co-financed by a cravat-wearing insurance worker, Robert Leo Gretton. Gretton had spent a month on a kibbutz in the mid-'70s, but on his return developed simultaneous sidelines as a soul DJ and a nom-de-brawl, the Scourge Of The Kippax, in honour of his exploits as a football hooligan for his beloved football team, Manchester City. But when, at the behest of future local punk galacticos Buzzcocks, the Sex Pistols came to the Lesser Free Trade Hall on June 4, 1976, something began to stir in the primordial swamp...

Two young Salford faux punks, Bernard Dicken and Peter Hook, were there. The next day, they formed a band. Soon they had a singer, Ian Curtis. When drummer Stephen Morris joined, they were complete. By January 1978 they were called Joy Division.

Hook had that Manc swagger, the one that the city's inhabitants had almost lost in the years of deprivation. You'd see it again in Manchester's next pop generation with Happy Mondays and The Stone Roses, and the one after that

6 Decades: Joy Division + New Order

Salford, 1974. "This is the way, step inside…"

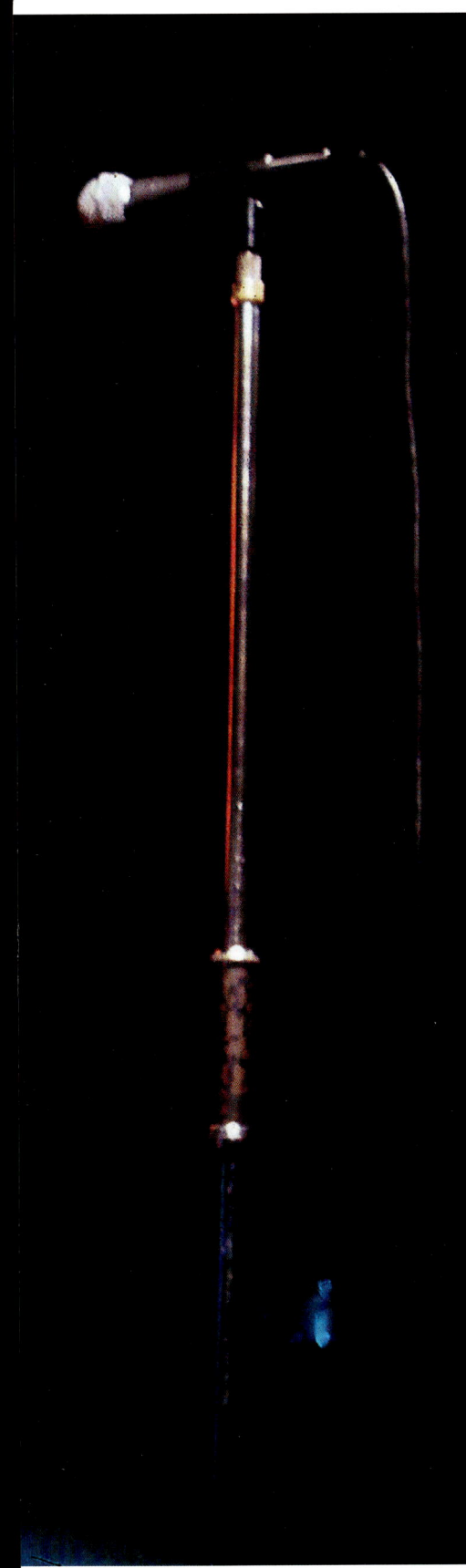

with the Gallagher brothers of Oasis, but Hook was the first since cheeky Peter Noone of Herman's Hermits. Aspiring to dominate the group's sound as Jean-Jacques Burnel did in The Stranglers, Hook's bass was slung low in honour of The Clash's Paul Simonon and if the indie scene normally eschewed rock star shapes and attitudes, he didn't. Part Andy Capp, part Viking warrior, he had a beard, he wore a vest and there was both a cheesy grin and an undercurrent of bare-knuckle boxing to his demeanour. In the very best sense of the term, he really didn't care.

In contrast, Bernard Dicken's guitar was strapped so high it sometimes resembled a giant ukulele. He wasn't a great player. Not when he became Bernard Albrecht in Joy Division, nor, when he morphed into New Order's vocalist and Bernard Sumner, would he be a great singer, but he would drive them through the dark days and bask in the days of light. Morris was the drummer, one of those quiet drummers (although no man who collects full-sized tanks and Daleks and took, so Hook claims, four hundred driving lessons to pass his test can be dismissed as ordinary), but Ian Curtis was the difference between Joy Division and the herd.

A young husband and father; a civil servant and an epileptic, like few other lyricists before or since, Ian Curtis meant it. Unremittingly bleak, he peered into his own heart of darkness and didn't flinch. This was method-writing. There were few story songs, almost no characters and certainly no digressions into whimsy or politics or love. As a result of him, Joy Division's influence is incalculable.

Their debut album, *Unknown Pleasures*, was anchored in '70s Manchester, but it was simultaneously futuristic, evoking those moonscapes whilst tapping into the maverick well of Can, Velvet Underground and Berlin-era David Bowie and Iggy Pop. Released on a small Manchester label, Factory, its ripples still resonate, not just in covers by acts as unlikely as Grace Jones and The Killers, but in the sound of bands from Nine Inch Nails and Depeche Mode to Editors and Interpol.

By the time the follow-up, *Closer*, was released, Ian Curtis was dead, killed by his own hand on the eve of their first American tour. Curtis's death – shocking but not a shock – left Joy Division musically complete. Their mystique bloomed from the moment one overwrought obituary declared, "This man died for you".

Without their golden ticket, others would have surrendered. Not Sumner (as he now was), Hook and Morris. They closed down Joy Division, rechristened themselves New Order, and recruited Morris's girlfriend Gillian Gilbert (she couldn't really play her keyboards, but that was the point). Sumner, tentatively at first, reinvented himself as singer and, later, leader.

It shouldn't have worked. In fact, after a disappointing first album, the Joy Division clone *Movement*, it looked like it wasn't going to work. They had reinvented everything but their music.

Slowly, they let the sun in. They discovered the electro dance music of New York, they discovered the United States, they discovered how to enjoy

Curtis the dervish, Hook the gladiator.

Introduction 9

New Order, New York, 1989 (from left): Peter Hook, Gillian Gilbert, Bernard Sumner, Stephen Morris.

themselves, although the price would be shockingly high. In return, the world discovered them.

Power, Corruption & Lies was the first peek into the future, but *Low-Life*, *Brotherhood*, and their first British number one, *Technique*, saw them embracing the dance zeitgeist, making music which appealed to the burgeoning club culture as much as indie mavens.

In an act of hubristic idiocy, they invested in a club – The Haçienda, Factory catalogue number FAC51. Manchester's finest band backing Manchester's finest club. What could possibly go wrong? As it happened, everything.

Still the records kept on selling. No 12-inch single sold more copies in Britain than "Blue Monday" and, when, in 1987, New Order assembled the *Substance* compilation, it became their American mainstream breakthrough.

10 Decades: Joy Division + New Order

Even when they took a sabbatical after 1993's *Republic*, ostensibly to focus on outside collaborations and for Morris and Gilbert to raise their children, nobody thought it would be permanent. It wasn't.

Back they came in 2001 with *Get Ready*. Although Gilbert would soon leave again, this time to deal with breast cancer, all appeared to be right with New Order's world. It wasn't.

The next split, in the wake of 2005's *Waiting For The Sirens' Call*, was more vicious entirely. Hook and Sumner, the schoolmates whose lives had been changed by seeing The Sex Pistols, fell out. This time the spat was nasty and seemingly permanent. Accusations flew. Counter-accusations flew back. Cases were taken to court. Cases were settled out of court. New Order carried on under Sumner's undisputed leadership and Peter Hook planted limpet mines on the mothership by finding new ways of flying his own and Joy Division/New Order's flags.

It's a tale of love, death, fall-outs, make-ups, hardcore bacchanalia, money gained, money squandered and some of the most remarkable and influential music of the '80s, '90s and beyond. You couldn't make it up: there's no need to.

Barney at Lollapalooza, Autodromo de Interlagos, Sao Paulo Brazil, April 6, 2014.

DIRTY OLD TOWN

DIRTY OLD TOWN

Back in 1950, the British magazine *New Statesman* visited Salford. Situated just west of Manchester city centre at the end of the Manchester Ship Canal, the route travelled in by cotton and out by the clothes made from it, Salford was dominated by docks and was Britain's largest inland port. It had escaped much of the extensive damage the Luftwaffe brought to its deepwater rivals, Southampton and Hull, but of the 50,000 houses, 35,000 were over 60 years old and inhabitants were considered toffs if they had running water. Ewan MacColl had just written "Dirty Old Town" about this dirty old town which would inform the work of the director Mike Leigh, the poetry of John Cooper Clarke (not least The Sopranos highlight, "Evidently Chickentown") and *A Taste Of Honey*, Shelagh Delaney's groundbreaking, gritty play. The intrepid but aghast reporter noted the "blackened crumbling brick, looking only as if its coating of grime held it together; streets so narrow that you hardly need to raise your voice to talk to your neighbour across the way; dirt everywhere and no water to fight it". This – or more precisely, as with MacColl, Leigh, Cooper Clarke and Delaney, the enclave of Broughton

John Cooper Clarke, Lass'o'Gowrie, Manchestrer, 1977. He wouldn't look like this for long...

14 Decades: Joy Division + New Order

Salford, 1974. Manchester United's Old Trafford ground in the background.

"IT DIDN'T MAKE ME ANGRY AND BITTER, BUT IT DID MAKE ME A LITTLE HARD-HEARTED."

BERNARD

Dirty Old Town 15

– was where Bernard Sumner was born on 4 January 1956 and Peter Woodhead six weeks later on 13 February.

Being poor – being really poor – is a rotten draw of the cards, but one of its less discussed side affects is how complicated it makes everyday life. And life for Bernard Dicken was very complicated indeed. He was born in the Crumpsall Hospital in North Manchester. He never knew his father. "It didn't make me angry and bitter, but it did make me a little hard-hearted," he confessed with the circumspection that marks almost his every utterance. His mother, Laura Sumner, was not as other mothers and not merely because she carried the still-acute stigma of being an unmarried mother. He took her surname of course. She had cerebral palsy, the movement-limiting disease with no known cause, let alone cure, and was wheelchair bound. Probably suffering from depression (these things weren't discussed, let alone diagnosed, but it's a disease Bernard is not immune from), she had a vicious temper which would inevitably escalate into violence; cerebral palsy or no cerebral palsy.

When Bernard was five, she married Jim Dicken. Jim formally adopted Bernard, who changed his surname and would later name one of his own sons James in tribute. Like his new wife, the calliper-wearing Jim Dicken was disabled and, just to complete the grimly gothic picture, the trio lived with Laura's parents, John and Laura, who was blind after a routine eye operation went horribly wrong. "Basically, they all became ill and I had to look after them, which I wasn't very good at," remembered Bernard. Complicated indeed.

The Dicken family moved to a terraced house, 11 Alfred Street, in Lower Broughton. It's demolished now but there was no bathroom, no indoor toilet and nothing approximating to luxury. Eventually, they fled to a flat in the Greengate district overlooking the River Irwell and a chemical factory. "It stank," remembers Bernard.

Bernard was a bright boy, not especially moved by music, although the first single he bought was T. Rex's "Ride A White Swan". He was late for everything (as he would be all his life), but he excelled at St Clement's Egerton (closed 2007) and passed his eleven-plus exam, receiving a bike as a gift from his startled parents. The British education system was formally segregated in the final year of elementary school. Those who passed the eleven-plus went on to grammar school – the gateway to a good job, ideally involving pens and paper. Those who failed went to secondary modern school – the gateway to a more manually inclined job, ideally not involving pens and paper. On Bernard's very first day at Salford Grammar, which had been the springboard to global acclaim for Albert Finney and Mike Leigh, he met Peter Hook, whom,

Marc Bolan: not one to play up those King Of Pop connotations.

16 Decades: Joy Division + New Order

with a certain reluctance, we must refer to as "Hooky", since everyone else does.

Irene Woodhead gave birth to her son Peter at the Hope Hospital (now the Salford Royal). His father, Jack, was a driver for Frederick Hampson, a glassworks company established by the eponymous former Mayor of Salford, who died in 1930. Jack liked the ladies and he loved a fight, so by the time Peter was four, the marriage was over. Enter Bill Hook.

Glass fitter Bill, took on the tribe and two years later, in 1962, they swapped Jane Street, Salford for Kingston, Jamaica when Bill secured a job with the Jamaica Glass Board and Irene found one with the local tourist bureau. There on Phoenix Avenue (today it's midway between the Peter Tosh Museum and the Bob Marley Museum) they lived the ex-pat life in excelsis: inside toilet, television, servants. Jack enjoyed the local culture a little too enthusiastically for Irene's tastes, and by 1966, they were back in Blighty, swapping luxury for 34 Rothwell Street, Ordsall on Salford's southern edges. Hooky was also no slouch on the intellectual front, for he also passed his eleven-plus. In 2005, Hooky reflected on his and Bernard's relationship to *NME*: "I've known him for thirty-eight years. You get less for murder. I met him on the first day of grammar school. We were friends for about 120 minutes. I've hated him ever since." He seemed to be joking.

The pair were thrust together. Whatever intellectual impetus had propelled them to pass their eleven-plus swiftly evaporated. "We were both bottom of the class," Bernard told *Uncut* in 2014. "We sat together. It wasn't

Bernard Sumner* in Salford 1974 (*not actual Bernard Sumner).

Cockney Rebel, 1974 (from left): Stuart Elliot, Paul Jeffreys, Steve Harley, Duncan Mackay, Milton Reame-James.

because of any great musical enlightenment we shared. We were the scum at the back of the class." They were, possibly not to the delight of their teachers, a pair of jokers. Bernard loves a practical joke, so long as it's not on him.

Hooky would emerge with a solitary O Level in English, Bernard with two, English and art. Still, the fact they stayed friends after school suggests Hooky is underplaying their camaraderie. Music began to loom. Bernard claims he was initially lured by Ennio Morricone's soundtracks to Sergio Leone's spaghetti western trilogy, but he loved nascent disco too.

They immersed themselves in what passed for Salford's youth culture. They were skinheads, they were mods, they were suedeheads and they acquired scooters: "better than getting a bus and good for attracting girls," reasoned Bernard. He had a Lambretta GP225, the ultimate mod machine. He'd ride it west to the nearby seaside resort of Blackpool or east to the rolling moors of the Pennines. He decorated it with a sticker of Santana, arguably the least mod act since

18   Decades: Joy Division + New Order

Sex Pistols, Free Trade Hall, Manchester, 4 June, 1976.

> "I'VE KNOWN HIM FOR THIRTY-EIGHT YEARS. YOU GET LESS FOR MURDER. I MET HIM ON THE FIRST DAY OF GRAMMAR SCHOOL. WE WERE FRIENDS FOR ABOUT 120 MINUTES. I'VE HATED HIM EVER SINCE."
>
> **HOOKY**

Pat Boone. Bernard was simply reflecting his favourite hangout, the North Salford Youth Club where one floor would play mod-tastic Stax and Tamla Motown; the other, the hairier, less kempt sounds of Free and Santana. He absorbed everything.

On leaving school, the pair hung around Pips (formerly Nice 'n' Easy), a basement club close to Manchester Cathedral which opened in 1972 and lasted for a decade before the drugs and the gangs forced closure and demolition. Fond of Cockney Rebel's gloriously overwrought "Sebastian", Hooky always had a more rock bent than Bernard and he was behind the pair seeing Deep Purple (Bernard went home early, claiming a headache), Wishbone Ash and, curing Bernard's love for them on the spot, Santana. Pips' Roxy Room introduced its clientele to the exotic sounds of David Bowie and Roxy Music. "Pips was outrageous," recalled Dave Booth, one of the club's DJs. "It was like walking into the lair at the end of James Cameron's *Aliens* movie, with stalactites and caves hidden in corners. It was loved by a lot of people."

There were menial jobs, the sort that those with no real idea of their path take. For Hooky there was a brief stint in the kitchens of Butlin's holiday camp in Clacton in England's deep south, before the family moved to the coal-mining suburb of Little Hulton. For Bernard, there was a clerical job at Salford Town Hall and, utilising his scooter, a runner's role at Greendow Commercials, the company owned by Simon Bosanquet, the director of Bryan Ferry's "A Hard Rain's A-Gonna Fall" video and nephew of beloved newscaster Reginald Bosanquet. Greendow soon closed and Bernard began to use his artistic bent at Cosgrove Hall Animation. The children's animated show, *Jamie And The Magic Torch*? Some of the backgrounds are Bernard's.

With hindsight it's easy to say they couldn't have gone on like this. But they could. They were natural drifters. But a musical cataclysm was afoot. On June 4, 1976, the Sex Pistols played the first of two dates, six weeks apart, at Manchester's Lesser Free Trade Hall. Tickets were fifty pence and Sex Pistols manager Malcolm McLaren would be at the door, collecting the money.

Dirty Old Town 19

THE WARSAW PACT

THE WARSAW PACT

Punk was a London movement, not a northern one. But in June 1976 even calling it a movement was a stretch. Manchester's Howard Devoto and Pete Shelley had formed Buzzcocks after meeting the Pistols in London and the canny pair arranged the two Manchester shows. The hall held around 150 people. Generous assessments suggest it was a third full at best, but the forty-ish people who were there included Mick Hucknall, who would later form Simply Red, Mark E. Smith (The Fall), Morrissey (The Smiths) and, of course Peter Hook and Bernard Dicken, who was accompanied by his future wife Sue.

The Pistols were traditionalists at heart, covering Dave Berry, Paul Revere, The Stooges, The Small Faces and The Who that night. But they were different too. Bernard's observation that "they were just a bunch of working-class twats like us" was part of it, but so was the DIY ethic he hadn't found in groups such as Wishbone Ash and certainly not Led Zeppelin, whom Hooky had dragged Bernard to see at Manchester Hardrock in 1972.

The next morning, Hooky went to Mazel Radio, on the approach to Manchester Piccadilly station and bought himself a guitar. Bernard already had one. They began to practice with their friend Terry Mason, who was soon demoted from guitar to drums. On July 20, the second Pistols show – they played a new song called "Anarchy In The UK" – was significantly more popular. Bernard and Hooky were there

22   Decades: Joy Division + New Order

Right: *Led Zeppelin: Manchester Hardrock, December 1972.*

Left: *Buzzcocks (from left): Steve Diggle, Steve Garvey, John Maher and Pete Shelley.*

again and, somewhere in the audience, there was an intense young man from Macclesfield called Ian Curtis and his wife Debbie.

Bernard was the first to see the future. The inchoate band needed a vocalist, so he placed an advertisement in the window of the Virgin Records store in Manchester. Who should telephone the Greengate flat, but the intense young man, recently part of a half-hearted band with Martin Jackson, who'd go on to drum with Magazine (Howard Devoto's post-Buzzcocks band), and Swing Out Sister.

When Ian told Bernard of his love for The Velvet Underground and The Stooges on that phone call, the job was his, whether he sang like Bing Crosby or Bill Cosby. Once Ian and Debbie returned from a hitch-hiking holiday to a punk festival at Mont-de-Marsan on the French side of the border with Spain (Ian discovered he was allergic to the sun, or so he told Debbie), rehearsals began in earnest in a room above the Grey Mare pub (closed 2012) in the Weaste area of Salford.

The Warsaw Pact 23

Sex Pistols, December 1976. They were not, technically, the antichirst.

The Sex Pistols returned to Manchester for a third time on December 9, shortly after they'd outraged the nation by swearing on early evening television. Not for the last time, where his career was concerned, Ian's intensity outweighed his chronic shyness. Although he hated all other bands on principle, he introduced himself to Buzzcock Pete Shelley, desperately seeking information on the practical side of making it to fame and its bosom buddy, fortune, as Buzzcocks had. Since Shelley's band had yet to release a record, the singer was nonplussed, but the kind-hearted soul did his best to oblige.

Terry Mason was back on guitar – second guitar to be precise – and he'd go on to become lighting man (briefly), manager (very briefly) and ultimately New Order's super-efficient, take-no-prisoners tour manager. Their new friends, Buzzcocks, even offered the band without a name a support slot at the Electric Circus on May 29, 1977. First, there was bonding to be done with the mysterious Ian Curtis. "We started out knowing precisely fuck all about music," Bernard admitted to *NME* in 1989. "We didn't start as musicians and that's a very creative thing." Hooky liked his rock, Bernard had a certain attachment to punk, but Ian would be their musical guide and the one who brought Kraftwerk records to rehearsals. He was the first among equals.

Whereas Bernard and Hooky were Salford lads with a certain street-tough sass, Ian was a Macclesfield boy. Thirty miles south of

> "WE STARTED OUT KNOWING PRECISELY FUCK ALL ABOUT MUSIC. WE DIDN'T START AS MUSICIANS AND THAT'S A VERY CREATIVE THING."
>
> BERNARD

Technique Burroughs of master a William cut-up was the.

Salford, Macclesfield was a hilly mill town. The Huguenots had started the silk industry which spawned those mills (the local soccer team, Macclesfield Town, are nicknamed The Silkmen). Later, in 1745, Scotland's rebel leader Bonnie Prince Charlie had passed through on his way, so he thought, to became ruler of England. Unfortunately, he brought six thousand of his friends with him and these less benign arrivals weren't in the mood to pay for their B&B or their fun. Those Maxonians who can trace their bloodlines back to the mid-18th century often find it part Scottish. By the time Ian Kevin Curtis was born on July 15, 1956 to father Kevin, a British Transport Police detective of Irish ancestry and mother Doreen, it had become a Manchester overspill town too.

In view of how Ian's life would end, it's tempting to hunt for clues to his demise in his youth. Tempting, but misguided. For reasons far from clear even then, the Curtis family moved from the relatively bucolic suburb of Hurdsfield to the Victoria Park Estate, a town centre tower block comprising of 543 flats. Cutting edge when it went up in the late-'60s, it was amongst the 7% most deprived areas in the UK by the mid-'90s and was demolished shortly after the turn of the century.

Yet, Ian was no ghetto child. He was bright, he read books and he was smart enough to win a scholarship at single-sex, fee-paying The King's School, a year ahead of Stephen Morris, who would be expelled. On the one hand, he couldn't have been more boyish: his peers nicknamed him Hammy on account of his hamster cheeks; he loved his speedway and, as a Manchester United fan, his soccer. He would leave with a war chest of qualifications. On the other, he leaned towards the right-wing Conservative Party – a rarity amongst his peers – and he loved William Burroughs (especially the *Junky* novel). His red jacket consciously evoked James Dean's character in *Rebel Without a Cause* and he smoked joints at lunchtime, often while devouring the counter-culture monthly magazine, *Oz*.

The Warsaw Pact 25

David Bowie, 1972. "Play The Laughing Gnome!" "No."

And then there was music – his real obsession and the one that derailed his academic potential. He'd smoke those joints while listening to Jacques Brel's eulogy to another kind of oblivion "My Death" and Throbbing Gristle. He even pretended to like Lou Reed's *Metal Machine Music*, but when he moved to Manchester to take A levels in divinity and history at St John's College (now The Manchester College), he only lasted a fortnight before dropping out to take a job at Rare, Manchester's most elite record shop. That didn't last either and he returned to Macclesfield to take a stall at the Butter Market, selling old records, or, more accurately, his own record collection. Customers were few, so he took proper jobs at the Ministry Of Defence's outpost in Cheadle Hulme between Manchester and Macclesfield; the Manpower Services Commission in Central Manchester and, back again in the local Job Centre in Macclesfield, with a special remit to assist disabled people.

Most astonishing of all, he was married and had been since he was a teenager. Deborah Woodruff wasn't like him. The erstwhile Macclesfield High School For Girls pupil was from Liverpool and as academically gifted as Ian. She loved music too. After he'd charmed her as she worked at the cheese and bacon stall in Macclesfield Market, their first date was a David Bowie concert at Manchester Hardrock in December 1972, shortly after Ian had his

26 Decades: Joy Division + New Order

stomach pumped following a (probably) accidental overdose. But while she was no volcano – she didn't even smoke cigarettes, let alone anything stronger – she would always be stronger than her husband.

Ian's conventional side saw them formally engaged in April 1974 and married sixteen months later at the distinctly gothic St Thomas's Church in Henbury on Macclesfield's west side. Many thought they were too young. They thought so too. Ian wore peach, they honeymooned in Paris and returned to live in his grandparents' terraced house in Stamford Street, Hulme, a southern Manchester suburb, before finding their own terraced house in Sylvan Street, Oldham, a satellite town north of Manchester, far away from family and friends.

Ian loved walking Candy, their Border Collie, but he would never learn to drive, so Debbie would chauffeur him in her Morris Traveller. Conventional or not, he loved to shock, hence their frequent trips to the hardcore reggae clubs – Ian adored reggae – of Manchester's gang-infested Moss Side. Yet Ian was a home bird too and by 1977, the couple were back in Macclesfield at Barton Street, close to the town centre. The walls of their lounge were sky blue.

Buzzcocks released their first record, the *Spiral Scratch* EP, in January 1977. Produced by Martin Zero, aka James Martin Hannett, a chemistry graduate with a penchant for chemicals, it galvanised the Manchester scene. Meanwhile, Bernard, Hooky and Ian were rehearsing themselves to semi-competence and when Iggy Pop released the David Bowie-produced *The Idiot* in March, Ian summoned Bernard to Macclesfield to share the experience. All they needed now was a drummer and a name.

Ian's milking of the genial Pete Shelley brought two rewards: a name and that gig supporting smart punks Penetration and Buzzcocks at the Electric Circus. Buzzcocks manager Richard Boon – in a later life a London librarian – suggested Stiff Kittens. It sounded right for the unmusical punks they still were. And that was the very reason Ian hated it. Like Bernard, he could see into the future, to a time when they wouldn't be Slaughter & The Dogs copycats. It just wouldn't do. Desperate to usurp Boon's suggestion, Ian looked to another of his heroes, David Bowie (who'd covered "My Death"), albeit no further than Bowie's current album, the ambient electronic masterpiece, *Low*. There it was, side two, track one. "Warszawa", or in English, "Warsaw". That very much would do. All they had to do now was stop sounding like Slaughter & The Dogs.

The gig in question wasn't a great success. Nobody knew they were Warsaw since they were billed as Stiff Kittens. Worse, those who didn't think they were Stiff Kittens assumed they were another support band, The Prefects. Bernard and Hooky had moustaches. Hooky even sported a leather cap – needless to say, in 1977 no other card-carrying heterosexual in the Manchester conurbation sported a moustache and leather cap – and there was even a drummer, Tony Tabac, a laid-back cove who'd been drafted in the day before when Terry Mason changed roles. Tony would last a month. The *NME* noted their "quirky cockiness", but the world stubbornly failed to stop turning.

Buzzcocks' Spiral Scratch EP.

Two days later, they played again, this time supporting the heroin-loving Heartbreakers at Manchester Rafters, a long, thin venue unsuited both acoustically and visually to hosting live music. Warsaw were granted an encore.

Much as they liked him, Tony Tabac wasn't the right man for drums. Neither was his replacement Stephen Brotherdale, prised from local punks Panik, who'd had a single produced by Rob Gretton. Brotherdale's first show, another Rafters support, this time to the Billy Idol-led Generation X. This show saw a new Ian, a man who, after he smashed a glass in frustration, crawled across the broken shards to attract attention, as if he was the Iggy Pop of Manchester. Brotherdale was a fine drummer, but not a fine fit. Shortly after Terry Mason was relieved of managerial duties after mis-taping a demo session and sending the unlistenable results to labels in July, Brotherdale departed in the wake of a show supporting Slaughter & The Dogs in Leicester during which he'd ambled to the front of the stage. Debbie Curtis recalls that they stopped the van after the show, asked him to check if the tyres were flat and drove off. Like so many who passed through the Joy Division/New Order axis, Brotherdale would struggle. He joined the band V2, but soon found himself serving at McDonald's. In 2009, he was jailed for stalking his ex-wife, Gillian Rochford. "He sent her a trilogy of books he had written – up to two hundred pages each – detailing his infatuation. The books had photos of Ms Rochford on the front depicted as an angel and later with devil horns," noted the *Macclesfield Express*.

Warsaw couldn't get traction, but they could get themselves a drummer who they liked and who could cut the proverbial mustard. Ian placed an advertisement in the window of Jones's Music Store in Macclesfield. Stephen Morris, the kid a year below Ian at school, replied.

Right: *Hooky, Warsaw, Manchester Rafters, 30 June, 1977. Cap? Tick. 'Tache? Tick. Vest? Tick.*

Below: *Slaughter & The Dogs: cranked up really high. Record sales really low.*

Steve Brotherdale, Warsaw, Rafters, Manchester, 30 June, 1977. Brotherdale was "let go" later that year.

Lora Logic and Poly Styrene, X-Ray Spex, 1977.

Stephen Paul David Morris was born in Macclesfield on October 28, 1957. Not for him the grinding Salford poverty of Bernard and Hooky or Ian's lower middle class scuffling. His father, George, was known as Cliff and he owned G. Clifford Morris, who distributed plumbing equipment. Stephen's mother Hilda (eleven years Cliff's junior) was a director. The Morrises had inside toilets and kept koi carp. Cliff was a jazzman who took his son to see Count Basie, but was sufficiently open-minded to accept Stephen's invitation to see Hawkwind. Stephen's audition was traumatic ("the most nervous person I'd ever met," chuckled Hooky), but everything felt right and they nicknamed him Son of Forsyth, after similarly impressively-chinned British entertainer Bruce Forsyth. What really counted were the facts that: a) Ian liked him and b) according to Hooky, he looked more like a geography teacher than a punk. Soon the jazzman's son was introducing his new bandmates to the delights of Charles Mingus. "He's a hard character to define," explained Bernard. "He doesn't like confrontation at all. He's quite eccentric, but drummers are odd people."

On August 27, Warsaw played their first gig with Stephen at Eric's in Liverpool, supporting X-Ray Spex. Only death would change the line-up now.

"HE DOESN'T LIKE CONFRONTATION AT ALL. HE'S QUITE ECCENTRIC, BUT DRUMMERS ARE ODD PEOPLE."

BERNARD

The Warsaw Pact 31

DARKNESS ON THE EDGE OF LUTON TOWN

DARKNESS ON THE EDGE OF LUTON TOWN

Now, things began to move apace. The Electric Circus closed over the first weekend in October and Warsaw played on the Sunday. Some of their performance would later appear on the mini-album *Short Circuit: Live At The Electric Circus*. They were rough and ready, but nobody would mistake them for run-of-the-mill punks and nobody else would preface a song (in this case "At A Later Date") with the incendiary call – Hooky claims it was Bernard; Debbie says Ian – "you all forget Rudolf Hess". They would never disown punk and as Bernard noted in 1988, "We come from punk roots. It didn't exclude anyone. It didn't matter what you looked like, whether you were fat, thin, ugly or beautiful. We didn't believe in snobbery or elitism. We still don't."

The sound hadn't fully taken shape, but the intensity was almost palpable. What really set them apart, though, was that their intensity was four-way. The key to Joy Division was there before they were even called Joy Division:

Hooky, Warsaw, Manchester Rafters, 30 June 1977.

Bernard, Hooky and Stephen all played as if their instrument was the lead and each managed it without trampling over the others or Ian. Martin Hannett, the man to turn that key, would see them for the first time the very next week at Salford College of Technology.

On December 14th, Warsaw went into Pennine Sound Studio, Oldham, to record the four songs that would become the *An Ideal For Living* EP. The band paid the £400 fee themselves and the one-day deadline meant the drums were recorded first, then the bass, then the guitar, then the vocals from Ian's vast lyrics bank which he carried around in a plastic bag. Those vocals were laid in one-take, the instruments were as close to one-take as possible but, luxury of luxuries, Hooky and Ian's backing vocals were added later, as time permitted. As someone once said, you get what you pay for.

Another problem was looming: the name. Warsaw sounded right – it still does – but there was another group, West London punks Warsaw Pakt. Unfortunately, not only had Warsaw Pakt released an album the month before Warsaw went into Pennine, it was on a major label and major labels had major lawyers. There was only one way ahead and on New Year's Eve, Warsaw played their final gig as Warsaw, at Liverpool's Swinging Apple, a third floor venue without a stage and where bands had to stand aside for punters wishing to use the toilet. They covered "The Passenger", highlight of Iggy Pop's new album, *Lust For Life*.

As the band gathered at the Morris family home in January 1978 to hand-stick the thousand copies of the *An Ideal For Living* sleeves, there was much to relish. The four songs had sounded immense in the studio and a name-change was nigh. Slaves Of Venus and Boys In Bondage had been considered (why they were considered must remain a mystery), but Ian had been reading *The House Of Dolls* the unsettling 1955 novel by Ka-Tsetnik 135633 (in English: concentration camp number 135633), the Auschwitz survivor formerly known as Yehiel De-Nur. It detailed joy divisions, the Jewish women who were kept for the pleasure of German soldiers, although sexual relations between Aryans and non-Aryans were forbidden in the Third Reich. Joy Division it was, then. No one seemed to grasp the implications.

Bernard designed the *An Ideal For Living* sleeve. Calamitously, it featured a Hitler Youth child thwacking a drum on one side and a

"WE COME FROM PUNK ROOTS. IT DIDN'T EXCLUDE ANYONE. IT DIDN'T MATTER WHAT YOU LOOKED LIKE, WHETHER YOU WERE FAT, THIN, UGLY OR BEAUTIFUL. WE DIDN'T BELIEVE IN SNOBBERY OR ELITISM. WE STILL DON'T."

BERNARD

German soldier pointing a gun at a boy during the Warsaw Uprising on the other. What was he thinking? He's never been clear. Oh, and he'd changed his name and was now Bernard Albrecht. "It was a bit of fun, a mishearing of Berthold Brecht," he claimed of that name-change, perhaps forgetting the SS headquarters were located on Berlin's Prinz-Albrecht Strasse. It was a lapse of taste Bernard – surely a man with no Nazi tendencies – would come to regret, before he quietly returned to Dicken.

Still, there was more good news. Factory, a Manchester record label named after a FACTORY CLEARANCE sign rather than anything to do with Andy Warhol was born in the Palatine Road flat of actor and label co-owner Alan Erasmus.

On January 25, Joy Division played their maiden show, at Bernard and Hooky's beloved Pips. The crowd were mostly Hooky's friends, they began with "Exercise One" and since there was a mid-set audience brawl, few begrudged Joy Division their £60. Wisely, they stopped gigging for a while, not least since there were Warsaw songs to discard of and since, of the songs they played that night, only "Day Of The Lords" would grace the debut album, there were Joy Division songs to write.

If Erasmus was the silent, enigmatic half of Factory, his business partner Tony Wilson was a brash, publicity seeking, narcissistic, brilliant, force of nature. He couldn't have been more different from Joy Division. An only child, Anthony Howard Wilson was born at Salford's Hope Hospital, like Hooky, on February 20, 1950. His parents, Sydney and Doris, ran a tobacconist in the Marple area of Stockport, another overspill town, south-east of Manchester. Like Rob Gretton and Martin Hannett, Wilson won a scholarship at Salford's Roman Catholic De La Salle School.

Left: *Bernard Albrecht, Warsaw, Manchester Rafters, 30 June 1977.*

Right: *Peter Saville, Tony Wilson and Alan Erasmus, Russell Club, Manchester, 1979.*

36 Decades: Joy Division + New Order

Darkness on the Edge of Luton Town   37

38 Decades: Joy Division + New Order

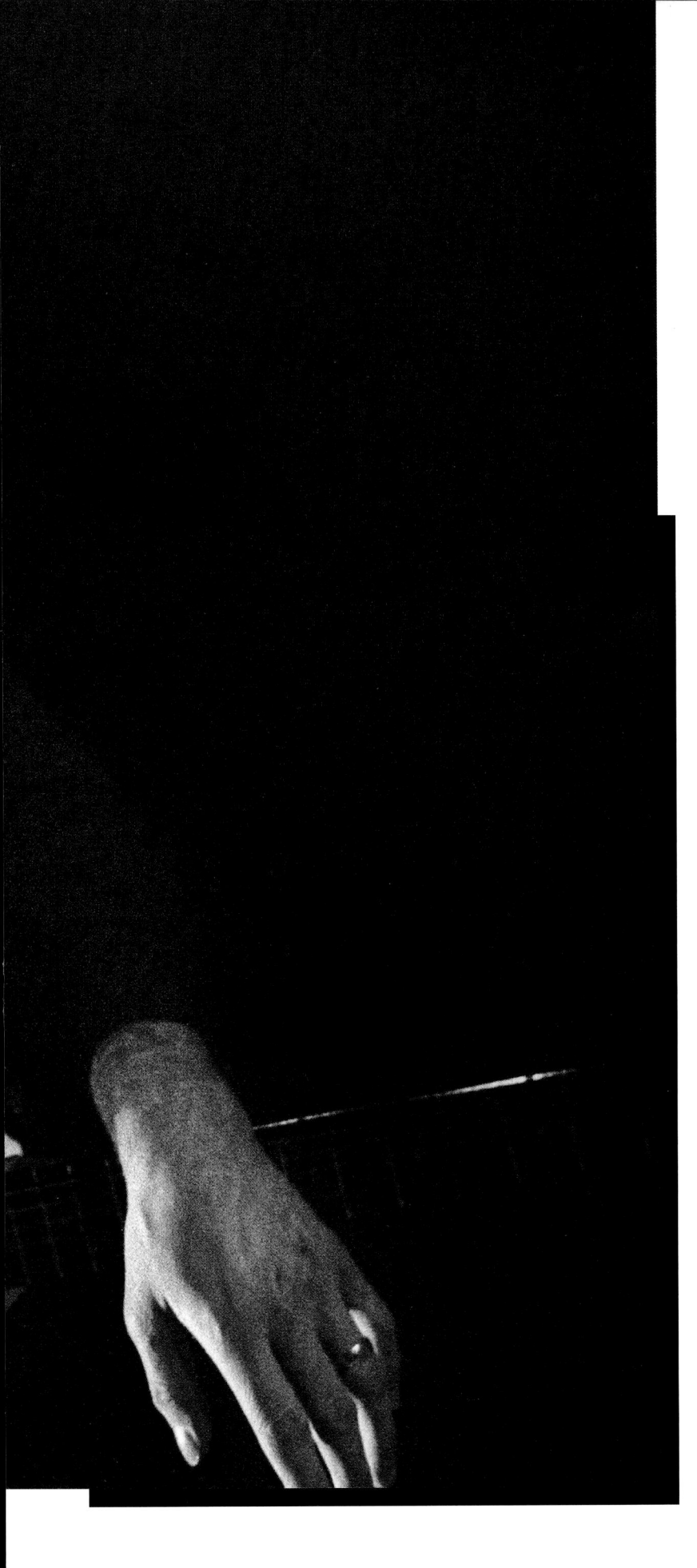

Unlike Bernard, Hooky and Ian, the super-bright Wilson fulfilled his academic potential and attended the elite Cambridge University. On his return to his beloved Manchester (and surely nobody loved Manchester more than Tony Wilson), the English graduate became a local television celebrity, presenting the arts programme *So It Goes* – where he introduced the rather startled burghers of Manchester to interviewees such as Leonard Cohen and Johnny Rotten – and the local news programme *Granada Reports*. Wilson had seen Warsaw at the Electric Circus and he saw Joy Division at their fourth gig, a battle of the bands (all seventeen of them) at Rafters on April 14.

There, Ian's more combative side emerged when he sent Wilson a note calling him "a fucking cunt" for not putting Joy Division on television. Wilson promised to rectify the omission and would declare on camera that "Joy Division are the best thing I have heard in Manchester for about six months". Rafters DJ, Rob Gretton, was there too and Hooky's girlfriend gave Rob an advance copy of *An Ideal For Living*. Having declared them "blazing madmen", the very next morning Rob bumped into Bernard in Manchester city centre, invited himself to a rehearsal and suggested he become their manager.

The rehearsal space, TJ Davidson's, was a room above family jewellers, Tony Davidson's. It was cheap (£1.50 a weeknight hour or £3 for three Sunday hours) and was used by Buzzcocks and Frantic Elevators, a punk band led by the very ginger Mick Hucknall. It was dark, industrial and cold, so very cold. Working in freezing conditions, surrounded by derelict factories and broken windows was peak Joy Division. This was the environment which spawned their music.

When Rob Gretton turned up at TJ's, nobody apart from Bernard knew who he was or why

Ian Curtis, LantarenVenster, Rotterdam, 16 January, 1980.

he was there. In a distinctly Bernard moment, he had neglected to tell the others that a coiled spring of a man with two front false teeth would be visiting. No matter, there being no competition, he was instantly appointed and his first decision was to sanction a run of Joy Division badges. From then, the quintet was bound together. Indeed, Rob Gretton would always be more messianic vis-á-vis Joy Division and New Order than Joy Division and New Order themselves.

There were starts, but they tended to be false. In one murky episode they were asked by the head of RCA's Manchester office to record a version of NF Porter's northern soul classic "Keep On Keepin' On" for a US soul label who wanted to sign a UK punk band. Other songs were recorded too with a view to perhaps signing to RCA and a session synthesiser player was recruited. Later it would cost £5,000 to buy back the tapes, although the unforgetting, unforgiving internet means they're easily accessible today. They are roughly how Joy Division would have sounded had they signed to a major label, something Ian always aspired to: fine enough, but with little hint of greatness.

If Joy Division were not being understandably mistaken for Nazis, there were other problems, not least when the finished *An Ideal For Living* arrived in time for its early June 1978 release. Those songs, "Warsaw", "Leaders Of Men", "Failures" and the *House Of Dolls*-quoting "No Love Lost", were the best they had (other than the jaw-dropping "Novelty", which would resurface soon) and while they were no life-changers, they oozed promise. However, when twelve minutes of music were squeezed onto two sides of a 7-inch single, those precious songs sounded like they had been recorded underwater. The band were devastated and since it had appeared on their own label, Enigma, there was nobody else to blame. Rob wisely suggested that *An Ideal For Living* would work better as a 12-inch. When the 7-inch sold

Rob Gretton, the Scourge Of The Kippax, at Rafters, 1979.

40   Decades: Joy Division + New Order

Tony Wilson on the set of So It Goes.

out in September, the 12-inch was rushed out in October. There were no Nazis on the sleeve anymore.

Short Circuit: Live At The Electric Circus quietly appeared a fortnight after the "An Ideal For Living" 7-inch and, to celebrate, Rob insisted the band buy a van, which Hooky would drive. Once again, for all that their local audience was growing and the sound was evolving apace – "Transmission" had made its live debut in May – traction remained elusive.

That same month, Tony Wilson finally came through and on 20 May, Joy Division made their television debut, on *Granada Reports*. Hooky dyed his hair, Rob bought them new clothes and they barnstormed through "Shadowplay", a performance missed by a certain young fan called Gillian Gilbert, who was in Liverpool on a school geography trip. Two days later, Joy Division played Huddersfield to an audience of one.

Next month, Tony Wilson came through again. He'd come into an inheritance and used it to properly start the Factory label. "Factory was more of an idea than a professional label," the writer Jon Savage, one of their earliest and most articulate champions, explained decades later. Factory had not actually got around to releasing anything or signing a band, although it had established The Factory Night at the Russell Club, where bands such as the Wilson-managed Durutti Column and Sheffield mavericks Cabaret Voltaire would perform.

Ever the conceptualist, Wilson thought of a title for the first Factory record, *A Factory Sample*, and built the disc around the idea. He offered two tracks apiece to Cabaret Voltaire, Manchester poet John Dowie, Durutti Column and – since the man still known as Martin Zero (fresh from an appearance on *Top Of The Pops* as part of Jilted John's backing band) agreed to produce them – Joy Division. The two tracks,

Darkness on the Edge of Luton Town 41

Cabaret Voltaire, Russell Club, Manchester, 1978.

"JOY DIVISION ARE THE BEST THING I HAVE HEARD IN MANCHESTER FOR ABOUT SIX MONTHS."

TONY WILSON

"Digital" and "Glass" were recorded quickly and some apparently magnificent dub mixes of both tracks have since been lost forever. Again, the tracks were fine enough, a further leap from Warsaw, but there was still no indication of what was to come. "They were a gift to a producer," smirked their producer. "They didn't have a clue. They didn't argue." The *Sample* went on to sell 4700 copies. Stephen was questioned as a suspect in the Yorkshire Ripper case after a show in Leeds and Bernard married Sue Barlow. The Curtises were invited (Ian was best man); Hooky and girlfriend Iris were not.

Still flirting with majors, Rob see-sawed between London labels, who didn't understand the band as much as the band didn't understand them. November saw a tour with The Rezillos and The Undertones, where new material could be tested on audiences outside Manchester who weren't their own, without consequences. Two dates into it, the headlining Rezillos fell apart and the tour was scrapped. Without a label, Joy Division were going nowhere.

A Factory Sample had been scheduled for December. That it didn't appear until 1979 was a warning nobody chose to heed, but in their first national feature in *Sounds* (closed 1991), Ian lamented "everybody calls us Nazis" without seeming to understand why.

Shortly after Jim Dicken had died of lung cancer in front of Bernard, 1978 had one last roll of the dice: their first London headline show on December 27th. The basement of the Hope and Anchor on Upper Street in pre-gentrified Islington was long past its pub rock zenith. Everything went wrong. Bernard had a debilitating flu, the promised audience of London hipsters eager to hear this new northern sensation failed to materialise in what is traditionally the worst week of the year for

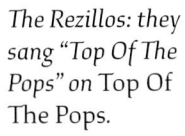

The Rezillos: they sang "Top Of The Pops" on Top Of The Pops.

Darkness on the Edge of Luton Town 43

Hooky, The Russell Club, aka The Factory, Manchester, 1979.

concerts. "It was one man and his dog," quipped Bernard, "and the dog didn't like us." Petrol costs came to £28.50. Door takings came to £27.50 and *Sounds*' Nick Tester was unimpressed: "I found Joy Division's 'tedium' a blunt hollow medium, comical in its superfluous angst." Then again, he did think the bassist was Peter Hooks.

Worse, much worse, was to follow as Peter Hooks drove them back up the M1 in the freezing van. As they passed Luton, Bernard and Ian began to tussle over a duvet. The moment that would change all their lives happened when the violence escalated to the point where Ian had some kind of fit and lashed out at the van as much as Bernard. Terrified – nothing like this had ever happened before – the band sped to the nearest hospital, the Luton & Dunstable, where Ian was medicated.

There had been hints of volatility. "Ian was a really polite, pleasant person, a delight to be around," noted Bernard perceptively. "He was funny, interesting and great company, but if he saw an injustice or someone wound him up, he'd blow up into these huge explosions like a Tasmanian Devil." But this was a new level of horror and after more attacks Ian was diagnosed with grand mal epilepsy at Macclesfield District General Hospital on January 23. It's a disease where, for reasons still not properly understood, the brain's nerve cells short-circuit. For many people, such as this author, it happens once and never reoccurs, but Ian's first fit triggered more. He was given anti-convulsants amongst medication so strong that he'd have violent mood swings for what little remained of his life. The attacks became more frequent and, understandably, his unworldly bandmates lacked the emotional maturity to deal with what was happening in front of them. It was a fatal aligning of the planets.

> "IAN WAS A REALLY POLITE, PLEASANT PERSON, A DELIGHT TO BE AROUND. HE WAS FUNNY, INTERESTING AND GREAT COMPANY, BUT IF HE SAW AN INJUSTICE OR SOMEONE WOUND HIM UP, HE'D BLOW UP INTO THESE HUGE EXPLOSIONS LIKE A TASMANIAN DEVIL."
>
> **BERNARD**

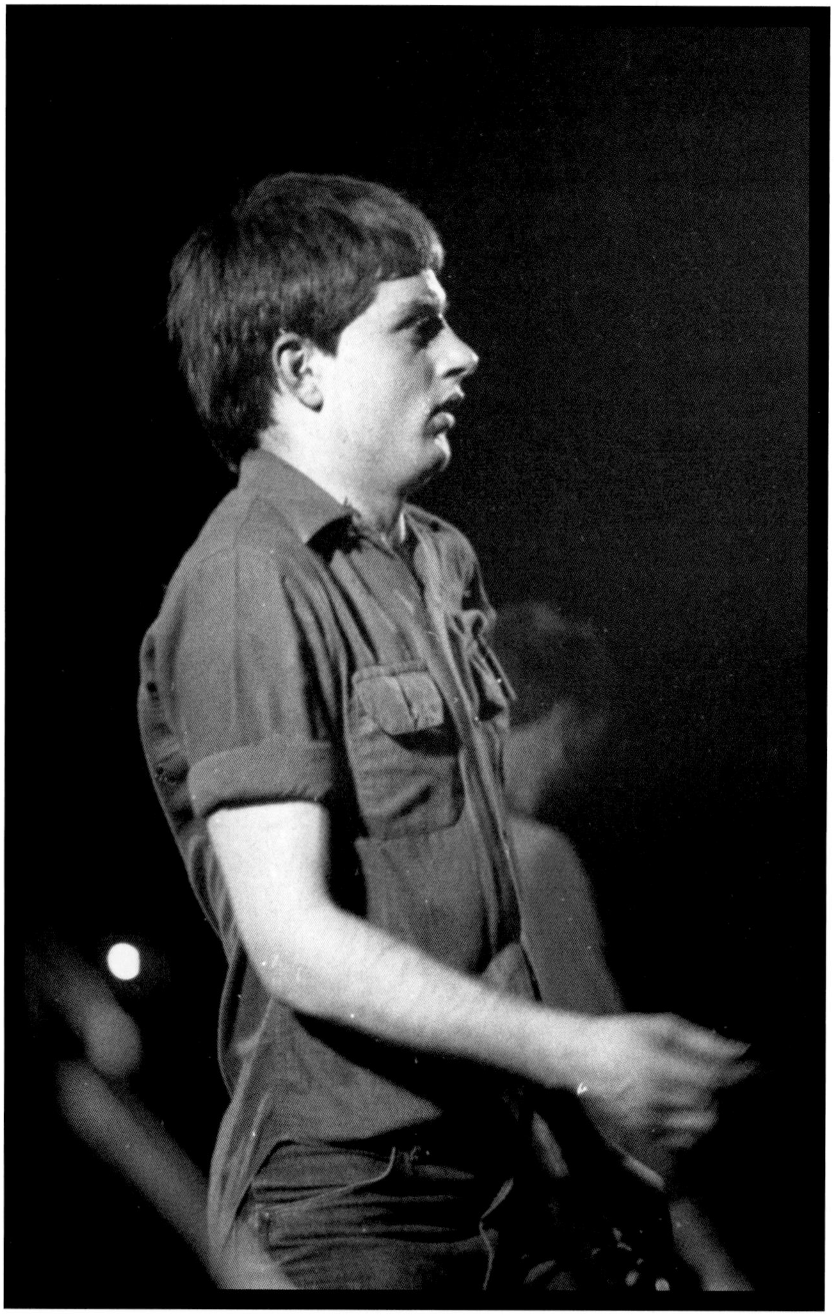

PLEASURES UNKNOWN

PLEASURES UNKNOWN

1979 would be Joy Division's year. Finally, almost apropos of nothing, they had that traction. The year began well, with Ian on the cover of the *NME* and a national radio session for the John Peel programme where "She's Lost Control" was introduced to the nation. They recorded with Martin Rushent, who'd produced the first two albums by now national contenders Buzzcocks and would go on to helm The Human League's phenomenally successful *Dare*. Rushent would go to his grave in 2011 believing his "Ice Age" was superior to Martin Hannett's speedier version, which would appear on *Still*. He was right too. After the session, the Genetic label offered them a five-album deal. They certainly needed the money. Their van was almost kaput, they were using a PA that had once been the property of local AOR hitsters Sad Café and they were existing on their day-job wages.

Re-enter Tony Wilson. He offered a deal that was light years away from anything proper labels would contemplate. Factory would pay the costs of an album and after said costs were recouped, everything would be split 50:50. There would be no contract and both parties would have what Wilson pronounced "the freedom to fuck off". Oh, and Joy Division would have absolute artistic control – in theory. Rob agreed, hands were shaken and Joy Division could make their album, their way – or at least Martin Hannett, née Zero's, way, since Rob and Tony had decided on the producer.

On March 31, band and producer decamped to Strawberry Studios where the weekend rates could accommodate their £8,000 budget. Owned by Graham Gouldman and Eric Stewart of 10cc, the great Manchester success story of the '70s, the 24-track studio had been used by Paul McCartney. Much later, The Stone Roses would enjoy its services and luxuries.

Work was remarkably speedy. The songs had been honed live, so in a schedule the great acts of the '50s would have understood, it took just three weekends for men with day jobs to record one of the finest debut albums of the 20th century: one to record the backing tracks; one for overdubs and vocals and one to mix. Later, New Order would take three years to make an album. In fact, sixteen songs were recorded for a ten-song album, so "Autosuggestion", "From

Martin Rushent, at home in Pangbourne, Berkshire, February 1981.

48 Decades: Joy Division + New Order

So much to answer for: Manchester, 6 January, 1979.

"ONE GENIUS AND THREE MANCHESTER UNITED FANS."

MARTIN HANNETT

Pleasures Unknown

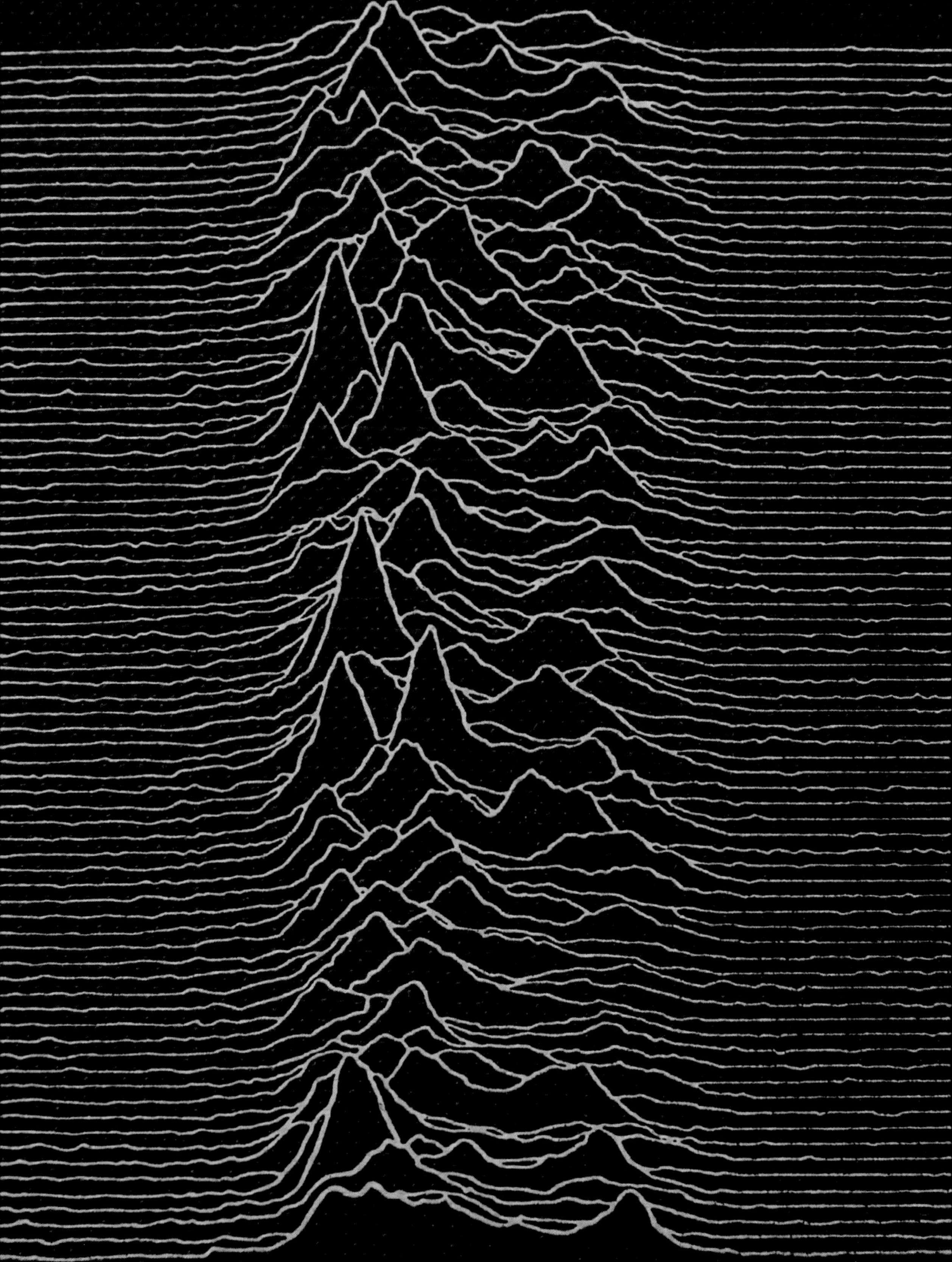

Safety To Where...?", "Exercise One", "The Only Mistake", "Walked In Line" and "The Kill" would be dumped. Hannett was at his most inspired, fashioning Joy Division's world in a way only Ian, his favourite, could truly appreciate. Midway through the sessions, Natalie Curtis was born. Her father, Ian, fainted at the birth, banging his head on the floor. His bandmates, Rob and Tony – all of whom Debbie claimed were far from welcoming during her pregnancy – were nonplussed. Everything and yet nothing had changed.

The cover which would launch a battalion of T-shirts for the next half century (although to the disbelief of the British tax authorities, the band wouldn't make money from them until 1994) was a Bernard masterstroke. Reading *The Cambridge Encyclopaedia Of Astronomy* (page 111, assuming you have the 1979 edition), he noted a black-on-white image of the radio pulsar, CP1919. Suitably inspired, he turned the idea over to designer Peter Saville, who inverted the colours. *Voila*.

Each instrument was recorded separately, before the vocals were added after Ian had rummaged around his plastic bag. The air conditioning was turned on full blast because the dope-guzzling Hannett thought a warm musician was a lazy musician. Stephen's drum kit was dismantled and re-assembled and a microphone placed in the bathroom to give extra echo. Naturally, Hannett didn't want any of what he incorrectly described as "one genius and three Manchester United fans" loitering when he remixed in the dead of night, in case they had ideas. He later confided that *Unknown Pleasures* was "the finest thing I ever had to polish," but Hannett was not as other men or other producers. As Tony Wilson said, "Martin could see sound, shape it and rebuild it."

Left: *The inverted radio pulsar that adorns T-shirts to this day.*

Below: *Curtis and Hooky, Bowdon Vale Youth Club, Altrincham, 14 March, 1979.*

Pleasures Unknown

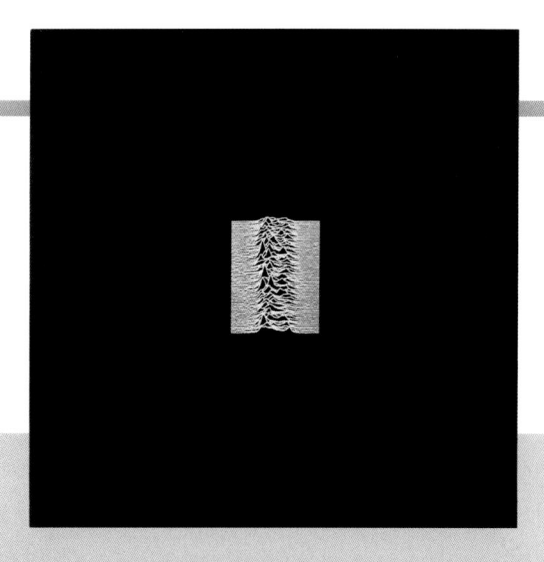

UNKNOWN PLEASURES

TRACK LISTING

Disorder
Day Of The Lords
Candidate
Insight
New Dawn Fades

She's Lost Control
Shadowplay
Wilderness
Interzone
I Remember Nothing

Released 15 June 1979
Label Factory – FACT 10
Recorded at Strawberry Studios, Stockport, England
Produced by Martin Hannett
Personnel
Ian Curtis: lead vocals (backing vocals on "Interzone")
Bernard Sumner: guitar, keyboards
Peter Hook: bass guitar, backing vocals (lead vocals on "Interzone")
Stephen Morris: drums, percussion
Cover Art Peter Saville
Notes
Factory Records did not release any singles from *Unknown Pleasures*, and the album did not chart despite the relative success of the group's non-album debut single "Transmission". It has since received sustained critical acclaim as an influential post-punk album and has been named as one of the best albums of all time by publications such as *NME*, *AllMusic*, *Select*, and *Spin*.

The opening to "Disorder" and *Unknown Pleasures* is one of the great moments in music. Echo-laden drums, bass as lead, outer space whooshing and then the actual lead guitar, before Ian entered with one of the finest opening lines of any album: "I've been waiting for a guide to come and take me by the hand/Could these sensations make me feel the pleasures of a normal man?". And it wasn't downhill afterwards. Already the die was cast.

Hannett added keyboards to "Day Of The Lords", previously known as "Moderation", without telling his clients. This time, the pace is slower, but the intensity is ratcheted up, like a Louis-Ferdinand Céline saga of childhood horror.

Hannett already knew which songs he wanted to jettison, but this left them one short, so they wrote "Candidate" at Strawberry. They felt it was unfinished and Bernard didn't want to play on it at all. Hannett knew otherwise and when Ian droned "I tried to get to you/ You treat me like this", it was clear the marital bed may not have been one of roses.

From the moment it began with the first of many opening doors, "Insight" was music from another planet. It would become Hooky's favourite Joy Division song. The keyboards, in the best sense of the word, are barbaric, but when Ian sings "I'm not afraid anymore", he sounds very afraid indeed.

Hannett began "New Dawn Fades" with a twisted sample from "Insight". Hooky still thinks it's too slow, but he's wrong again. With his bass crashing against Bernard's guitar, it's Joy Division at their most grandstanding, but it's also the first time Ian directly dealt with his suicidal impulses and his feelings of utter numbness. Even now, it's horrific and perfect.

Ian was so deep inside himself, he didn't need to tell stories, but "She's Lost Control" is just that. The woman in question was a client of Ian's disabled resettlement work at the Job Centre, before he knew of his own condition. She would have seizures in Ian's office. When

Joy Division in an art and furniture shop, Manchester, 6 January, 1979. Hooky's polo neck pictured. Unfortunately.

she stopped visiting, he assumed she'd secured employment. But, in fact, she'd died following another epileptic fit.

Bernard loosely channelled The Velvet Underground's "Ocean" for "Shadowplay", another tale of suffering, abuse and humiliation at the hands of unspecified others in the setting of moonscape Manchester.

The musically busy "Wilderness" finds Ian time-travelling. What does he find? Not entirely unpredictably, he finds Christ being crucified. Even Rob thought this was too much.

Short and sharp and based upon their take of "Keep On Keepin' On", the brutal "Interzone" was the moment where Warsaw's punkiness flowered. Hooky did most of the singing, with Ian relegated to backing vocals. He didn't mind: it suited the song better. Corny as it may sound, that really was all he cared about.

There would be no respite from darkness, unless Ian bringing a whoopee cushion into the studio counts. And it does. "I Remember Nothing" was Hannett at his most unfettered. Broken bottles abounded and Ian was at his most Frank Sinatra-esque, hence the reference to "strangers". Tony had given him a hits collection and Ian had immediately latched on to the bleakness and the loneliness of Sinatra at his most bleary eyed.

The smashing glass, the recording in a lift shaft, the samples, the space-age keyboards were the results of one man in his sonic playground, but the songs were the band's. Expecting an extension of the live show, the Salford lads weren't overly impressed: "We hated it," admitted Hooky, who declared it a Martin Hannett record rather than a Joy Division one. "Me and Bernard wanted it to be so much more rocky." Bernard concurred: "I felt Martin had robbed us of our power. It was drained and weedy." They were spectacularly wrong.

The critics were more on the ball, especially *NME*'s Max Bell, who invited his readers to "investigate these confined spaces, these insides of cages, this outside of insanity", while in *Melody Maker* (closed 2000), Jon Savage argued "what gives Joy Division their edge is the consistency of their vision." Joy Division had created their own world. They had made an album beyond time and space.

Hooky and Tony Wilson collected the initial run of 10,000 and stored them in actress/presenter Margi Clarke's flat. *Unknown Pleasures* – the first Factory album – initially failed to chart, although in the wake of Ian's death it sailed to seventy-one in the British charts, a big thing in an era where majors had the industry and the chart machine sewn up. When the album sold

"INVESTIGATE THESE CONFINED SPACES, THESE INSIDES OF CAGES, THIS OUTSIDE OF INSANITY."

MAX BELL, *NME*

At TJ Davidson's, 19 August, 1979.

15,000 copies in six months, there was a profit of circa £40,000 to go round. There was no time to take stock, especially for Ian, whose fragility was becoming increasingly apparent. Even so, within a fortnight of the album's release, Ian was looking ahead. "No matter how many songs you do," he told *NME*, "you're always looking for the next one." As soon as July, they were back in the studio for the first of two sessions at Central Sound (cheaper than Strawberry) with a clutch of oldish ("Transmission", "Novelty") and newer ("Atmosphere", "Dead Souls") songs to grapple with. They were back on television, rattling through "She's Lost Control" on *So It Goes*, as presented by Tony Wilson and Margox, aka Margi Clarke.

Now that more press wanted to speak to them, Rob and Tony tried to cultivate mystique: few interviews, no encores, no autographs.

Ian was fairly loquacious, but while Bernard and Stephen said little, Hooky brought oikish menace to the table. It didn't quite work. Dave McCullough, the man from *Sounds*, didn't bother to discover Bernard, Hooky and Stephen's names, but he wasn't impressed: "manager Gretton (obviously assured of his own cleverness) and the bearded bassist gave the impression they suffered from serious mental deficiencies as they groped about in the dimness of their 'attitudes'." The *NME* was kinder, perceptively describing Hooky as "blunt, wary"; Bernard as "quiet, easy-going", Stephen as "mischievous" and Ian as "shy, fragile, polite".

They toured hard, but such was their rate of progress that *Unknown Pleasures* tracks would comprise less than half the set as "Atmosphere", "Colony" and "Dead Souls" were unveiled. At London's Nashville Rooms on August 13, Annik

Pleasures Unknown

Honore, was there. The twenty-one-year-old Belgian police inspector's daughter had recently moved to London to take a secretarial job at her country's embassy. She was also a writer for the Belgian fanzine En Attendant and she interviewed the band a couple of weeks later. From there, the darkness of Joy Division would turn a whole lot blacker.

"Both Bernard and I had a go at bagging Annik," admitted Hooky, rather unchivalrously. Somehow spurning the opportunity to be "bagged" by the Salford lads, she and Ian began an affair: "I saw beautiful eyes, a soft look, a person suffering, fragile," she said in 2010. "Affair" is a problematic word. Until her death from cancer in 2014, Annik maintained the relationship was never consummated and Hooky, offering too much information, claimed erectile dysfunction was a side effect of the industrial-strength medication Ian was taking. "It was a completely pure and platonic relationship," Annik insisted. "Very childish, very chaste. I did not have a sexual relationship with Ian. He was on medication, which rendered it a non-physical relationship. I am so fed up that people question my word." Debbie Curtis would always believe otherwise, but the tug between wife-and-child and the other woman would escalate Ian's stress levels to fit-inducingly stratospheric.

In August, they were invited onto the now genuinely successful Buzzcocks' national tour and the day jobs were over. Better still, they made their first appearance on national television on September 15, romping through "Transmission" and "She's Lost Control" on the BBC2 programme, *Something Else*, a remarkable achievement for a band on a

Above: *Leigh Open Air Festival, 27 August, 1979.*

Right: *Bowden Vale Youth Club, March 1979. Nobody had shinier shoes than Ian.*

"I SAW BEAUTIFUL EYES, A SOFT LOOK, A PERSON SUFFERING, FRAGILE."

ANNIK HONORE

barely functioning, inchoate indie label. This was getting serious.

The tour began in October and coincided with the first Joy Division single. "Transmission" had been recorded during the RCA sessions, but Martin Hannett speeded it up and added magic, as he did to the superior "Novelty" which offered the prescient question "What you gonna do when it's over?". It could have charted, but Hannett told Tony Wilson that "Transmission" didn't need a radio plugger because the "dance to the radio" line would automatically ensure airplay. Lack of airplay prevented it from being a hit and of the 10,000 initially pressed, 3,000 were sold.

There was more: Scottish label Fast Product released *Earcom 2: Contradiction*, an EP featuring Thursdays, Basczax and Joy Division's "Autosuggestion" and "From Safety To Where...?", cast-offs from the *Unknown Pleasures* sessions.

Things moved quickly in post-punk Britain and Buzzcocks' buzz was already beginning to fade, despite a fabulously inventive, Martin Rushent produced third album, *A Different Kind Of Tension*. They played the same set every night and roadies would stand side-stage turning over giant cue cards for Pete Shelley to sing the album's stream of consciousness title track. Relishing the chance for national exposure and the challenge of wooing someone else's crowd, Joy Division were staggering. Those of us rammed at the front of the stage at Sheffield Top Rank on October 21 understood instantly that Joy Division were special. It wasn't great collective insight: it was obvious that this was a band like no other. Hooky, Bernard and Stephen were supremely tightly drilled and not just in comparison with their sub-standard indie peers, but Ian was something else, a force of nature dressed as a bank clerk, reaching into the very depths of his soul. He had to be helped off stage at the end. Nobody knew, or cared, why. Nor did they a few days later when Ian actually fitted on stage at Bournemouth Winter Gardens and ended the night in hospital.

58　Decades: Joy Division + New Order

Left: *Ian and Hooky, Electric Ballroom, London, 26 October, 1979; a headline show during a break from the Buzzcocks tour. The Distractions and A Certain Ratio supported.*

During the Buzzcocks tour, they recorded the definitive versions of "Atmosphere" and "Dead Souls" at Cargo in Rochdale. When Ian cut his hand and couldn't play his occasional guitar at a headline show at Liverpool Eric's, Gillian Gilbert, from all-girl punk band The Inadequates, stepped in. To round off the year of their great leap forwards, there was another John Peel session, where they introduced a song occasionally aired on the Buzzcocks tour, "Love Will Tear Us Apart", with its perhaps revealing line "Just can't function no more".

Americans were beginning to notice. At the end of 1979, Warner Brothers offered Factory $1m for distribution rights to Joy Division. In his first – but far from final – act of financial and career sabotage, Tony Wilson sent – of all people – Martin Hannett and Peter Saville to negotiate. "That's why it never happened," said a still-rankled Stephen in 2010. "We'd have taken it."

Joy Division were everywhere, even places they shouldn't have been such as the Dutch television show which captioned Gang of Four as Joy Division. They were paid for a show at Preston Warehouse in frozen chickens. "Love Will Tear Us Apart" was recorded at Pennine on January 7 and 8. The burst of drums was meant to evoke The Clash's "Safe European Home" but Martin

Pleasures Unknown   59

> "HE DIDN'T WANT THE RESPONSIBILITY OF THE DECISION TO LEAVE HIS WIFE AND DAUGHTER. THE LONGER HE WAS LOCKED IN INDECISION, THE MORE HARM IT WAS DOING HIM MENTALLY."
>
> BERNARD

Hannett struggled to decide on the definitive mix or whether the song was deceptively complex or deceptively simple. Everyone would try again at Strawberry in March.

They played Paris the week before Christmas, but they were soon off on their first European tour, a ten-day, small venue jaunt around the Netherlands, West Germany and Belgium. They would never play out of England again. The atmosphere was different now. Annik's presence (wives and girlfriends were hitherto taboo and not merely for budgetary reasons) transformed Ian. She despised their laddishness – imagine Lisa Simpson trekking around sophisticated Europe with Nelson Muntz's gang – and, as someone put it, turds and birds had been usurped by Burroughs and Dostoevsky. When a run of sub-standard accommodation was broken by a relatively comfortable brothel in Antwerp, Annik forbade the band to stay there.

On their return, Hooky had a skinhead haircut and Ian started cutting himself. "He didn't want the responsibility of the decision to leave his wife and daughter," mused Bernard. "The longer he was locked in indecision, the more harm it was doing him mentally." But Ian and Rob still found time to produce Section 25's "Girls Don't Count" single and when the two Factory bands shared a bill, they'd play the song together.

Apparently, Ian told Debbie about Annik shortly after the European tour.

She smashed his copy of *Low* and then gave away Ian's beloved Candy. In March, the single "Atmosphere"/ "Dead Souls" was released. The astonishing thing – and it beggars belief even now – was *how* it was released. With Factory's cheery acquiescence, two of the finest songs in Joy Division's canon – and "Atmosphere" defines them as much as anything they did – were tossed off in a limited edition (just the 1,578 copies), mail-order release on tiny European label, Sordide Sentimental as *Licht Und Blindheit* (Light and Blindness). It was almost impossible for their burgeoning, increasingly fanatical fanbase to acquire. But, my, what music…

Initially titled "Chance", the haunting, funereal and ice-cold, "Atmosphere" was the sound of a man coming to terms with the end of a relationship and possibly himself, while it simultaneously sounded like the hushed soundtrack to the end of civilisation. Decades later, James Blake's live cover showed that it packed a hefty emotional punch for a generation who weren't born when it was recorded. Its title taken from Nikolai Gogol's 1842 novel, the impossibly dramatic "Dead Souls", with its two-minutes, twelve-seconds introduction, was Ian speaking to the dead, to himself, to Debbie, to Annik. It's almost too much to bear.

Ian and his William Faulkner T-shirt, Paradiso Amsterdam, 11 January, 1980.

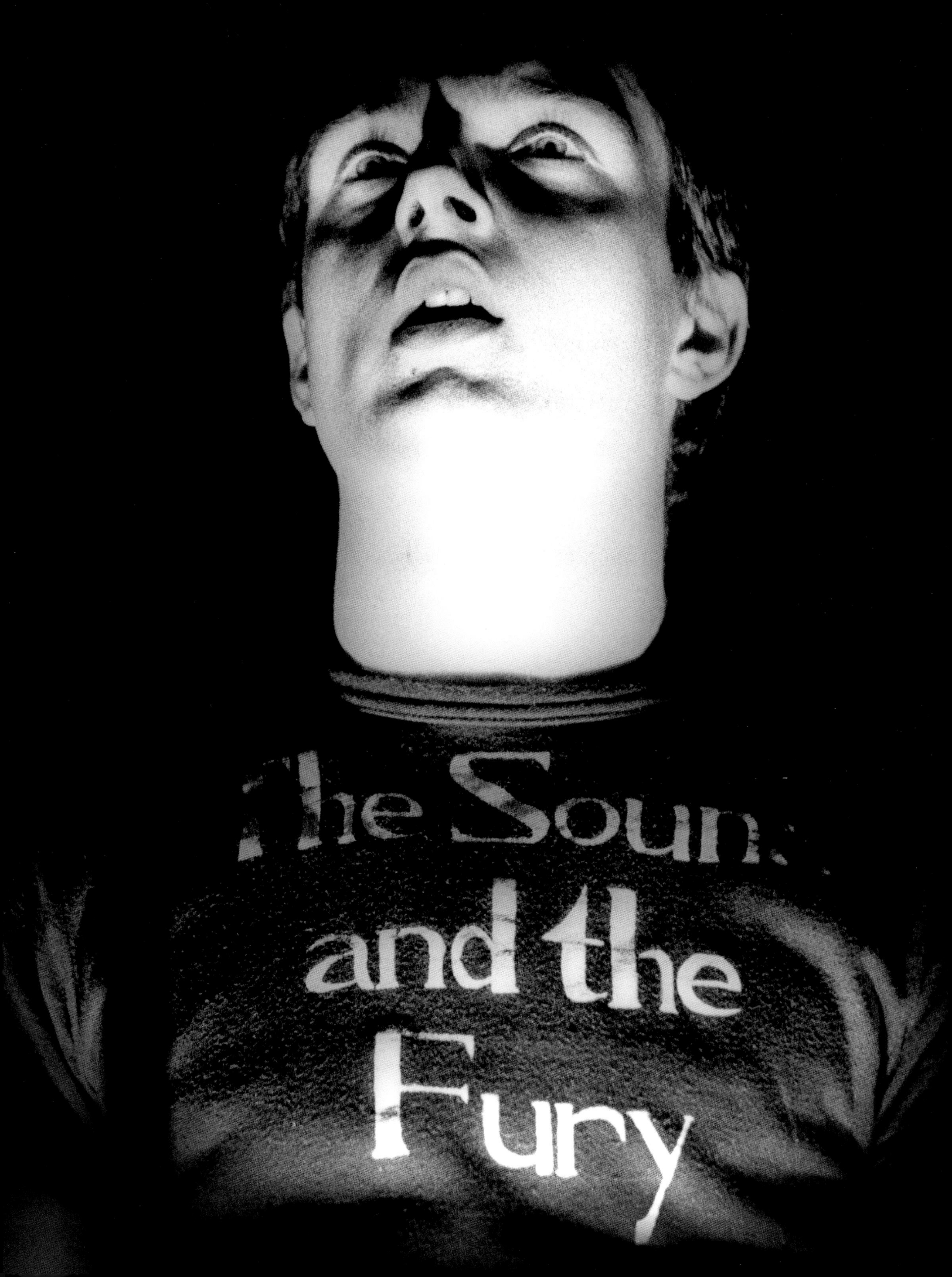
and the
Fury

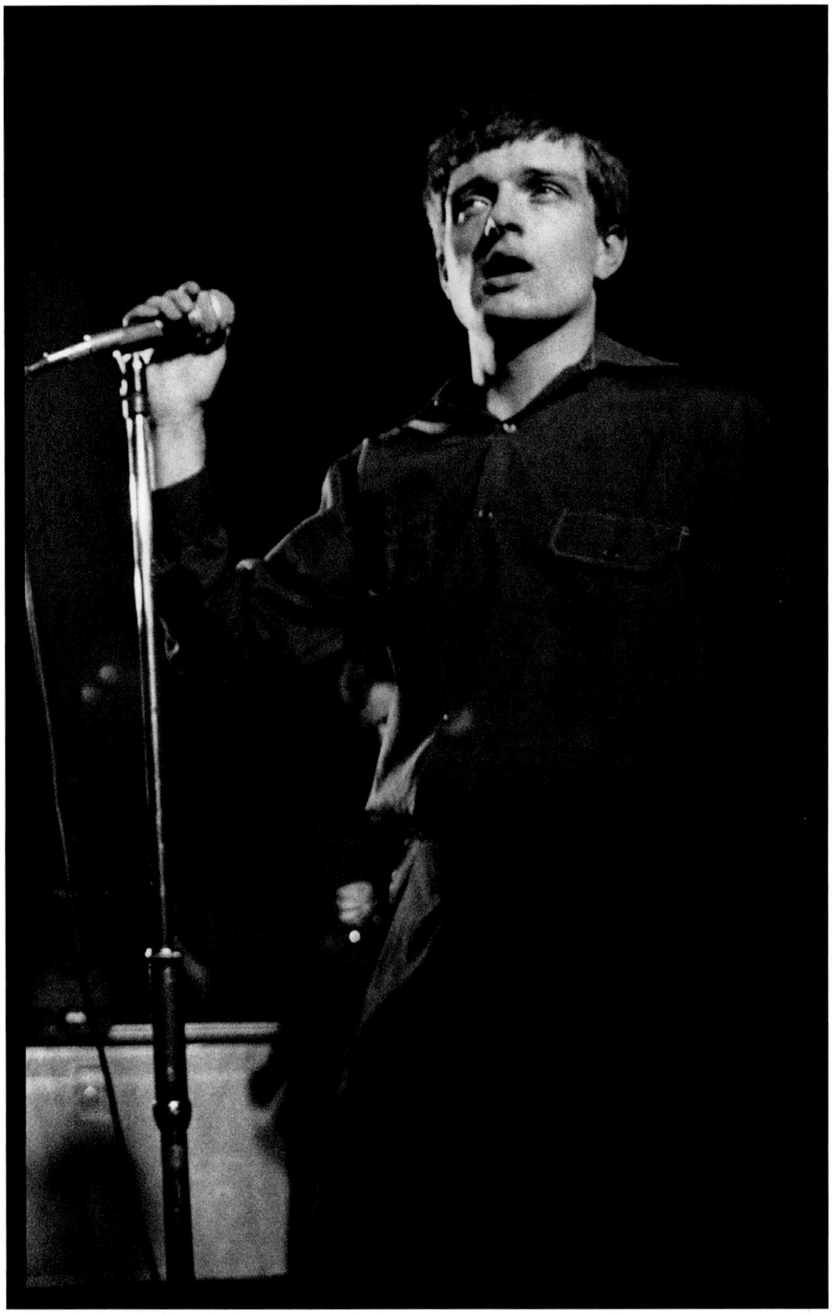

THE END

THE END

On March 17, 1980, Joy Division began to record their second album. Strawberry had been the initially favoured location, but instead they settled on Britannia Row in London, at the opposite end of Upper Street from the Hope And Anchor. The studio was owned and mostly used by Pink Floyd. Ian needed to get away from Macclesfield, while Martin Hannett's drug use had spiralled out of control in Manchester and he was supplementing his marijuana with heroin. None of this was going to end well.

They rented two flats in York Street, a few miles away in Marylebone. The party flat housed Rob, Stephen and Hooky. The intellectual flat housed Ian, Annik and Bernard. "They were boorish; we were the creative background," sniffed Bernard.

"We were always messing about and Annik hated it," remembered Hooky of the indie John and Yoko in 2010. "Every time she and Ian went out, we'd tip the beds up and string her knickers off the lights. She was going fucking apeshit."

The twain did meet from time to time. Beneath his little boy lost exterior ("He's funny. He just sits and looks at you like he's a little kid or something," noted Echo & The Bunnymen singer Ian McCulloch), Bernard was always into bacchanalia, but he hated mess as much as Annik. And since Annik was trying to turn Ian

LantarenVenster, Rotterdam, January 1980. Joy Division always sent their audiences wild.

64 Decades: Joy Division + New Order

The End 65

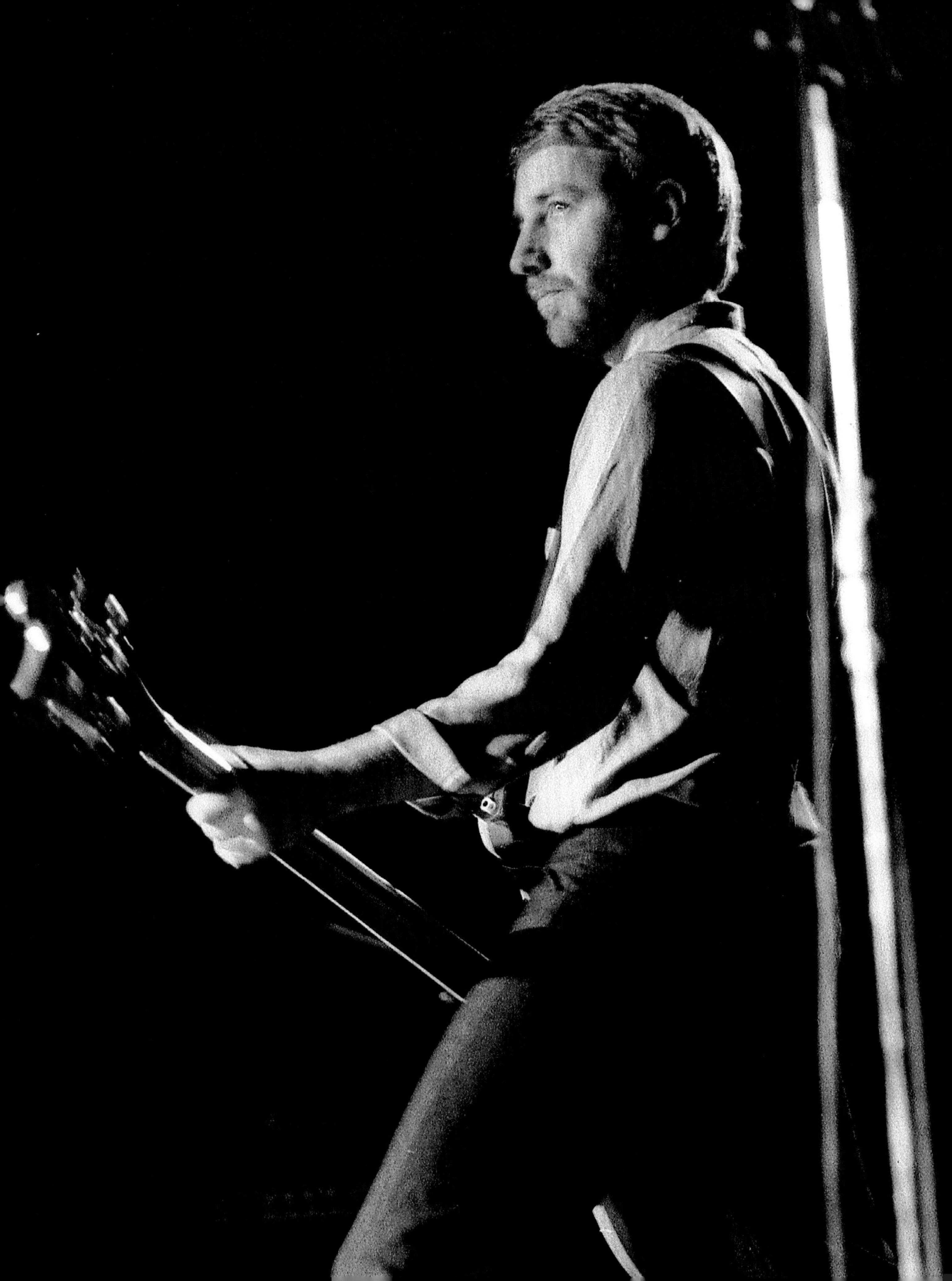

vegetarian, the singer had to pop over to share the party flat's lamb kebabs. Martin Hannett chain-smoked joints in the studio at nights and enjoyed his heroin in his hotel room during the day.

There were visitors. One night a bunch of bedraggled Dubliners turned up to pay homage and to entice Martin Hannett into their world. They were "practically bloody shaking," chuckled Hooky. U2 left a tape. In an act of atypical largesse, Rob gave the wives and girlfriends £20 each and told them to get themselves on a train to London. Debbie demurred, citing an overdue electricity bill. The others arrived at Euston Station at just after 9 p.m. Just after midnight, Stephen finally rolled up to collect them. It was not an overly joyful reunion. "It didn't get off to a good start and then it went downhill," admitted Stephen, who always claimed he'd been given the wrong time. "Every one of us had a fight with our respective girlfriend," chuckled Hooky, "probably because of the guilt of Annik being there."

They worked hard though. Joy Division always worked hard. Hannett and Ian would spend long hours together, working on his vocals after Ian had finished tweaking his lyrics in the studio, but Joy Division was still a four-way tie. Half the songs, the more guitar-based ones, had been road-tested. The other half, synthesiser based after Bernard had upped his game in that department after soaking up as much Giorgio Moroder as he could, were more recent compositions and they were cut from a similar cloth to "Atmosphere", which, of course, was never considered for inclusion. "We were growing into a different band while we were making that record," claims Stephen. "We were all very much about the future. We couldn't wait to get there."

One night, Ian disappeared. Hooky found him in the bathroom: he'd fitted and banged his head on the sink. In quieter moments, Ian talked wistfully of moving to Bournemouth to open a bookstore. With which woman wasn't clear. But more important to all of them, he and his bandmates knew they had made an album every bit as strong as *Unknown Pleasures* and their first American tour was booked. Ian was a few weeks away from death. Hooky remembered that time when speaking to *Mojo* in 2020: "Ian had two formats: 'Well Ian' and 'Ill Ian'. 'Well Ian' was full of life, energy, ambition and positivity for the future. There was nothing more scary than 'Ill Ian'."

They hung around in London, buying clothes for the US tour and playing dates, including a support for The Stranglers, whose leader, Hugh Cornwell, was in prison for drug possession. Their wretched treatment at the hands of the Stranglers' crew would reap an unlikely harvest.

Things began to move too quickly. On their return from London, Joy Division played off the beaten track in Great Malvern. On returning home, Ian tried to kill himself in his marital bed by overdosing on his prescribed medicine, phenobarbitone. He left a note declaring his love for Annik. He came out of hospital to play a show in Bury and moved in with Tony Wilson and his long-suffering wife Lindsay Reade, at their home in the beautiful Pennine village of Charlesworth. Wilson was working at his day job, so it was mostly the boss's wife and the boss's protégé. "He was obviously very

Hooky, Lyceum, London, 29 February, 1980.

"IT DIDN'T GET OFF TO A GOOD START AND THEN IT WENT DOWNHILL."

STEPHEN

The End

depressed," she remembered. "We drove each other around the twist." Tony's father was gay. He and his partner, Tony Connolly visited. Connolly was the first to openly predict that Ian would kill himself.

That gig at Bury's Derby Hall was a dangerous disaster. Stephen and Hooky were adamant that Ian was in no state to perform so soon after his suicide attempt, but the band needed money for the American tour and Rob was adamant the show must go on before a crowd of six hundred – two hundred over capacity. Bernard booked Alan Hempsall of Factory's Crispy Ambulance as a stand-in. Ian managed to sing new songs "Decades" and "The Eternal", but Hempsall's offerings went down less well and, after an abortive attempt at The Velvet Underground's "Sister Ray", a pint glass shattered a chandelier. Rob threw himself into the crowd and a full-scale riot followed. Five people were hospitalised and only the roadies saved Hooky from a pummelling. Ian sat backstage in tears, muttering, "It's all my fault." Still nobody saw the signs – nobody said "stop". "We shouldn't have done Bury," sighed Hooky later. "It was a really bad mistake."

Three nights later, Joy Division played a Factory club night. Debbie and Ian argued over Annik. Her view, that Annik struggled to engage with Ian's health issues and treated him like a lapdog, was a view not without sympathy within the inner circle.

Ian left the Wilsons' sanctuary and bounced between his parents' house in Failsworth near Oldham and Bernard's home in Worsley, a notch on the Manchester commuter belt. Ian missed Natalie's birthday on April 16. On April 22, Ian, Debbie, their respective parents, plus Tony and Lindsay, gathered for a marriage summit. Ian's parents learned of their son's suicide bid and, after the summit, Debbie telephoned Annik to say divorce was imminent. Ian joined his muse in London before she went on holiday to Egypt. They would never meet again.

Debbie instigated divorce proceedings, but the business of Joy Division continued. It seems almost barbaric in hindsight, but even Ian wasn't trying to halt the merry-go-round. There was a low budget video for "Love Will Tear Us Apart", shot at their old rehearsal room, TJ's. The hand at the beginning is Rob's and Ian looks unshaven, but most of all he looks – in that word used by Annik – "fragile". As they rehearsed for the States, they still managed to write and play two new songs, "Ceremony" and "Little Boy", later retitled "In A Lonely Place". Nothing, it seemed, could stop their creative flow.

On 2 May, they played what would be their final concert at the University of Birmingham's High Hall. Jon Savage popped by to say hello before the show. He noticed nothing untoward. It was no wonder Savage failed to detect a problem: there didn't appear to be one. Bernard's keyboards on "Isolation" were almost prog-like in their heaviness, "Ceremony" was aired and "Shadowplay" was especially transcendent. But the next night's show at Liverpool's Eric's Club was cancelled as were subsequent dates in Scotland.

Ian attended his final epilepsy clinic appointment on May 6 and on May 13, the last photograph with Natalie was taken. He looks haunted, but he didn't on May 15 when Bernard took him to the pub. They saw the comedy-magician, Amazing Noswad (Bernard's friend Paul Dawson) and Ian laughed like a drain. Afterwards Bernard walked him through graveyards "to try to bring home the reality of death".

With America just hours away, what would be Ian's last day was meant to have been spent in Blackpool, water-skiing with Bernard and Section 25. Instead, Ian went to the marital home at 77 Barton Street. Since Debbie had to work shifts at a bar, their paths barely crossed, but when they did there was the inevitable row. That day the bar held an afternoon disco and an evening wedding reception and Debbie worked both.

Ian drank whisky and coffee and watched Werner Herzog's *Stroszek*, a tale of a European

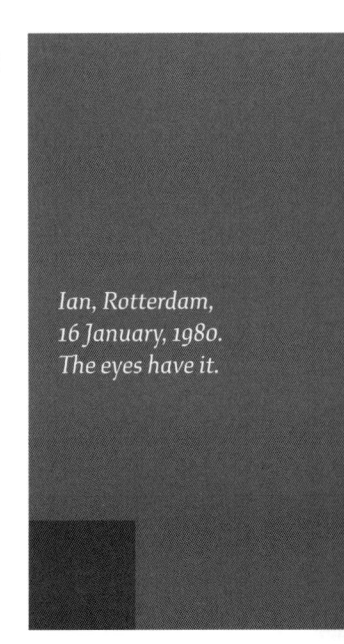

Ian, Rotterdam, 16 January, 1980. The eyes have it.

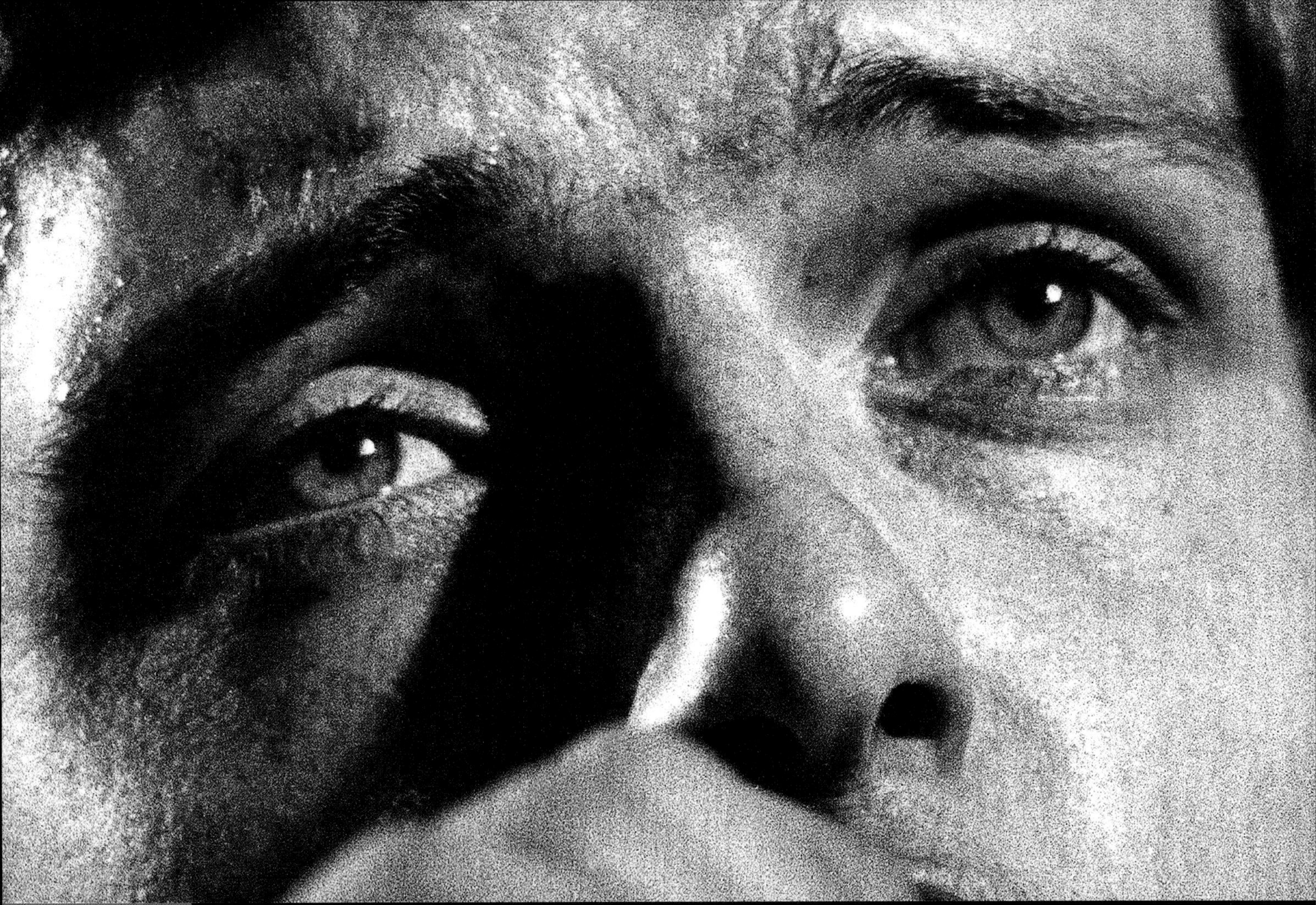

> "ON SUNDAY MORNING I WAS TURNING MY TROUSERS UP; MONDAY, I WAS SCREAMING. EVEN AFTER HE ATTEMPTED SUICIDE, IT DIDN'T SEEM HE WAS THAT HELL-BENT ON DESTRUCTION."
>
> STEPHEN

musician who kills himself in the United States. After her nightshift, Debbie went to her parents' home. Ian listened to Iggy Pop's *The Idiot* over and over. Some time in the early hours of Sunday May 18, he hanged himself in the kitchen. He was just twenty-three.

Debbie found him when she returned home in the morning and a neighbour, Kevin Wood, took on the gruesome task of cutting Ian down. Not everyone was as unsympathetic as Durutti Column's Vini Reilly ("I wasn't surprised when it happened, his personality was completely fucked up"), but nobody was more surprised than the men who were close enough to see it coming. Tony Wilson, as ever, was so right, but so wrong: "We're just left feeling sorry for ourselves, which I suppose is the wrong kind of emotion."

Stephen was more apposite. "On Sunday morning I was turning my trousers up; Monday, I was screaming. Even after he attempted suicide, it didn't seem he was that hell-bent on destruction." Hooky was enjoying Sunday lunch when the police telephoned. When he put the receiver down, he carried on eating until his partner Iris asked him who'd called. "He never, ever led me to believe for one moment that he was depressed," claimed Hooky. It seems absurd, but since they hadn't read Ian's lyrics – an astonishing assertion that nobody has dissented from – it seems true too.

Rob telephoned Bernard, who was still in Blackpool: "I came to terms with it straight away because I thought I could understand why he'd done it, but after he died we did listen to his words and thought 'this is someone who sounds like they're in a lot of trouble emotionally'."

What Joy Division actually talked about remains unclear. "We never talked about music ever," claims Hooky. "Just 'We need another fast dancey one'."

And so it continued. John Peel told the nation of Ian's death on his Monday night radio show. In the *NME*, Chris Bohn struck the wisest note of all, noting Ian's death "didn't bring their journey to an abrupt halt as much freeze it for all eternity at the brink of discovery." Joy Division has been discovered over and over again since Ian's death, but Bohn was right: they are paused forever at the moment of their transformation from minor to major.

In *Sounds*, Dave McCullough, the writer who didn't know their names, went for demented gold: "His death was poetically beautiful. The industrial pyre you made for him is now your

Deborah Curtis: "I knew a different Ian to the Ian the band knew."

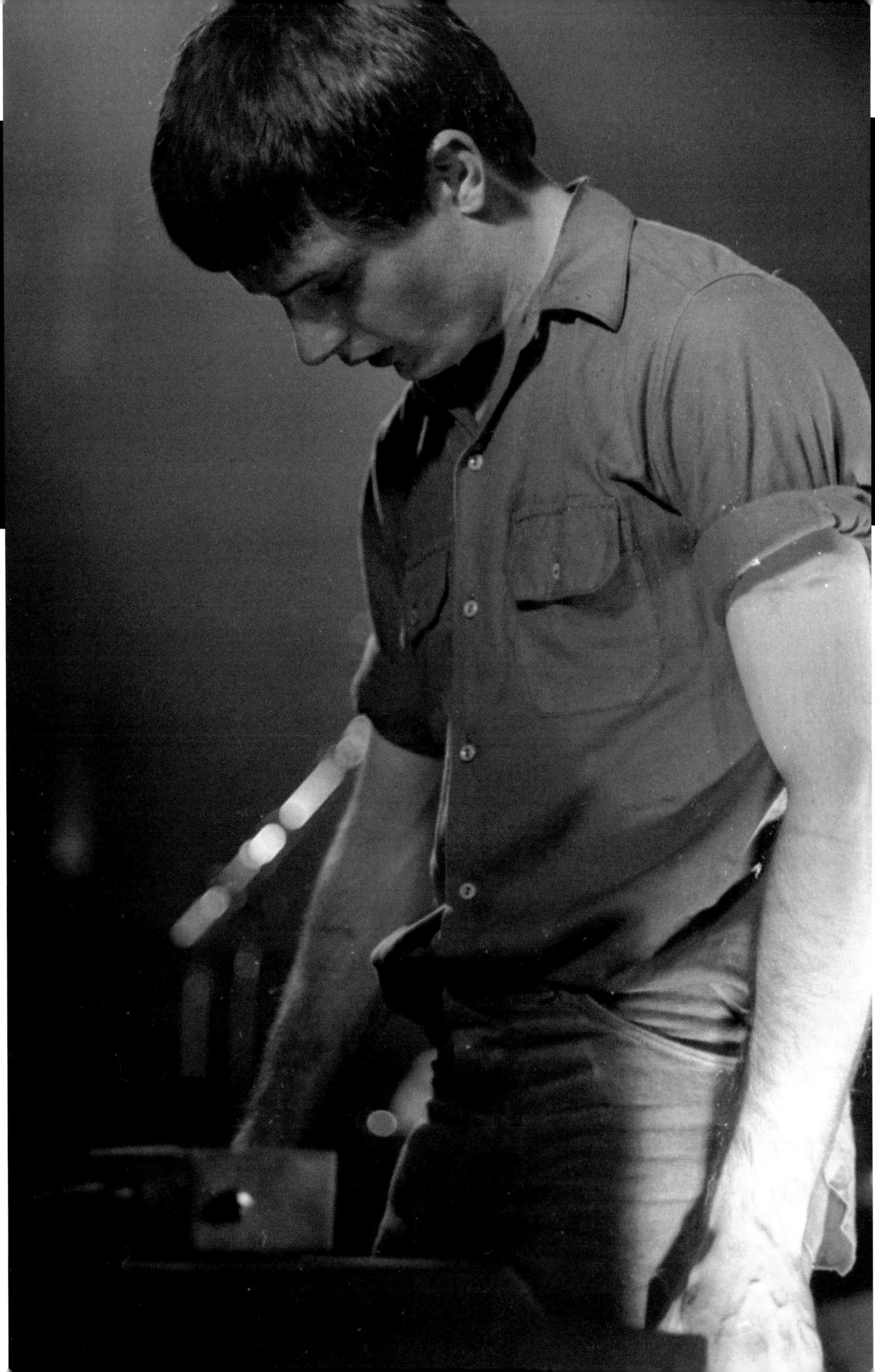

"PEOPLE ADMIRED HIM FOR THE THINGS WHICH WERE DESTROYING HIM. HE WAS A DIFFERENT PERSON TO EVERYONE HE MET."

DEBORAH CURTIS

own pyre, your own guilt, your own stupidity, your own way of evading the simple truths... that man cared for you, that man died for you."

Debbie got it, of course, citing the many Ians who *were* Ian Curtis: "People admired him for the things which were destroying him. He was a different person to everyone he met. I truly believe I knew a different Ian to the Ian the band knew. My problem wasn't the other woman, it was that he told me he didn't love me and wouldn't let me have a divorce."

On May 21 the US (and Toronto) tour alongside Cabaret Voltaire, with Martin Hannett as sound-man was meant to begin at Hurrah, New York, where David Bowie had filmed much of the "Fashion" video. Ruth Polsky was the booking agent. Instead, Ian's funeral took place on the May 23. It was, as Hooky noted, "a truly miserable affair." Before Ian was cremated, Hooky and Bernard couldn't bring themselves to look at the body. Afterwards, there was drinking and a wholly inappropriate viewing of the Sex Pistols film, *The Great Rock 'n' Roll Swindle*. Nobody knew how to behave.

What to do? Objectively, there was no point carrying on. For all the four-way equality, an integral part of the band had died. Ian was the singer, the lyricist, the one with the ambition, the obsession and the vision. Yet, as Bernard confirmed, "There was never serious consideration of our not carrying on." That forced flippancy might suggest the survivors were losers who had nothing better in their sad lives and there was some truth in that, but these were also three colossally stubborn men, who'd invested their very existence in Joy Division being great. They had become brilliant at what they did, only to find tragedy had taken it from them. Perhaps a better question would have been, *why shouldn't* they carry on? The Monday after Ian's funeral, they went back to work. Hooky had even written a new song, "Dreams Never End". As Stephen said with characteristic unsentimental bluntness: "We were still alive, so we thought we'd carry on."

Carrying on looked so wrong – so crassly insensitive – but it was, unquestionably, the right thing to do. In 2020, Hooky told *Rolling Stone* with the perspective of forty years that "the first thing we did was disown Joy Division, in a really weird, grief-driven way. Now, it amazes me that we didn't take time off. When you're young, you feel if you don't do something quickly, someone's going to snatch it off you. Truth is, we could have had time off and New Order wouldn't have suffered. But we were drowning. We felt we needed to grasp at straws. I never had the thought – and I was surprised our manager did – that Joy Division would be more popular in five, ten, twenty, thirty, forty years, like The Doors. I just told him to fuck off."

There would be no immediate escape. As planned, "Love Will Tear Us Apart" was released in June. Martin Hannett was still so unsure of the best version that he insisted two went on the 7-inch, alongside the unusually mundane "These Days". "Ian sung it like Frank Sinatra to fuck us off," smiled Bernard. Designed before Ian died, with words etched by acid on metal, the sleeve was meant to look like a gravestone.

Despite misguided criticism of that sleeve, the song became the hit Ian had so desperately desired, reaching number thirteen. The mainstream was still alien territory. Radio 1's Dave Lee Travis (aka The Hairy Cornflake; catchphrase "quack, quack, oops") played the song on his breakfast show, Britain's most listened to radio programme. Having not heard the news that the song's singer had killed himself, he made a quip about how gloomy it was. Later, to his immense credit, he returned to the topic and apologised. And when the children's television programme Fun Factory aired the video of "Love Will Tear Us Apart" (kids' television! Ian would have been thrilled), the presenter cheerily reminded us that "Joy Division isn't a female vocalist, it's a band." Needless to say, they didn't mention the band's singer was dead.

On July 18, *Closer* was released and with it came immortality. Again, its sleeve did nobody

Bernard, LantarenVenster, Rotterdam, 16 January, 1980.

any favours. Bernard Pierre Wolff's photographs were of the Appiani family tomb in Genoa's Monumental Cemetery of Staglieno, a place where rich people competed with each other in death as they had in life. Designer Peter Saville hadn't heard a note of the album, but Ian had and he'd approved the sleeve.

It's possible to see *Closer* as a suicide note and not just in hindsight. If that seems too trite, it is, at least, one very troubled man confronting his demons. Although there's an argument that it's too much, too self-absorbed – again, Ian meant it like few others had meant it. But he had left adolescent misery behind: this was grown-up despair. *Closer* is not just Ian Curtis, though, Joy Division never was. Behind him: Bernard adding keyboards to some breathtakingly inventive guitar playing; Hooky far more subtle and intuitive than he chose to let on and Stephen, utilising electrodrums when the song took him there, but vying for prominence every step of the way. *Closer* marked the beginning of the end for Martin Hannett. This time, both Hooky and Bernard began to have reservations during rather than after the recording and, having found their studio feet, they both sparred with their overly controlling producer. Overall, the tempo was slower than *Unknown Pleasures*. This was deliberate and calculated: Ian was less likely to fit on stage during less frenetic songs.

"Atrocity Exhibition" took its title from a novel by JG Ballard, theoretically one of Ian's favourite authors, although he hadn't actually read most of the shape-shifting collection of interlinked tales. Hooky played guitar and would hate what he saw as Martin Hannett's reduction of it to "like someone strangling a cat." Bernard played bass, but the real star beyond Ian's chilling invocation of "this is the way, step inside" was Stephen's repetitive, circular drumming.

There was no guitar on "Isolation", just Hooky's bass, Bernard's impressive synthesisers (albeit toned down from the live incarnation) and Ian intoning to his mother "I'm ashamed of the things I've been put through/I'm ashamed of the person I am". What he felt he'd been put through wasn't clear, but again he was part victim, part perpetrator. "I remember thinking it was raw," Stephen admitted decades later. "But we thought he was writing dystopian science fiction, a future where everything is going wrong."

Hooky used a six-string bass on the deceptively lugubrious "Passover", a finger-pointing litany of betrayal, given added drama by Stephen's drumming at its most hypnotically metronomic, Bernard spraying magic everywhere and Hannett providing the musical claustrophobia.

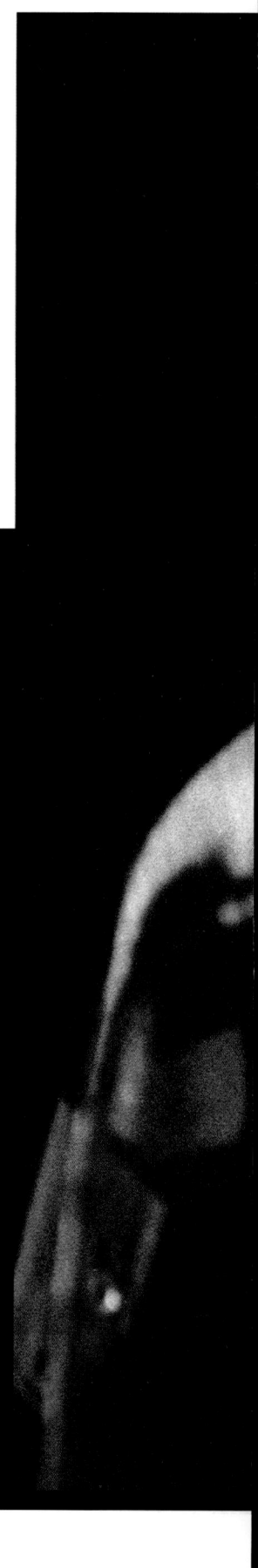

Right: *"Ian was something else, a force of nature dressed as a bank clerk, reaching into the very depths of his soul."*

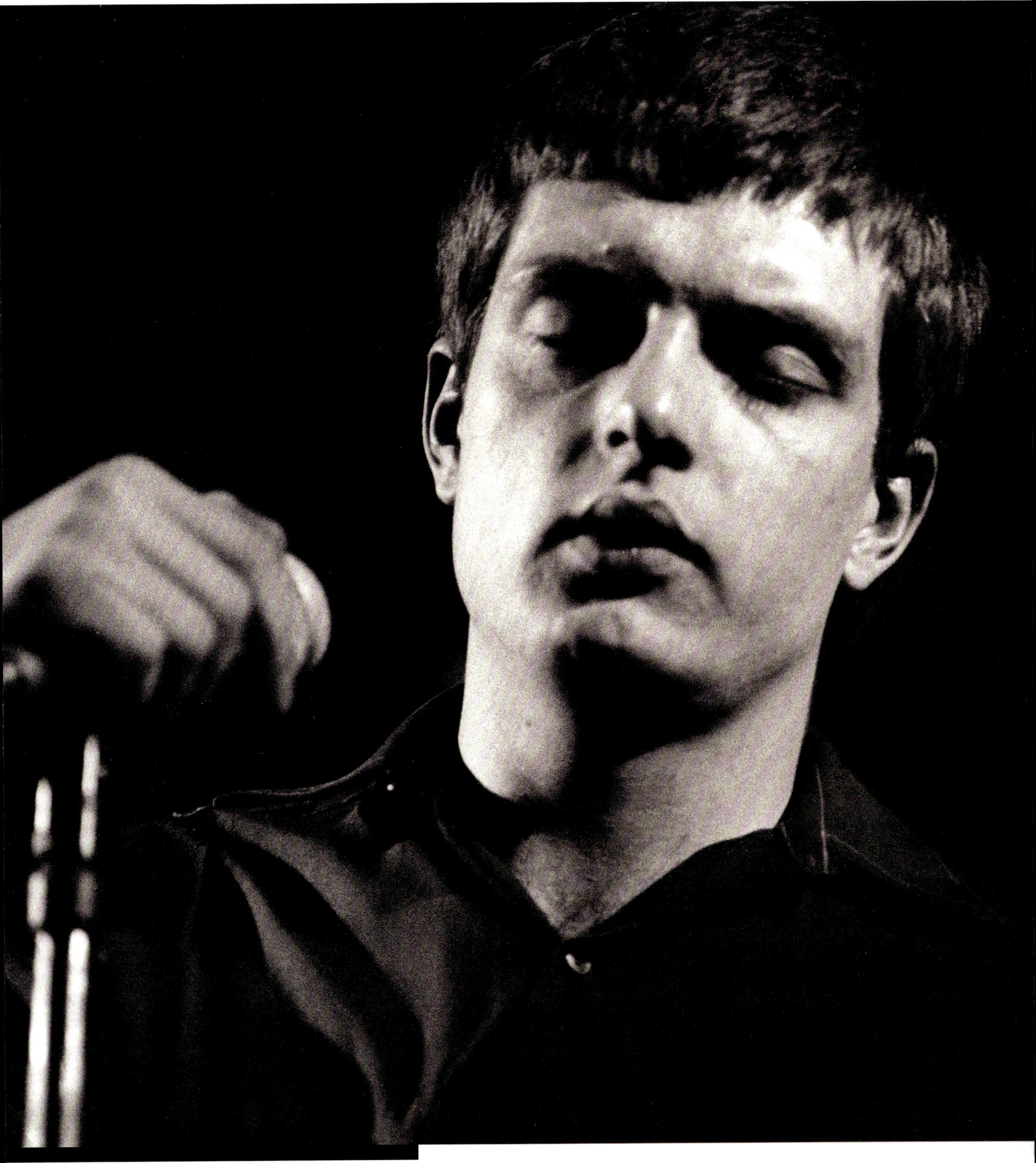

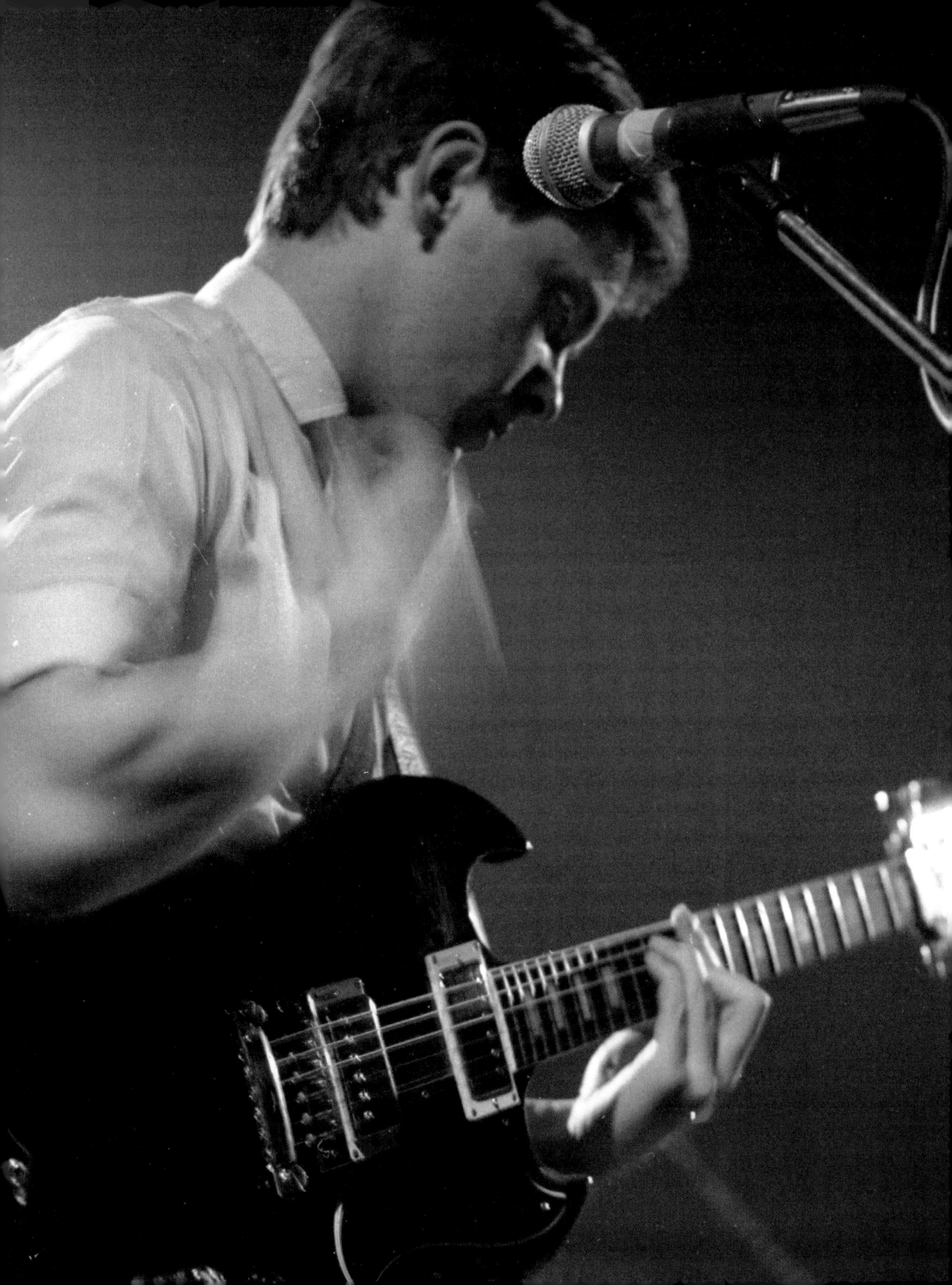

CLOSER

TRACK LISTING

Atrocity Exhibition
Isolation
Passover
Colony
A Means To An End

Heart And Soul
Twenty Four Hours
The Eternal
Decades

Released 18 July 1980
Label Factory – FACT 25
Recorded at Britannia Row, London, England
Produced by Martin Hannett
Personnel
Ian Curtis: lead vocals, guitar (track 6), melodica (track 9)
Bernard Sumner: guitar (all except tracks 1 and 6), bass guitar (track 1), synthesizers (tracks 2, 6, 8, and 9)
Peter Hook: bass guitar (all except track 1), guitar (track 1), 6-string bass guitar (tracks 3, 6, and 8)
Stephen Morris: drums (all except tracks 2 and 9), electronic drums (tracks 2, 4, 8, 9), percussion (all except track 2)
Cover Art Peter Saville
Notes
The album was voted number 1 in the 1980 Albums of the Year poll conducted by music magazine *NME* and was listed as number 157 upon the *Rolling Stone*'s list of the 500 Greatest Albums of All Time. In addition, *Q* magazine placed *Closer* at number 8 in a list compiled of the 40 greatest albums to be released in the 1980s. In 2012, *Slant* listed the album at number 7 in their compiled list of the best albums of the 1980s.

"They were supremely tightly drilled and not just in comparison with their sub-standard indie peers."

Franz Kafka's "In The Penal Colony" was a gruesome short story encompassing humiliation, torture, execution, abandonment and self-inflicted death. It loosely influenced Ian's lyrics to "Colony", another song detailing the very point of break-up and one of the two written before they went to London. Stephen's drums – a discreet homage to Captain Beefheart & The Magic Band's John French – are similar to the circular refrain of "Atrocity Exhibition", Bernard is unusually jagged and Hooky holds the whole thing together.

The pace quickened on "A Means To An End" which Hooky always interpreted as a pop song and not without good cause. Bernard had never strummed in such an anthemic fashion, Stephen's drums were disco ("It was us listening to Giorgio Moroder and not quite figuring out how to do it") and, while Ian was picking over the detritus of a crumbled relationship, he did accept that at one point "our vision touched the sky." Debbie or Annik or Joy Division? He never said and the band never asked.

"Heart and Soul" was Stephen at his most subtle; Ian at his most vocally hushed and on rudimentary guitar; Hooky at his most subdued and Bernard at his most glistening. It's rhythmic in a way Joy Division had never been, but New Order most certainly would be. They might have gone this way with Ian. After all, he couldn't have written a suicide note for too many more albums.

If *Closer* has a centrepiece it's "Twenty Four Hours", the second pre-written track. It's an astonishing achievement which starts slowly, builds into a torrent of despair before slumping back into acceptance of, in possibly Ian's best line, "a valueless collection of hopes and past desires". Like no other song, it's Joy Division all at once. Hooky's remorseless James Jamerson-style bass, the punky squall of Warsaw, Ian at the point of despair, Bernard going his own way and the collective ability to craft an earworm.

The longest tracks come at the end. Although the pace is typical of *Closer*, "The Eternal" is Martin Hannett rekindling the kid in the musical sweet shop who masterminded *Unknown Pleasures* and his demanding that Bernard play a grand piano was a master stroke. Perhaps uniquely on *Closer*, it's not wholly personal. One of Ian's childhood neighbours was a mentally disabled boy. On a return visit to Macclesfield, adult Ian saw the boy again. Although the neighbour boy was now a man, his world, his backyard and his mind remained unchanged. Eternal even.

Finally for *Closer* and finally for Joy Division, "Decades" was the only track they struggled to write and, since they used an electronic bass drum, to record. "A fucking struggle, it wasn't going anywhere," admitted Stephen. "Then it suddenly turned into a Martini advert. It was quite James Bondish." Perhaps, perhaps not, but *Closer* closed with the line "Where have they been?" and, although they didn't know it, Joy Division's recording life was over.

As with *Unknown Pleasures*, the band were disappointed, again blaming Martin Hannett.

Stephen said it was "a fucking disaster" and having heard the finished product before he died, Ian had written Rob a letter where he too used the word "disaster".

Outside the bubble, the reaction was universally positive. Again, *NME* was on the case: "Where they had presented a gleaming chiselled surface, now they are wreathed in mist. If Ian Curtis were still living, it would sound no less haunted. This music deals with terror and confronts it. It is as magnificent a memorial as any post-Presley popular musician could have." With the mystique already building around Ian, *Closer* sped to number six in the UK, becoming Britain's fastest selling indie album at the time.

George Michael, always a wise observer of what was happening musically around him, was full of reverence and the misplaced doubts of an outsider: "The second side of *Closer* is just beautiful. Their image was pretentious and contrived and it did have fascist elements to it. The way they were elevated after Ian Curtis's death was sick."

As ever, Hooky felt his bass had been downgraded, but by 2020 he was less paranoid. "Because of what happened, *Closer* always felt detached," he told *Rolling Stone*. "After a couple of years, it felt like the LP was by somebody else. I was only able to listen to it years later. It was really, really strange, but it became one of my favourite records."

"Debbie, Annik or Joy Division? Ian never said and the band never asked."

"THIS MUSIC DEALS WITH TERROR AND CONFRONTS IT. IT IS AS MAGNIFICENT A MEMORIAL AS ANY POST-PRESLEY POPULAR MUSICIAN COULD HAVE."

NME

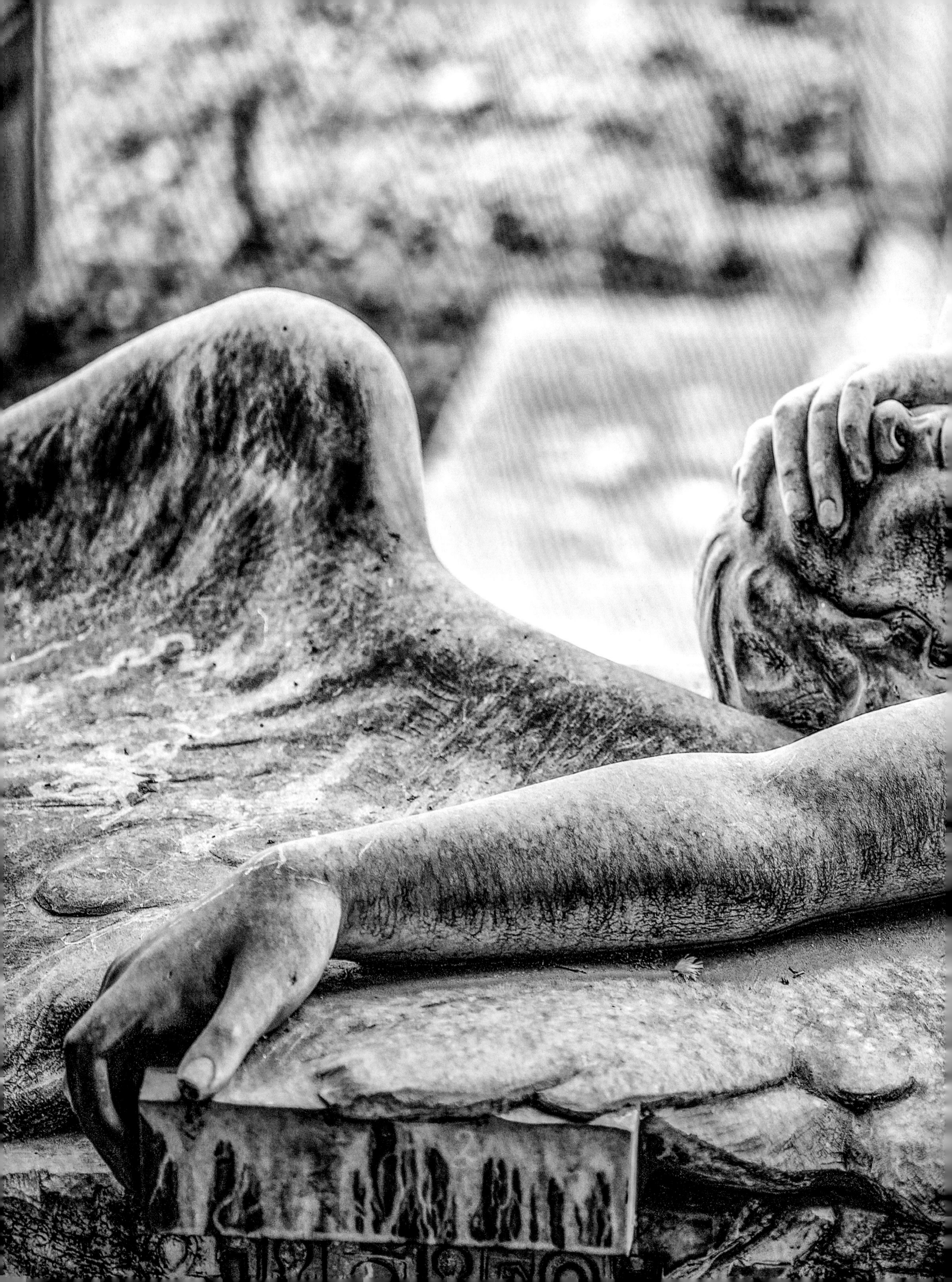

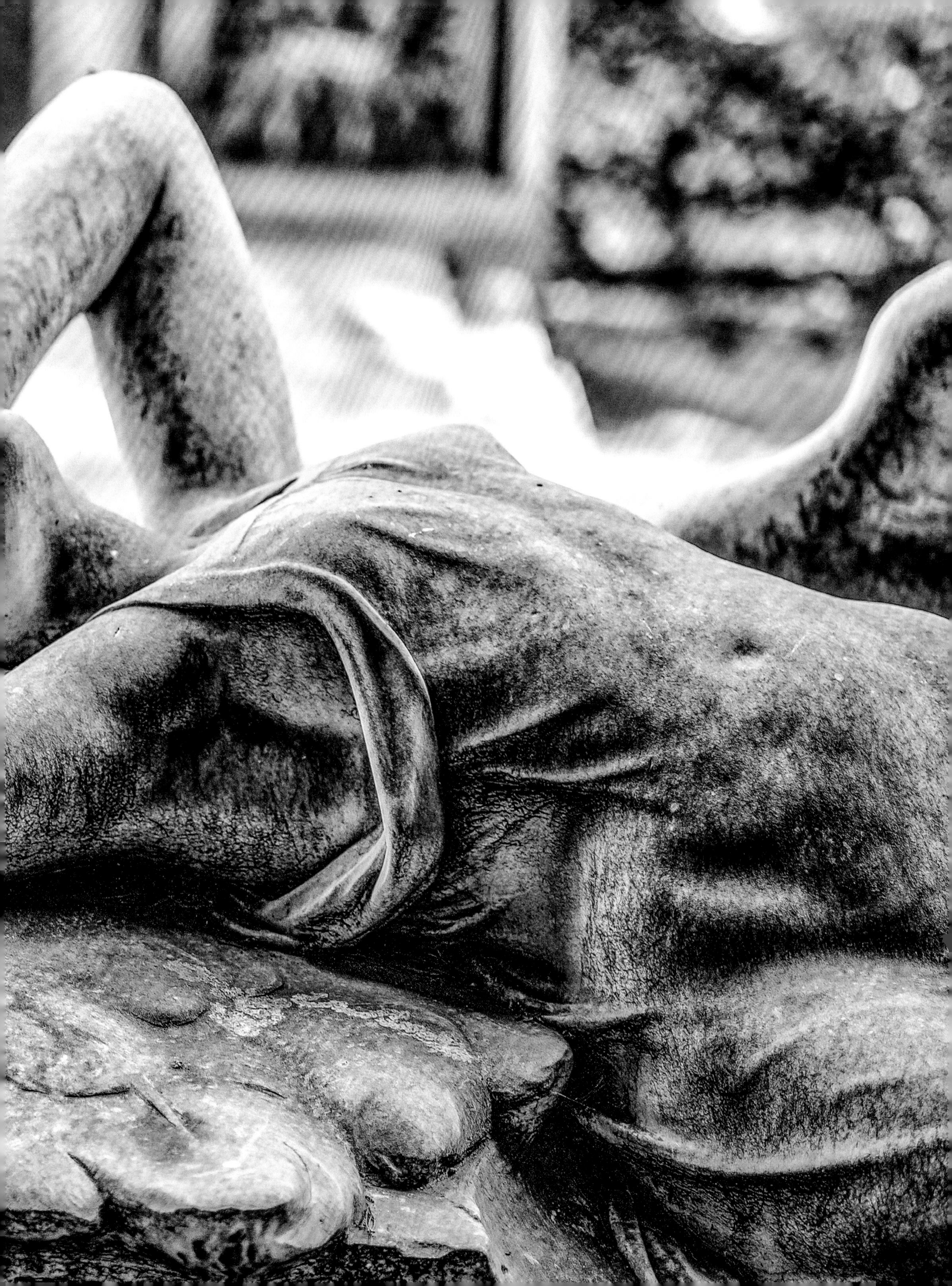

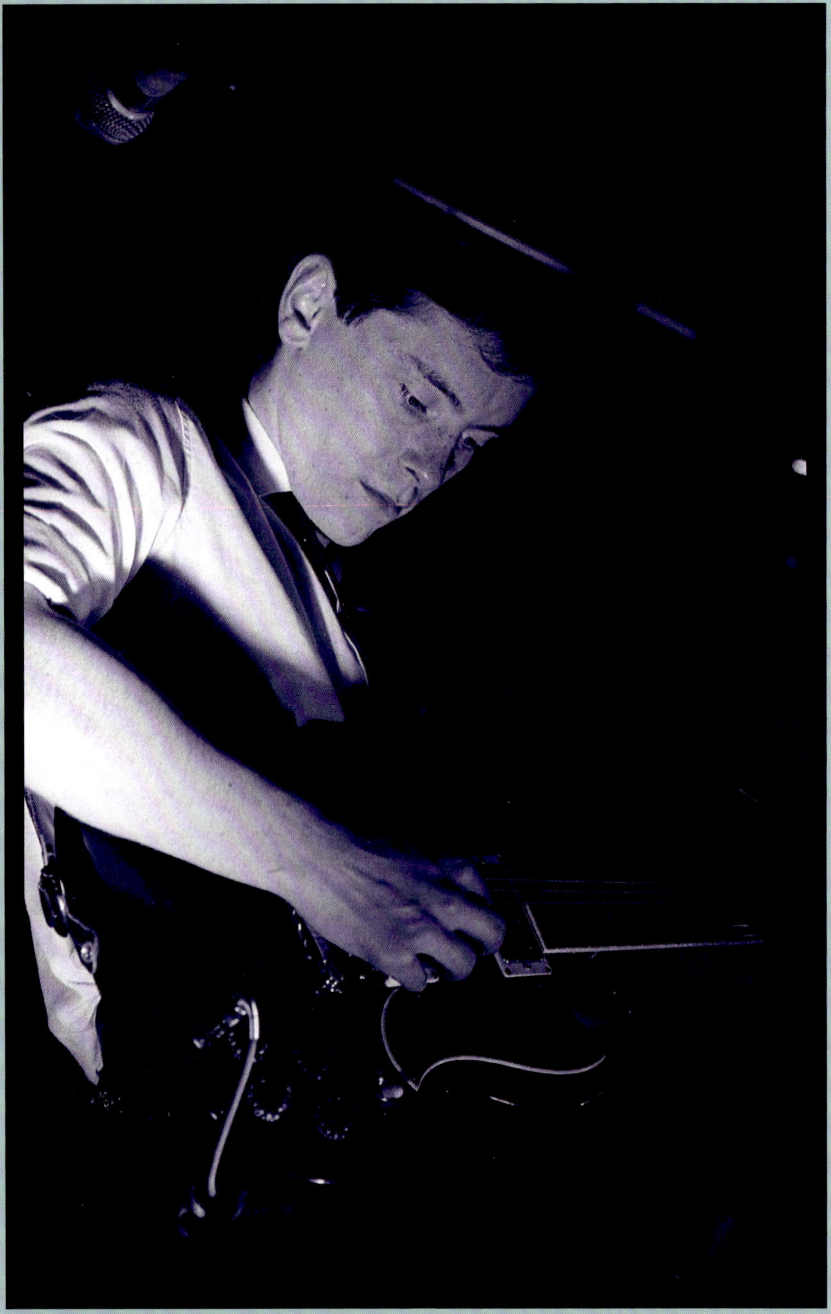

THE BEGINNING

THE BEGINNING

Before *Closer*'s release, but after Ian's inquest (Stephen and Hooky attended; Bernard did not), the threesome and Rob had gathered at Pinky's rehearsal space in Salford to take the formal decision to continue. Joy Division were indie behemoths, but the post-Ian rump were underdogs: they didn't have a singer, they didn't have a lyricist, they didn't even have a name.

Anyway, they rehearsed and Factory's Kevin Hewick, was tried out as singer on the day "Komakino", backed with "Incubation" and "As You Said", a free Joy Division flexi disc of passable but inconsequential *Closer* out-takes, was released in the first of two runs of 25,000.

Hewick was Tony Wilson's idea. The misunderstanding was mutual: the singer assumed they were backing him on his songs and the band assumed Hewick was auditioning for their singer's role. "I was picked up at Piccadilly Station by Bernard and Stephen in a really old car. They were friendly, good humoured and I soon felt at ease. For a while," Hewick recalled. He suggested one of Bernard's guitar solos was Buzzcockian and Bernard bizarrely took offence, but their version of Hewick's "Haystack", found its way onto the

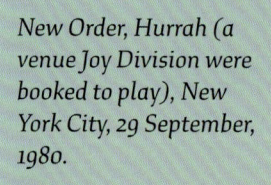

New Order, Hurrah (a venue Joy Division were booked to play), New York City, 29 September, 1980.

Grace Jones: very much in control.

84 Decades: Joy Division + New Order

From Brussels With Love cassette compilation in November. It is, by any yardstick, a shocker, not so much under-produced by Martin Hannett, as unproduced. A second song, "A Piece Of Fate" would be revisited by Hewick many years later as "No Miracle".

Later in June, the first Joy Division cover version appeared, when Grace Jones grappled with "She's Lost Control" and put it on the B-side of her first British hit, "Private Life". The eight-minute version finds Jones talking and then screaming over Alex Sadkin's dubby but unashamedly Hannett-esque way with a sound tableaux.

Seven weeks after Ian's death, the trio decided to chance a low-key gig in the early hours of July 30 at Manchester's sand-free Beach Club's Oozits night. They were meant to share the bill (not the stage, since there wasn't one) with Factory Benelux's The Names. "Even I was nervous," admitted Gillian Gilbert, Stephen's girlfriend, who was in the audience. When The Names pulled out, Bernard, Hooky and Stephen became No Names. "We were like Joy Division,

The Beginning 85

Hooky, Hurrah. Bass booming, beard burgeoning.

but with a big gap where Ian should have been," admitted Stephen. Rob insisted on drum machines but no backing tapes and no Joy Division material. Refusing to play Joy Division songs was as brave as it was foolish. "It seemed high and noble," rued Bernard, "but it made things much more difficult for us." There were drum machine failures, but "In A Lonely Place", "Ceremony", "Dreams Never End", "Truth" and a song nobody claims to remember offered what Bernard called "a glimmer of hope." Stephen sang three songs, while Bernard and Hooky had one apiece. If their aim had been to make a quiet return, they had unquestionably succeeded.

It was time to christen themselves. They sat in the Dover Castle pub (closed 2010) and mulled over assorted names of terrorist groups, Shining Path, Khmer Rouge, Black September, plus Sunshine Valley Dance Band. Eventually, the headline to a *Guardian* article about the Khmer Rouge was chanced upon: "The People's New Order of Kampuchea". New Order it was, then. "We just thought it sounded good," shrugged Hooky.

Once again, they were either wilfully courting controversy or they were genuinely ignorant of New Order being the term Adolf Hitler used to describe the potential future world run by him and his party. It was hard to sympathise with their having to fend off yet more accusations of far-right affiliations, although accusations of stupidity would have been closer to home.

The name sorted, it was now time to find a singer and lyricist. Eventually it would turn out to be the same man. The three-way vocal split wasn't really working, although Stephen did a memorably fine job with "Ceremony" at the next-but-one show in Blackpool's Scamps on September 3.

The following week they took themselves off to Sheffield to record some demos in a relaxed fashion at Cabaret Voltaire's Western Works studio. The relatively sophisticated Sheffielders introduced the New Order to curry. "In A Lonely Place", "Dreams Never End", "Procession", "Mesh", the remarkably jaunty "Homage" and "Truth" with a drum machine were developed, as was "Are You Ready For This", a slice of distorted electronica written with Cabaret Voltaire with Rob on unintelligible faux vocals – its obscurity is well-deserved. There was another issue, one which the band weren't ready to see yet. Joy Division had spawned a slew of copyists, but none more obvious than the band containing the former members of Joy Division.

All the same, they were ready to take another run at the United States. This time nothing would stop them. In New York, they met up with Tony Wilson and Martin Hannett who were recording Factory act A Certain Ratio's *To Each...* album in New Jersey. Ruth Polsky was now ensconced as their US booking agent. They stayed in the Iroquois hotel (Bernard, Hooky and Rob shared a room) alongside The Clash and British Airways lost everyone's bags except for Bernard's. Hooky claims they were on $3 a day, but after their first gig on American soil, at Maxwell's in Hoboken, New Jersey, they had $10,000 of equipment stolen from their van and when Rob admitted to the insurance company it hadn't been properly secured, the loss could not be recouped.

Replacement equipment was hired and Ruth Polsky, New York's Queen of Clubs, introduced these wide-eyed, unworldly Brits to the city's nightlife: Peppermint Lounge, Danceteria, Mudd Club, The Tunnel. "You had to wear a suit and tie to get in Manchester clubs and no trainers," Bernard mused. They even had a go at recording "Ceremony" with Martin Hannett. Bernard sang, but he'd never written Ian's lyrics down, so he guessed them. And his voice was so winsome, that Hannett had to use all sorts of studio skulduggery to render

A Certain Ratio, Heaven, London, 7 September, 1981.

him audible. Either way, the trip – especially the show at Hurrah, a venue Joy Division had been booked to play – was therapy, but also an early indication that they were in it for the long haul. On their return, it was decided that Bernard would be the singer, although lyrical contributions would still be three-way. Hooky claims Bernard elbowed his way into prominence. That seems a rather churlish view, although less disingenuous than Bernard's explanation for his ascension: "I have no idea why." In 2017, he was still ploughing the same furrow: "I never dreamed of being a singer, it never appealed to me. I didn't want to be the centre of attention. There was no alternative, other than fall into a life of nothingness."

Losing their equipment was a covert blessing. "A clean slate," said Stephen. They needed replacements, but the band were so intoxicated by the New York club scene, that they purchased in homage to it, going for syndrums and synthesisers rather than standard rock furniture. The results would change their lives, but not just yet.

Other than Rob buying new Alfa Romeos for Hooky and Bernard and a Volvo for Stephen, there was one further repercussion from the American trip. Bernard couldn't sing, play guitar and play keyboards live and he had no inclination to do so in the studio. They needed a fourth member, ideally on keyboards. Rob thought Stephen's girlfriend, Gillian Gilbert, the erstwhile "Inadequate" who'd been a member of Joy Division for one Liverpool night and whose band had loaned them equipment occasionally, could be the missing link. There was a major factor in her favour: she was musically inept. Others may have regarded it as a deal-breaker, but for New Order, it was a deal maker.

"We'd seen her, so we knew she couldn't play," chirped her boyfriend. The idea was that she would learn on the job, thus ensuring she was the perfect fit. After having learned the songs on her sister's Bontempi organ, she wouldn't be able to play any other way. "So long as it wasn't my girlfriend, she was easy to ignore," harrumphed Hooky, ungallantly. He did indeed mostly ignore her for the next three decades, but she was hardly a token member. "I was made to feel equal, so I didn't feel like an outsider. I was paid equally and my opinion was sought after," Gillian recalls. Years later, Stephen was less guarded: "It was awkward but the fact a lot of Joy Division fans didn't like it – 'they shouldn't be enjoying themselves!' – was a great thing to me."

"Nobody expected a girl," Gillian admitted in 2020. "They expected another singer. It got better, but going to Japan in the '80s for

"I WAS MADE TO FEEL EQUAL, SO I DIDN'T FEEL LIKE AN OUTSIDER. I WAS PAID EQUALLY AND MY OPINION WAS SOUGHT AFTER."

GILLIAN

photoshoots was a real shock because they didn't want to talk to me. They'd say to the male members, 'Can you tell her to move?' That was how they treated women. I was in the background a lot of the time."

Born on 27 January, 1961 in Manchester's Whalley Range suburb, Gillian Lesley Gilbert's family had moved to Macclesfield when she was a girl, but once she'd graduated in graphic design from Stockport Technical College, she moved into the twilight world of the Manchester indie scene. By the time she joined New Order, she was living with Stephen in the Salford district of Peel Green.

Gillian Gilbert, Bedford Boys Club, 21 March, 1981. "She couldn't really play, but that was the point."

On October 25, one day after Factory became a limited company (New Order's 20% shareholding was held in Rob's name: other shareholders were Tony Wilson, Alan Erasmus, Martin Hannett and Peter Saville), their first gig as a fourpiece took place at Manchester's The Squat, supporting Durutti Column. With a set list of just seven songs spread over twenty-one minutes (short shows would become the source of much fan disgruntlement as the years passed), it was hardly a big deal and such was Bernard's nervousness at having to sing, he overdid his favourite tipple, Pernod. However, less than six months after Ian's demise, Joy Division's survivors had regrouped, found a name, found a singer, played the United States and found the line-up which would bring them global success. To celebrate, they had another go at recording "Ceremony" at Strawberry, this time with Gillian. All they had to do now was stop sounding like Joy Division impersonators. That would take more time.

The first New Order release, "Ceremony" (with a B-side featuring "In A Lonely Place", arguably the most suicidal of Ian's lyrics: "The hangman looks round as he waits/Gullet stretches tight and it breaks"), appeared in January 1981. The less bassy version with Gillian on guitar would be released in September. That they went with two Joy Division songs – albeit two wonderful ones – was the first indication that there was musical trouble brewing.

As if to show just how hard Joy Division's shadow would be to cast off, the esteemed writer Julie Burchill, unaware of their author, derided the lyrics to "Ceremony" as not being

90 Decades: Joy Division + New Order

Barney, Bedford Boys Club: takeover imminent...

up to Ian's standard. The song itself was a glorious, elegiac statement of intent, which both mourned the past and embraced the future. It stumbled to number thirty-four in the UK charts. In 2020 Hooky offered real perspective. "Ian left us with a wonderful present: 'Ceremony' and 'In A Lonely Place'. They burn with that question of what Joy Division could have gone on to achieve. I always loved Bernard's very, very fragile vocal to 'Ceremony', because it didn't take over, it was just an integral part of the music."

Now it was time to make the debut album. There were portents that it might not be as easy or as quick as the Joy Division albums. "Haystack" was a pointer to where those problems might lie. Martin Hannett, always Ian's biggest fan, had sneered at the Kevin Hewick sessions. "Fairport Convention" was his mildly bonkers assessment and he spent more time asleep under his desk than working. His drug intake had not diminished. Oh, and these new songs New Order were writing and playing... Can we be blunt? They weren't as good as Joy Division's.

No matter, they all assembled at Cargo, Rochdale, in January with the road-tested material. The whole grim process would trundle on for seven months. There would be distractions such as recording overdubs on Joy Division's "The Kill" and "The Only Mistake" at Britannia Row. There would be gigs such as Heaven in London where Martin Hannett's attempts at live sound were catastrophic and the one in Sheffield at Romeo & Juliet's which Annik and this author attended. That Annik was present and would later promote New Order shows in Belgium, suggested there had been some softening of opinion on both sides. That Sheffield show was a nervy affair, dominated by the songs they didn't play – that is anything by Joy Division. Neither band nor respectful audience knew quite how to behave during the brief, awkward set. As Stephen had intimated, we were all overpowered by the space where Ian should have been.

There was a European tour with all-girl group Malaria: "great because we copped off with most of them," claimed Hooky and there was almost a riot in Hamburg when the local skinheads were somewhat disappointed by a thirty-five minute set with no encore. They invaded the band's dressing room and invited them to return to the stage. One lengthy, jam-tastic version of the new "Everything's Gone Green" later, and everyone was happy-ish.

There were outside productions: Hooky for Blackpool's Tunnelvision, who'd supported New Order in Sheffield; Bernard for more Section 25 after he'd supplied guitar for Martin Hannett's production of Pauline Murray and The Invisible Girls' lovely "Searching For Heaven" single; Stephen and Gillian for Thick Pigeon.

And at the newly named Glastonbury Festival, they were second on the bill to Hawkwind on Saturday night. They used new promoter Michael Eavis's farmhouse as a dressing room. They played just eight songs, stubbornly omitting "Ceremony", but including the obvious step-forward from Hamburg, "Everything's Gone Green". It wasn't a great success. "We'd never played anything as huge before. It was so big I couldn't look at the audience," remembered Gillian.

"Glastonbury was nothing like it is now," added Stephen. "The Pyramid Stage was built

**NEW ORDER
CEREMONY
IN A LONELY PLACE
FAC. 33**

The Beginning 91

on top of the cowsheds, the backstage area was half a dozen Transit vans parked up and we all had a cup of tea at Michael Eavis's house after we finished. But it did have that special atmosphere. Unfortunately, Bernard over-imbibed on Pernod again and halfway through one song fell over and started playing guitar on his back."

In between all this, Hannett's increasingly bizarre behaviour – he refused to commence working until a gram of cocaine had been secured – and the band's lack of confidence combined to ensure recordings at a succession of studios went badly.

Ian's producer had come to terms with Ian's death less successfully than Ian's band.

"Martin was bombastic, bitter and antagonistic," explained Hooky. "He kept saying 'I wish you'd died instead of Ian' to us."

There were musical differences too. In March, the band declared themselves unhappy with Hannett's work. The former master of the drum sound hadn't put enough drums in the mixes. Crucially, Rob backed the musicians for the first time and from there the balance of power shifted irrevocably. Increasingly addled, Hannett spent his days hiding in a cupboard, refusing to emerge unless he heard something he liked.

On May 8 at Reading University, New Order granted their first encore. Later that month, they granted *Melody Maker* their first proper interview.

Hooky: the fondly remembered zips on pockets phase...

"MARTIN WAS BOMBASTIC, BITTER AND ANTAGONISTIC. HE KEPT SAYING 'I WISH YOU'D DIED INSTEAD OF IAN' TO US."

HOOKY

Rob was never happy when his charges spoke. "Rob did not speak much," explained Hillegonda Rietveld, wife of Haçienda booker and future M-People leader Mike Pickering, a one-time football-watching friend of Rob's. "Partly due to shyness, but also because the 'non-marketing' of New Order had shown the less you say, the more the myth will develop."

Still battered by Ian's death, they veered between Hooky at his most blasé: "I didn't really take a lot of notice of Ian. I couldn't give up just because he died." And Bernard at his most considerate: "I will never be able to cope with Ian's death. It will affect me now and forever. Some people are hard-skinned about life, but Ian was not. He was a good person, he wasn't a twat. That's how you should judge people: whether they're a good person or a twat." In July, the album was finally finished.

First, though, there was other business to attend. Inspired by the success of the Factory night at the Russell Club and the dip into New York club culture which had the air of an office outing, Factory decided to acquire themselves a nightclub. The band didn't look at the financial implications any more than they had looked at Ian's lyrics. Of the Factory shareholders, Rob and Tony Wilson were heavily in favour. The band was passive. Alan Erasmus (quietly) and Martin Hannett (noisily) were against it. Peter Saville had the casting vote. He said yes and in July 1981, leases were signed on a former warehouse on Whitworth Street West. The Haçienda – catalogue number FAC51 – would be the gift that never gave.

In September, a new single, "Procession" reached number thirty-eight in the British charts. Recorded during the album sessions, Martin Hannett had insisted on over forty vocal takes and when the band assembled the *Retro* box set in 2002, a still-traumatised Bernard claimed never to have heard the song, let alone sung on it. Stephen played keyboards and wrote most of the lyrics, while Gillian added divine backing vocals. The B-side was "Everything's Gone Green". Bernard played Ian's guitar, but it ended their relationship with Martin Hannett, who walked out halfway through the torturous sessions ("We said we wanted more drums, more drive, he said 'fuck off' and walked out") as the battle between the act's punk and electro inclinations and the producer's quest for texture began in earnest. "We had a totally different sound in our heads," mused Bernard.

They would write better, less dense, more nimbly produced, more successful songs, but this pivotal release heralded a new New Order and Tony Wilson claimed "Everything's Gone

"I WILL NEVER BE ABLE TO COPE WITH IAN'S DEATH. IT WILL AFFECT ME NOW AND FOREVER. SOME PEOPLE ARE HARD-SKINNED ABOUT LIFE, BUT IAN WAS NOT."

BERNARD

Green" was "the most important song in the modern world." It was their first sequencer-driven sortie into electronic dance and when the initially instrumental "Temptation" made its live debut in Helsinki on September 19 as work began on the Haçienda site, the way ahead became clear. "I felt frustrated I couldn't play and sing at the same time, but I could programme a sequencer to play what I couldn't," acknowledged Bernard.

As a further distraction, on October 8, there was another Joy Division album, the bootlegger-quashing, but completist-thwarting *Still*, which was a number five hit in the UK. A double, initially with an unpleasant to touch hessian sleeve, it gathered out-takes from assorted sessions, such as the recently overdubbed "The Kill" and "The Only Mistake". There was "Dead Souls" (but scandalously not "Atmosphere") and a live splurge through The Velvet Underground's "Sister Ray" from London's Moonlight Club, where Ian made a joke of sorts afterwards "you should hear our version of 'Louie Louie', whoa."

Morbidly, there was also that last Joy Division concert in Birmingham. The recording is patchy ("Ceremony" starts halfway through) and only a fabulous "Isolation" and Ian's death elevate it to essential. *Still* is no *Unknown Pleasures* or *Closer*, but it enhanced rather than diminished the legacy.

There was another trip to the United States, where Simple Minds played some supports. The ever-priapic Hooky began an affair with Ruth Polsky ("She was the first person to give me cocaine," remembered Hooky. "I blew it all over the floor, Woody Allen-style") and the band began a long-term relationship with Michael Shamberg who would become Factory's man in the US and play cupid between New Order and directors Kathryn Bigelow and Jonathan Demme. The absence of an encore ignited (another) riot, this time in Boston, but perhaps more importantly, in San Francisco, Hooky discovered an exotic new food: pizza.

Bernard and Stephen, Hurrah, New York: the guitarist on melodica; the drummer on sytnthesiser...

On their return, the debut album, *Movement*, was released in time for the Christmas market. It would only reach a desperately disappointing thirty in the British charts. By the time *Movement* reached the shops, New Order had outgrown it and were no longer stodgy Joy Division soundalikes. Reception was muted and they missed Ian so very, very desperately, although it's far from the lumpen disaster it was perceived as in 1981.

Peter Saville's cover – so delayed that Hooky was dispatched to London to encourage him to finish – was based on a design by the Italian futurist, Fortunato Depero, but the music was regressive. There was no room for the singles of course and the overall sense was of Joy Division wannabees attempting to flee Martin Hannett's murk.

Hooky sang "Dreams Never End", the song he'd written immediately after Ian's death. There's optimism in the "No looking back now, we're pushing through" line, some cheery, Cure-style guitar and the sense that things might work out. As an opener it established a template for a mood which failed to appear again.

The dystopian "Truth" is so Joy Division-esque it could have been an out-take from either album. There's a melodica, Bernard's buried vocals and, for the first time, a drum machine. Ian's genius was the missing X factor

The Beginning 95

and the survivors had lost their melodic way. "Stephen was very resistant to drum machines and synthesisers, but when he realised it wasn't going to put him out of a job, he embraced it and became extremely proficient," remembered Bernard.

Oddly, since it was the only time he built a soundscape, Hannett was especially averse to "Senses", one of the *Movement* moments that did look forwards. With hindsight, it was the bridge between *Closer* and "Blue Monday". The drums – the bone of contention between band and producer – were immense, the bass floor-quaking and the guitars wild.

"Chosen Time" was recorded mostly live apparently and its urgency would form part of the electronic sea-change to come, but Bernard is barely audible on vocals.

"ICB" was rumoured to stand for "Ian Curtis Buried". It sort of did. In fact, it came from the company tasked with transporting New Order's flight cases on the first American jaunt. Hooky made the off-colour gag and a song title was born. Fragments were written in the Joy Division era and it sounds like something they were working up for *Closer* which didn't quite make the cut.

According to Hooky, Bauhaus built their breakthrough "Bela Lugosi's Dead" on the bassline to "The Him". He might have a point, but when it gets busy, it gets better. Suggestions it's about Ian seem fanciful.

Hooky's second vocal, "Doubts Even Here" was formerly titled "Tiny Tim" and Bernard didn't like it at all. Stephen wrote the lyrics but refused to sing them, Gillian did a spoken word

Michel Duval of Les Disques du Crepusclue and Michael Shamberg of Factory US.

turn in the background and the lugubrious pace gave it a seeming depth it didn't really justify.

The closing track, "Denial" began with upbeat drums and chiming guitar, but like so much of *Movement*, it doesn't really go anywhere beyond its opening flurry.

The reception for *Movement* was lukewarm but respectful. Not because the new direction had only been fleetingly embraced – it was only one little-heard single at this point – but because Joy Division were untouchable and by extension New Order were owed autopilot reverence. Even so, nobody pretended *Movement* was a classic and *Trouser Press*'s Stephen Grant said out loud what others were thinking: "it is unlikely New Order will ever shake off Joy Division's shadow." The *NME*'s Danny Baker's met head with nail when he said of *Movement*: "it's terrifically dull."

The band knew. Album tracks often comprised less than half the songs played on the US dates and as the years rolled by, their

> "IT IS UNLIKELY NEW ORDER WILL EVER SHAKE OFF JOY DIVISION'S SHADOW."
>
> STEPHEN GRANT, *NME*

MOVEMENT

TRACK LISTING

Dreams Never End	ICB
Truth	The Him
Senses	Doubts Even Here
Chosen Time	Denial

Released 19 November 1981
Label Factory – FACT 50
Recorded at Strawberry Studios, Stockport, England
Produced by Martin Hannett
Personnel
Bernard Sumner: vocals, guitars, melodica, synthesizers and programming
Peter Hook: 4- and 6-stringed bass, vocals ("Dreams Never End" and "Doubts Even Here")
Stephen Morris: drums, synthesizers and programming
Gillian Gilbert: synthesizers and programming, guitars, spoken words ("Doubts Even Here")
Cover Art Grafica Industria + Peter Saville
Notes
The artwork, by Peter Saville, is based on a poster by Italian Futurist Fortunato Depero for the 1932 exposition "Futurismo Trentino". Saville adapted it so that the 'F' stands for Factory and the 'L' (Roman numeral) for 50. The album colour in the UK was blue with blue artwork, while in the US it was white with burgundy artwork.

The Beginning

true feelings emerged. Bernard: "*Movement* did my head in... people were interested in us because we were Joy Division. The burden was that we couldn't actually be Joy Division." Stephen: "It was horrible to make, I couldn't listen to it for ages."

Hooky was more considered. "It's bad because of the production, not the songs. *Unknown Pleasures* bothered me a lot more because I had very strong ideas and it ended up completely different. Everybody thought it was bloody great which was even more upsetting. The end product of *Movement* was diabolical though. Listening to it was like Ian dying all over again."

There wasn't a great re-appraisal of where New Order were going, not least since New Order weren't ones to appraise in the first place. More crucially, there was nothing to re-appraise, since they already knew where they were headed. "Everything's Gone Green" re-emerged as an A-side in thrillingly extended fashion, albeit in mainland Europe only, alongside "Cries and Whispers" – where Martin Hannett's quest for vocal perfection had forced Bernard himself to flounce out – and the uninspiring "Mesh". Factory muddled up the order of the B-sides on the sleeve.

So, while 1981 was a let-down, it was catharsis too. 1982 would be the year they cast off their fetters and began to enjoy themselves. "We knew we were getting somewhere when Joy Division fans were disgusted with us," chuckled Stephen.

With his Factory shareholder hat on, Martin Hannett rebelled and took out a lawsuit, citing financial mismanagement – not least spending £50,000 on The Haçienda rather than £30,000 on a Fairlight synthesiser – and board practices which took place "without Hannett's consent or knowledge." The suit attempted to have Factory wound up. It would be settled in 1984 with a £40,000 payment to Hannett and it was given its own Factory catalogue number, FAC61.

Bernard and Hooky, Manchester Polytechnic, 6 February, 1981.

98   Decades: Joy Division + New Order

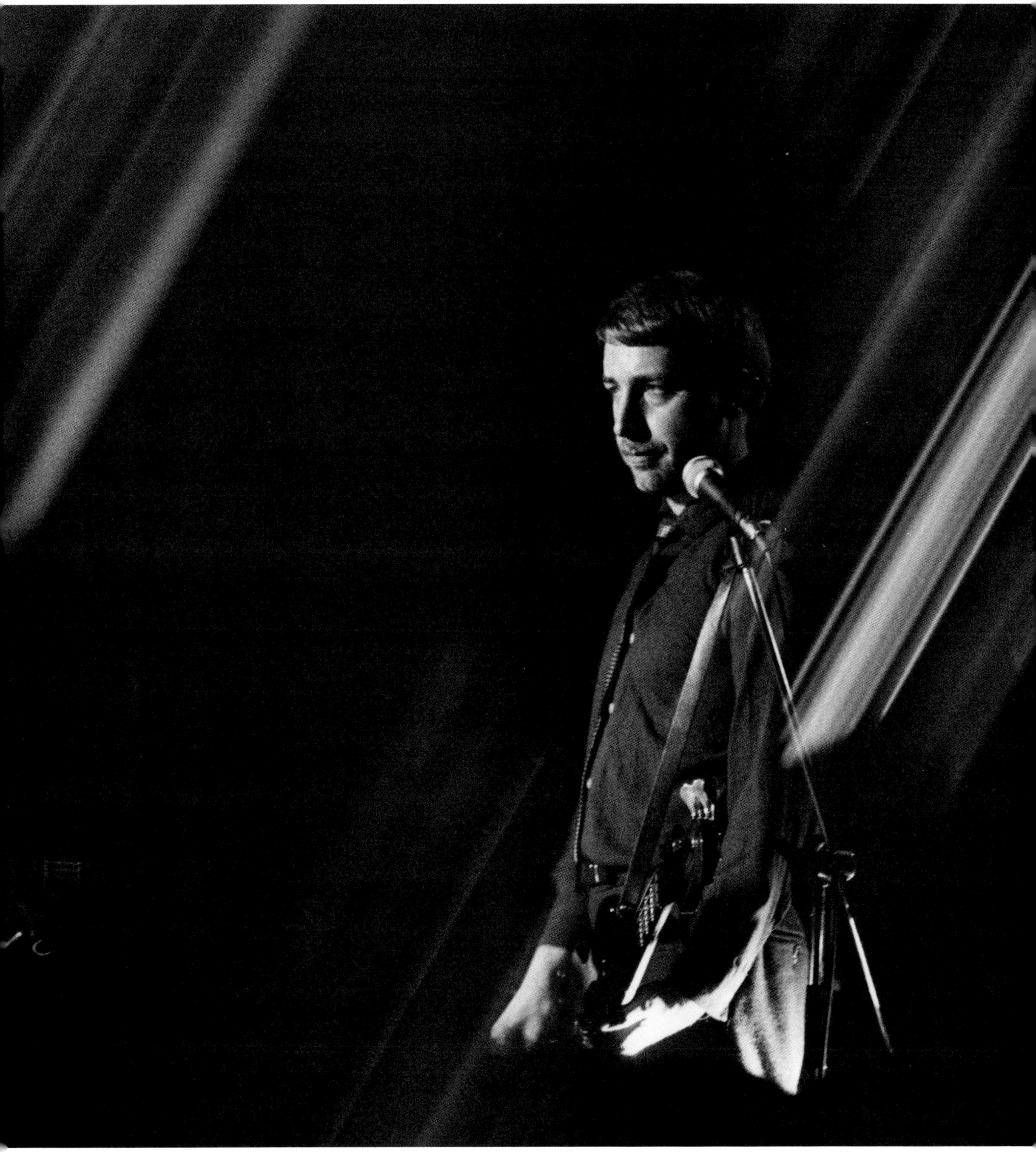

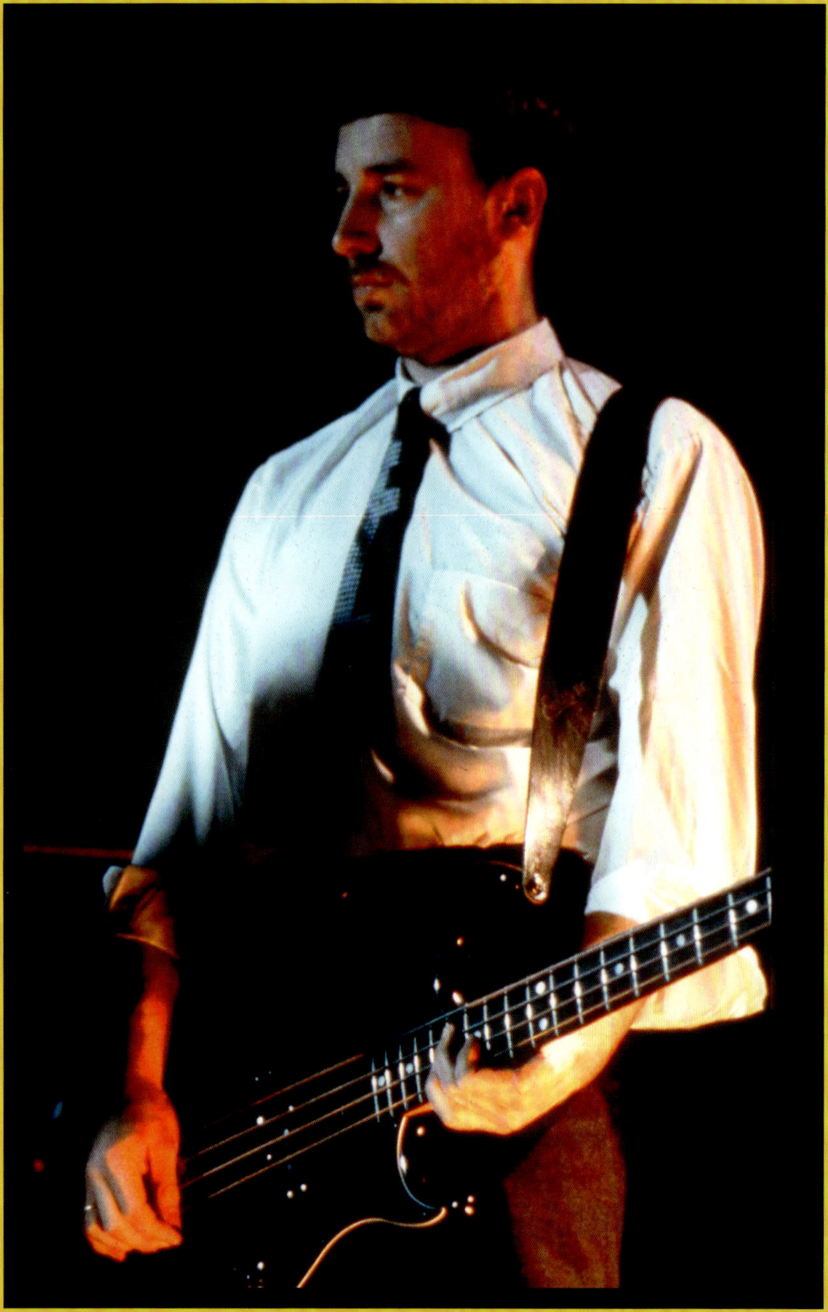

MONDAY
MONDAY

MONDAY MONDAY

Now it was time to self-produce and to make flesh their dreams of indie dance revolution. As he had during the making of *Closer*, Bernard had been listening to the clean, yet always emotional, work Giorgio Moroder had crafted with Donna Summer and Sparks, whose magical, Moroder-produced "When I'm With You" would be a very occasional New Order cover.

"Temptation" would change everything and despite its improvised lyrics and the fact that it only reached twenty-nine in the UK charts, it remains their most played song live. Stephen quickly tired of it and Bernard would come to see it as more curse than blessing, but when he described it as "transcendent and exultant" he was right. Such was the feeling of freewheeling joy in the camp at the time of recording that when Bernard, mindset slightly altered after ingesting some LSD, squealed after Hooky stuffed a snowball down his shirt in the studio, it made the final cut. Significantly, the song was a regional hit in New York as it rose to sixty-eight in the Billboard Dance Chat. A tiny step, but a step all the same.

The Haçienda opened in May, "like a spaceship had landed in Manchester," purred Bernard. Joy Division's miserable Stranglers support slot resonated and, as a result, bands who performed there were treated excellently, which at least offset how terrible they sounded. The club needed 200 people a night to cover lighting and heating, but, as ever, Hooky had his own rationale: "I never used to get in anywhere. This was the first club you could get in dressed as you liked. And I had to fucking open it."

Haçienda DJ, Dave Haslam, possibly the most erudite and trustworthy chronicler of New Order's Manchester, summed up The Haçienda years in *Barmcake* in 2020. "There were three phases. 1982–87 was gigs, mostly good bands but not very full. 1987–90 saw the rise of the DJs and it was a different world: DJs not bands; acid house rather than alternative rock; upbeat instead of dour; busy instead of empty. 1991–97 was a slow death, with a few bright moments like the monthly gay night, *Flesh*."

Donna Summer (left) and Giorgio Moroder.

"I NEVER USED TO GET IN ANYWHERE. THIS WAS THE FIRST CLUB YOU COULD GET IN DRESSED AS YOU LIKED. AND I HAD TO FUCKING OPEN IT."

HOOKY

Sparks singer Russell Mael, London, 1979.

For now, though, it was back to the day job. A John Peel session (such was New Order's new clout, it was recoded in Manchester rather than London) featured a melodica-infused, dreamy cover of Keith Hudson's "Turn The Heater On" which honoured Ian's love of reggae and "Too Late", which they would never play live and was subsequently discarded forever. Hooky claimed Bernard didn't like the bassist's vocal take, but the great lost New Order song isn't actually that great a loss.

In June there were dates in the Joy Division stronghold of Italy, where audience members held Ian Curtis placards. In the pre-internet days of the '80s, music videos were big. August saw *A Factory Video*, to which New Order provided so-so live versions of "Ceremony" and "In A Lonely Place". Later, in September, Joy Division's *Here Are The Young Men* included performances from two October 1979 Manchester Apollo shows and selections from another in Eindhoven three months later. The *NME* were in the mood for a scathing backlash. They rightly cited the shoddy camerawork of something that was never really intended to be commercially available, but idiotically claimed that "Ian Curtis was not the most charismatic of performers" and berated the "lapses into the ponderous dirge for which the group is often remembered."

A second album seemed like a good idea. In October, New Order rented a flat at 15 Basil Street, Kensington, close to Hyde Park, but the other side of London from Britannia Row, which still met their needs as a studio. The commuting distance would cause problems. Hooky was a man of regular working hours, Bernard preferred to work from midday to 2 a.m. The band were splitting into camps for the first time.

"After 'Everything's Gone Green' and 'Temptation', we knew how we wanted to sound," said Gillian to *NME* in 2020. "We wanted to move it along in our own way rather than how a producer might. We were left alone and came up with our own sound. Recording in London meant we could concentrate more because we were in our own little world."

Recording took seven reasonably harmonious weeks ("our honeymoon period," remembered Hooky) although since they wrote the music first, the still-collectively created lyrics were rather rushed. They emerged with an album and a lively track called "Blue Monday".

November saw the release of *1981–1982*, a calling card EP for the American market with a sleeve painting by Martha Ladly, Peter Saville's then girlfriend, once one of the two Marthas in Martha and The Muffins and later a Professor of Design back in her home, Toronto. The track listing took in "Temptation", "Everything's Gone Green", "Procession", "Mesh" and "Hurt" – the clattering B-side to "Temptation" which was formerly, and more impressively, titled "Cramp".

There were dates in Australia and New Zealand and a free Christmas flexi disc comprising "Rocking Carol" – a hideous synth plink with distorted vocals threatening "We will rock you, rock you, rock you" – and a similarly twisted, vocal take on Beethoven's "Ode to Joy". "Guaranteed to ruin anyone's Christmas," quipped Stephen. There were few arguments there.

Bernard's son James (after his stepfather, Jim) was born in early 1983. Bernard himself was now legally Sumner again, an upgrade on his

> "AFTER 'EVERYTHING'S GONE GREEN' AND 'TEMPTATION', WE KNEW HOW WE WANTED TO SOUND."
>
> GILLIAN

Stephen Morris, Bernard Sumner, Peter Hook and Gillian Gilbert, 1982.

Monday Monday 105

previous surname that was mostly convenient slang for penis or the other that honoured the location of the SS's headquarters.

In February, at the suggestion of Michael Shamberg, they went to New York to record with producer Arthur Baker. Fresh from Afrika Bambaataa and The Soul Sonic Force's groundbreaking collaboration, the Kraftwerk-drenched "Planet Rock", Baker was arguably the world's hippest producer. New Order relished the opportunity to work with an outsider they unreservedly admired. Baker's motivations were more complex: "the fact they make depressing sounding records isn't what attracted me, but I do not write happy music myself. My songs are based on reality, on human emotions and that's what I liked about their stuff."

The band had to wait while Baker finished Freeez's "IOU" and when they finally began work his methods were alien to the Brits. The far from Stakhanovite New Order wanted to remix a new album track, "586". Baker told Michael Shamberg it was "shit" and wanted a new song. Baker won: he sat them down and ordered them to write something on the spot. They panicked and presented him with ten unedited hours of music, assuming Baker would sift through the lot and select what he fancied. He had been expecting a snappy chorus and a title.

First, though, "Blue Monday", the moment New Order changed the course of music. Mostly written at their oft-burgled new rehearsal base at Cheetham Hill set in the heart of North Manchester's ganglands, its title came less from Fats Domino's classic song and more from *Breakfast Of Champions*, the Kurt Vonnegut novel Stephen had been reading. The novel had

Hooky, Capital Theatre, Sydney, 29 November, 1982. John Cooper Clarke supported.

Kraftwerk, SF Festival, Rotterdam, 21 March, 1976.

an alternative title, *Goodbye Blue Monday*, which referred to washday.

Lyrically, it was the first time Bernard embraced the sea as a place of refuge and escape, but its genesis was practical. To counter the negative, sometimes violent, audience response that refusing to play encores brought, they intended to play it without being present, inspired by Kraftwerk who had replaced themselves on stage with robot replacements when they played their single "The Robots". Early versions of "Blue Monday" had a soon-to-be-dumped robot voice. Hooky played bass, Bernard played synth-bass and they were influenced by a cornucopia of delicious sounds: the beat to Donna Summer's "Our Love"; Sylvester's mighty "You Make Me Feel (Mighty Real)"; fellow Mancunians Gerry & The Holograms' "Meet the Dissidents"; Kraftwerk's "Uranium" which was sampled; and Klein & M.B.O's "Dirty Talk". Reaction was overwhelmingly positive. "I nearly burst into tears," sighed Pet Shop Boy Neil Tennant. "This was so much what we were trying to do."

"People said it didn't sound like New Order, which was a great confidence boost. It was like when Bob Dylan went electric," declared Bernard. "We got a lot of backlash after Joy Division, because we weren't very good. 'Blue Monday' shut everyone up." What could possibly go wrong? Only at Factory…

Deadlines meant that Peter Saville's sleeve had been sent to the printers with very little in the way of formal approval. Meant to mimic the new-fangled floppy disc, the holes in the first pressing of the sleeve had to be punched individually. This meant that the label lost 10 pence (Tony Wilson claimed 5 pence) on each

"WE GOT A LOT OF BACKLASH AFTER JOY DIVISION, BECAUSE WE WEREN'T VERY GOOD. 'BLUE MONDAY' SHUT EVERYONE UP."

BERNARD

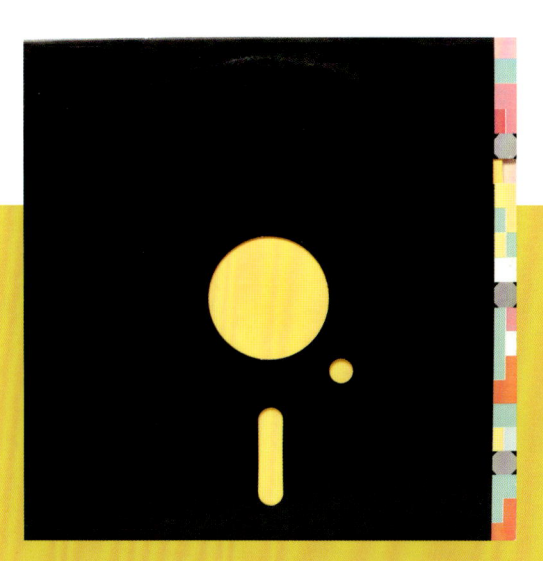

Left: *Performaning "Blue Monday" on Top Of The Pops, 30 November, 1983.*

copy. Naturally, this wouldn't have mattered if it had sold like "Procession". But it didn't: "Blue Monday" would become the best-selling 12-inch single in music history, finding its way into over a million British homes. "Blue Monday" was a global hit "and I couldn't pay my fucking gas bill," rued Hooky. "'Love Will Tear Us Apart' connects with people because of the emotional content of the song," noted Bernard. "But 'Blue Monday' connects because of its startling lack of emotional content. If I could properly explain it, I'd write another."

There was a wretched live appearance on the normally mimed *Top Of The Pops*, where Stephen played synthesisers and Hooky syndrums. Perhaps uniquely, the greatest promotional opportunity British music could offer sent the record tumbling down the charts the following week.

"Other bands such as Orchestral Manoeuvres in the Dark, Kajagoogoo and The Human League would apologise for miming," argued Stephen. "We just didn't want to. Not because of any convictions or commitments. We'd have felt like complete and utter prats."

The band were ambivalent about "Blue Monday" after it had changed their world. "People said it was a great leap forwards, but it wasn't, other than sales-wise," shrugged Hooky. "It was never that special to us." In time, they would play it regularly as, of all things, an encore, and inevitably their golden albatross became a burden. "I call it 'Fucking Blue Monday' now, because I'm sick of it," admitted Bernard. Stephen was more philosophical: "I remember seeing the bloody Troggs in Sweden in the '80s. They played 'Wild Thing' three times. I thought it must be terrible having to do that, but 'Blue Monday' turned into our 'Wild Thing'."

"Blue Monday" only reached number nine in the UK charts, but it was a stayer and spent seventy-four weeks in those charts. The slow burn meant New Order's fortunes were transformed steadily. Unsurprisingly, they refused to put "Blue Monday" on album number two, but when *Power, Corruption & Lies* was released in May 1983, expectations were different. They were no longer the ultimate Joy Division soundalikes, they were a band at the cutting edge in their own right.

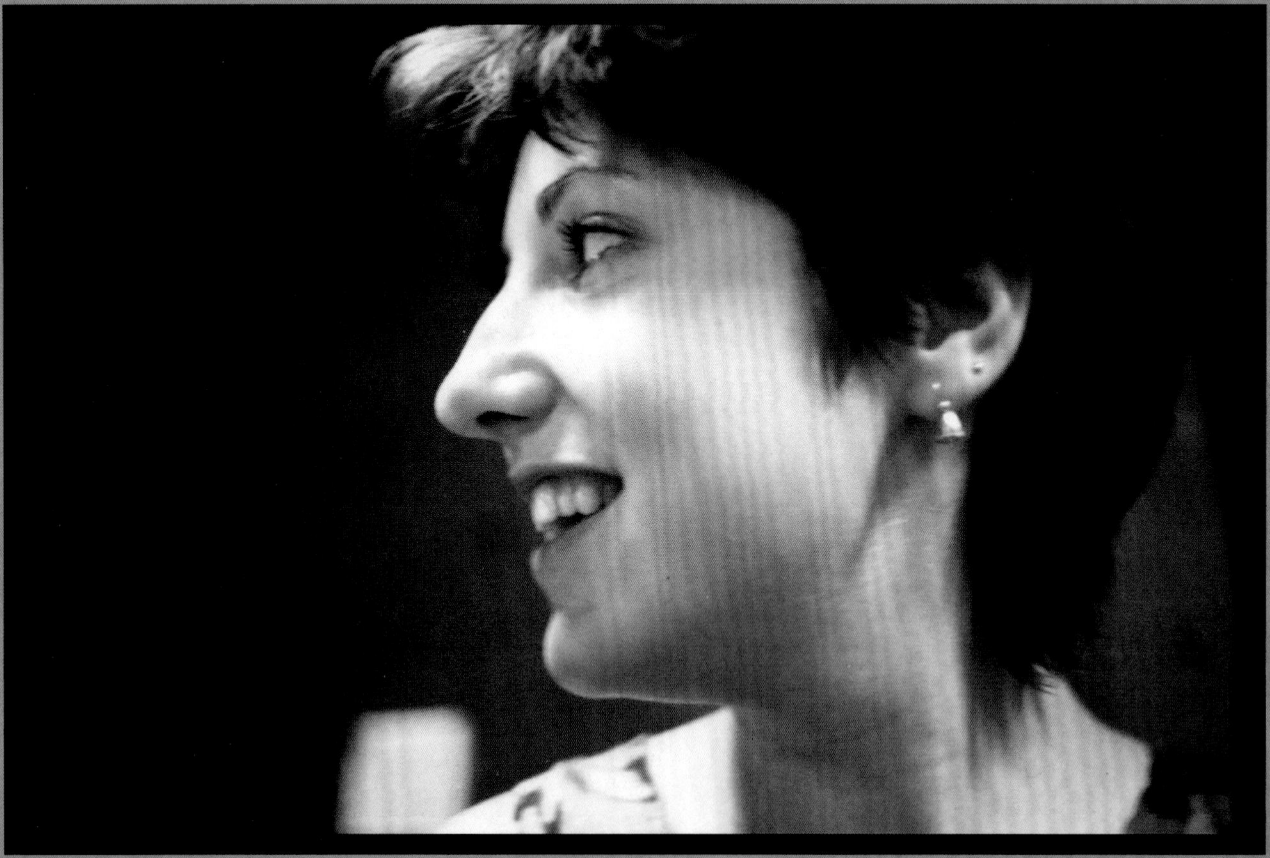

HELLO MAINSTREAM

HELLO MAINSTREAM

Depending on whom you believe, the second album's title came from graffiti outside Cologne's Kunsthalle or a *Daily Telegraph* article on George Orwell's *1984* (or perhaps *Animal Farm*) that Hooky had read which pronounced the novel "a startling tale of power, corruption and lies."

Still refusing to have such fripperies as the band's name or photograph on the sleeve (or even album and track titles), the cover was 19th century French painter, Henri Fantin-Latour's *A Basket Of Roses*, which Peter Saville had discovered in the National Gallery. The painting's owners, the taxpayer-funded National Heritage Trust, denied permission to use it until silver-tongued Tony Wilson suggested that, as a taxpayer, he was a co-owner of the painting. They relented.

Lyrically, Bernard was beginning to dominate and while the music was, again, completed long before the rushed lyrics, he changed his approach: "I tried writing serious lyrics, but I was self-conscious coming after Ian and I was shit at it. For *Power, Corruption & Lies*, I wrote down whatever I felt like." Joy Division were almost wholly expunged, but New Order were still too canny to go down the electro route without a safety net.

From the moment "Age Of Consent" opened with a gleeful guitar riff that swung like Joy Division or New Order had never previously swung, New Order showed they could be a pop band. Stephen reused some of the drums from the "Love Will Tear Us Apart" sessions. The title came from a *Sunday Times* article about lowering the age of consent and when Bernard intones the coda "I've lost you, I've lost you, I've lost you", it may have been something Ian would have sung, but he wouldn't have sung it with such a spring in his step.

A distant cousin of "Decades", "We All Stand" moved like a galleon, but Bernard's assured vocals were a giant leap forwards from anything on *Movement*. Stephen's percussion is otherworldly and it's the first moment that Bernard evokes the military in a lyric – his cousin was in the army and he claimed he'd have joined up for the Falklands War, "I'm a patriot" – but in this dreamlike journey to rendezvous with a soldier, there is always three miles to go.

"Temptation" wasn't on the album, but it was there in the spirit of "The Village" which had a titular reference to the cult television series *The Prisoner*. The songs had similar choruses, structure, pace and lyrics, although "Temptation" didn't end with such alarming abruptness. It's a very good rather than a great song, but it did show how comfortable the newly assured New Order sounded.

That abrupt ending paved the way for the slow moving, bass-free "586", which might well have benefited from some Arthur Baker remixing, although it wasn't "shit" as he claimed. One of the first tracks to be mooted for *Power, Corruption & Lies*, it faded in gently, a homage to Sparks's Giorgio Moroder-produced "The Number One Song In Heaven" and began

Gillian and Barney, Salford University, 17 April, 1985.

"IT'S WHEN WE STOPPED BEING JOY DIVISION AND FOUND A NEW DIRECTION THROUGH TECHNOLOGY AND DANCE MUSIC."

STEPHEN

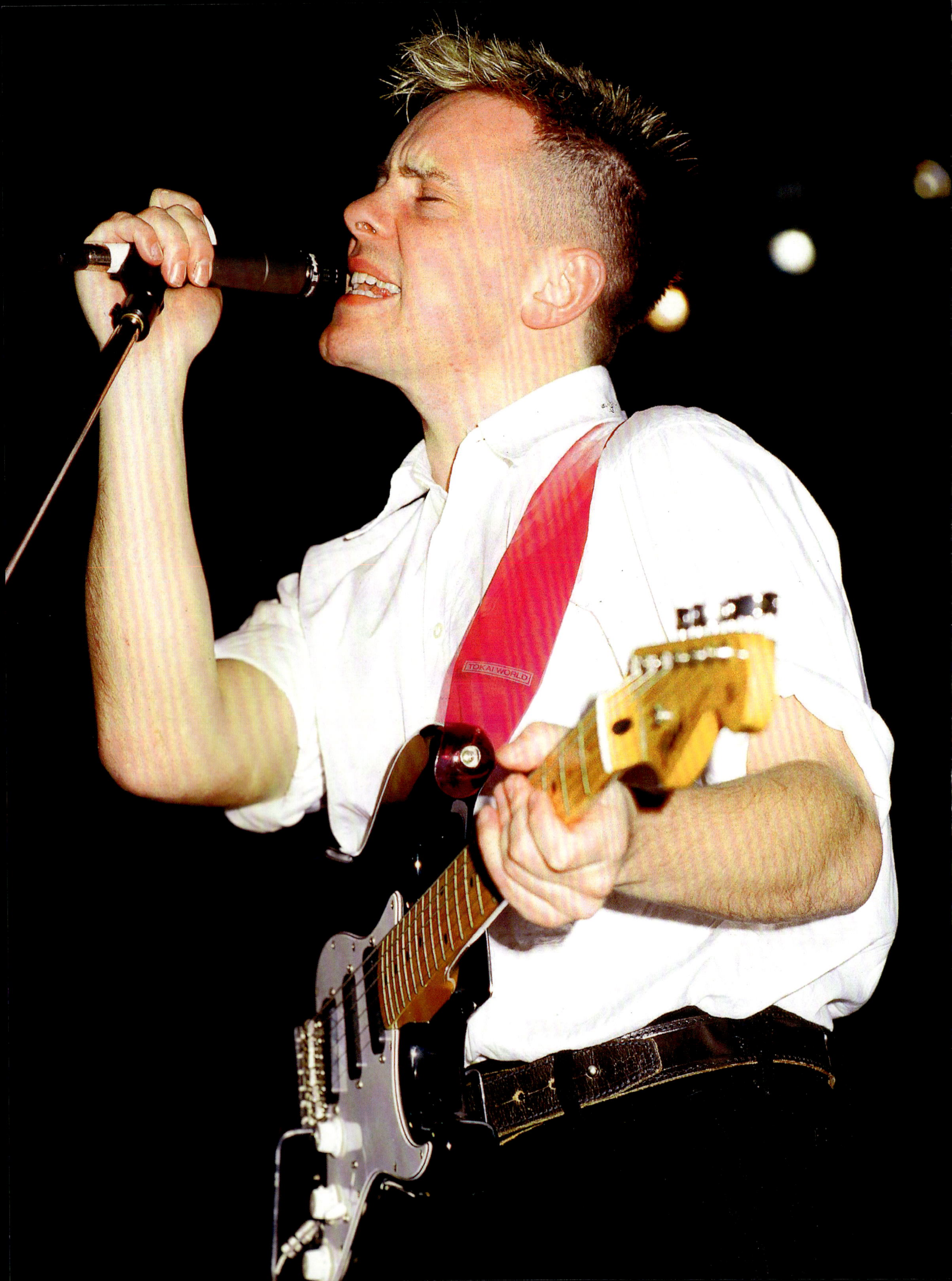
TOKAI WORLD

in almost prog fashion, before exploding into the part-template for "Blue Monday" that it actually was. The title was a musician's joke, its motif – one it shared with "Ecstasy" – was five bars, then eight bars, then six bars. There were also snippets of it in "Video 586" (aka "Prime 586" which had already made a surreptitious appearance on *A Factory Video*), a lengthy instrumental made to be played over The Haçienda's PA which they had gifted to the cassette magazine, *Touch* in 1982. It would be snuck out as a single in 1997.

"Your Silent Face" is *Power, Corruption & Lies*' heartbeat, even if the initial swathes of keyboards could have graced *Closer*. Its similarity to Kraftwerk's "Europe Endless" was acknowledged in its early title, "KW1", although early takes of something mostly written in the studio had more spaghetti western guitar. Bernard was back on the melodica and there was oboe too. As *Melody Maker* noted, "if you have any heart left, it'll tear it out." Yet, they couldn't let their beautiful baby lie and this gentle, lovelorn song ends with "You've caught me at a bad time/So why don't you piss off?". As Stephen confessed "it was a very majestic piece and we thought, 'ah, it's getting too serious'." In fairness, Ian was probably laughing rather than turning in his grave.

Its title a nod to *A Clockwork Orange*, on "Ultraviolence" Stephen reckoned he was seeking a percussive effect akin to the gloriously deranged "Bat Chain Puller", by his "Colony" inspiration, Captain Beefheart & The Magic Band. Stephen was right too. They had never been quite so unashamedly rhythmic.

Bernard was on unintelligible vocoder for "Only The Lonely", a harsh instrumental which had been retitled "Ecstasy". It seemed like an anomaly or filler at the time. It still feels like filler, but it was no anomaly: this was one route they would take again.

Bernard: as Stephen told *Uncut*, "democracy never works in pop bands".

POWER, CORRUPTION & LIES

TRACK LISTING

Age Of Consent
We All Stand
The Village
5 8 6

Your Silent Face
Ultraviolence
Ecstasy
Leave Me Alone

Released 2 May 1983
Label Factory – FACT 75
Recorded at Britannia Row Studios, London, England
Produced by New Order
Personnel
Bernard Sumner: vocals, guitars, melodica, synthesizers and programming
Peter Hook: 4- and 6-stringed bass and electronic percussion
Stephen Morris: drums, synthesizers and programming
Gillian Gilbert: synthesizers, guitars and programming
Cover Art Peter Saville
Notes
The cover features a reproduction of the painting "A Basket of Roses" by French artist Henri Fantin-Latour, which Saville found on a postcard he bought at the National Gallery. His then girlfriend Martha Ladly (of Martha & The Muffins) asked him if he was going to use it for the cover. Peter Saville's design for the album cover has a colour-based code, similar to the singles "Blue Monday" and "Confusion".

The closing "Leave Me Alone", the only synthesiser-free track, took its musical cue from "Ceremony", but its lyrical thrust was born of F. Scott Fitzgerald's *Tender Is The Night*, which Hooky was reading. "It feels just as melancholic," he explained of what would become his favourite New Order moment. There it was: the first great New Order album and their first top five album in the UK. "It was the first real New Order record," contends Stephen. "It's when we stopped being Joy Division and found a new direction through technology and dance music."

The critical response to an album dwarfed by a track that wasn't on it was significantly less reverential than it had been in the aftermath of Ian's death. "Vigorous and exhilarating, brisk and stripped of undue preciousness, New Order are just getting on with it, simply, efficiently and enjoyably," suggested *NME*'s Paul Du Noyer. While *Melody Maker* admitted "there are moments time stands still", *Record Mirror* (closed 1991) heard only "a rather sluggish journey through familiar territory, with little tension or edge. It's remarkably sedate."

Bernard too was not entirely happy. Without saying precisely what, he detected "something missing," although surely he was being provocative when he sneered that *Power, Corruption & Lies* was "a pound, shillings and pence album, wink, wink."

Also in May, there would be The Haçienda's first birthday to celebrate – without Stephen and Gillian who had been turned away at the door one night and never came back informally – although its debt of around £1 million and £10,000 a week losses gave those celebrations a rather hollow ring. From here on, New Order's record sales would keep The Haçienda afloat.

An American tour in June and July had its share of awkwardness, since Hooky and Ruth Polsky were no longer lovers ("I broke her heart on several occasions"). But things had changed and not just because they'd started playing "Thieves Like Us", an unfinished product of the Arthur Baker sessions. New Order had never been angels, but as the mood lightened, the rock 'n' roll lifestyle began to take hold. "The biggest mistake people make about us?" asked Bernard rhetorically in New York. "Thinking we're serious."

Stephen was more expansive. "People associate doom, death and suicide with us, but it's an albatross. We are not trying to get across the mood of the times. We are not talking the unemployment blues."

Cracks were beginning to appear. They played the prestigious New Music Seminar in New York where Bernard changed the lyrics of their best-loved song to "How does it feel to stand in front of a bunch of fucking cunts like you?". The following day, an uproariously drunk Hooky missed his plane to Washington, turned up desperately late for the show at the capital's Ontario Theater (Rob had sort-of deputised in his absence) and announced his arrival with a cheery "Hello shitheads". These days he remembers it as "one of the best tours we ever did."

After the final date in Trenton, NJ, they reunited with Arthur Baker to test the finished version of "Confusion" at New York's hyper-hip Funhouse club. The band didn't recognise their own song. There was a "Confusion" video to be filmed, partly at the Funhouse, directed by the unlikely figure of Charles Sturridge, who'd helmed the epic television version of *Brideshead Revisited*. According to Hooky, Bernard's escalating Pernod consumption rendered him a less than ideal working companion. The band weren't keen on being filmed, but they were even less keen on a photo session for *Rolling Stone* magazine. Rob lounged on the hotel roof, chain-smoking joints, while refusing to summon the band for the increasingly irate photographer and his platoon of assistants. The horror show was still a topic of discussion in the *Rolling Stone* office a decade later. Having cast off Joy Division's shadow, it now seemed they didn't care. About anything.

Back home, there was the cover of style bible magazine *The Face* (closed 2004) to be posed for (style bible or not, Stephen's sister cut his hair) and the release of "Confusion" in August. Of the

Not just any night out, a night out at Paradise Garage, New York City, 7 July, 1983.

hours of jamming and water-treading the band had dumped on Arthur Baker's desk ("It gave him a bleeding heart attack," chuckled an unrepentant Hooky), he selected twenty-eight minutes and split them into four versions. It made number twelve in the UK and sped to five in the US dance chart, but there was something unsatisfying about the whole marriage of inconvenience. Both parties appeared to be saving their best efforts for elsewhere and the perfunctory song wasn't strong enough. Acquiescing to Baker's insistence on dumping Stephen's work in favour of his own drumbeats was a concession the band didn't need to make. Hooky buried his misery by receiving £150 in exchange for a sizzling bassline on Martha's (as in Martha Ladly) deliciously poppy "Light Years From Love".

Elsewhere, there were little things to keep the machine ticking over. Named after the Ukrainian poet, *Taras Shevchenko* was a nine-song video of a 1981 New York show at the Ukrainian National Home. "Chosen Time" was listed as "ICB". In October, another video, *A Factory Outing*, saw the label's roster playing The Haçienda. Parts of "Video 586" soundtracked some Haçienda construction footage and the version of "Your Silent Face" was majestic, but James's "Stutter" wasn't bad either.

The same month, "Love Will Tear Us Apart" was re-released and went to number nineteen in the UK. It was a belated response to Paul Young's much-maligned (but really rather excellent) version which featured on his triple platinum album, *No Parlez*.

1984 looked promising – all years looked promising for New Order then – and in January they were back at Britannia Row recording "Thieves Like Us", the other track

Hello Mainstream 117

Madonna, 1984: shortly after telling New Order to "get stuffed".

written during the Arthur Baker interregnum, shortly before a young American singer played The Haçienda for the princely sum of £50. Madonna's two songs, "Burning Up" and "Holiday" were delivered from the dancefloor rather than the stage and filmed for *The Tube* television programme. Madonna later claimed her hotel room had been robbed. She fled Manchester when filming finished at 6 p.m. "We asked her to play again that evening for another £50," remembered Hooky. "She told us to get stuffed. Didn't even turn around."

Co-written by Arthur Baker who claimed to have seen the phrase written on a wall, the sublime "Thieves Like Us" was released in April in very different form to the lo-fi New York demo. More likely, the title came from Robert Altman's film of Edward Anderson's bank robbers novel and the cover from Greek/Italian surrealist Giorgio de Chirico's *The Evil Genius Of A King*. The random numbers were meant to resemble the cover of the 19th-century board game (deep breath), *The New & Fashionable Game Of The Jew*. "If Arthur had produced it, he wouldn't have put a four-minute intro on it," chuckled Stephen to *Record Collector* in 2020.

"Thieves Like Us" itself was backed by the bass-driven, Elvis-acknowledging "Lonesome Tonight" which had been premiered on the previous year's US dates and featured Hooky coughing up phlegm towards the end. Owing debts to The Human League and Hot Chocolate, it was a delight which reached number nineteen in the UK. It failed to secure an American release.

A few weeks later, for reasons never adequately explained, the good people of Belgium were treated to "Murder", backed with a lengthy, laborious instrumental version of "Thieves Like Us", the last release of 1984. The sleeve was another Giorgio de Chirico painting surrounded by more random numbers in the style of *The New & Fashionable Game Of The Jew*. Recorded during the *Power, Corruption & Lies* sessions, the near-instrumental "Murder" featured dialogue from the films *2001: A Space Odyssey* and *Caligula*. It would have made a passable B-side, but Bernard did wear a white lab coat while recording it.

Barney, Seaside Festival, De Panne, Belgium, 11 August, 1984: he'd bet his shirt on "Blue Monday" turning a profit.

118 Decades: Joy Division + New Order

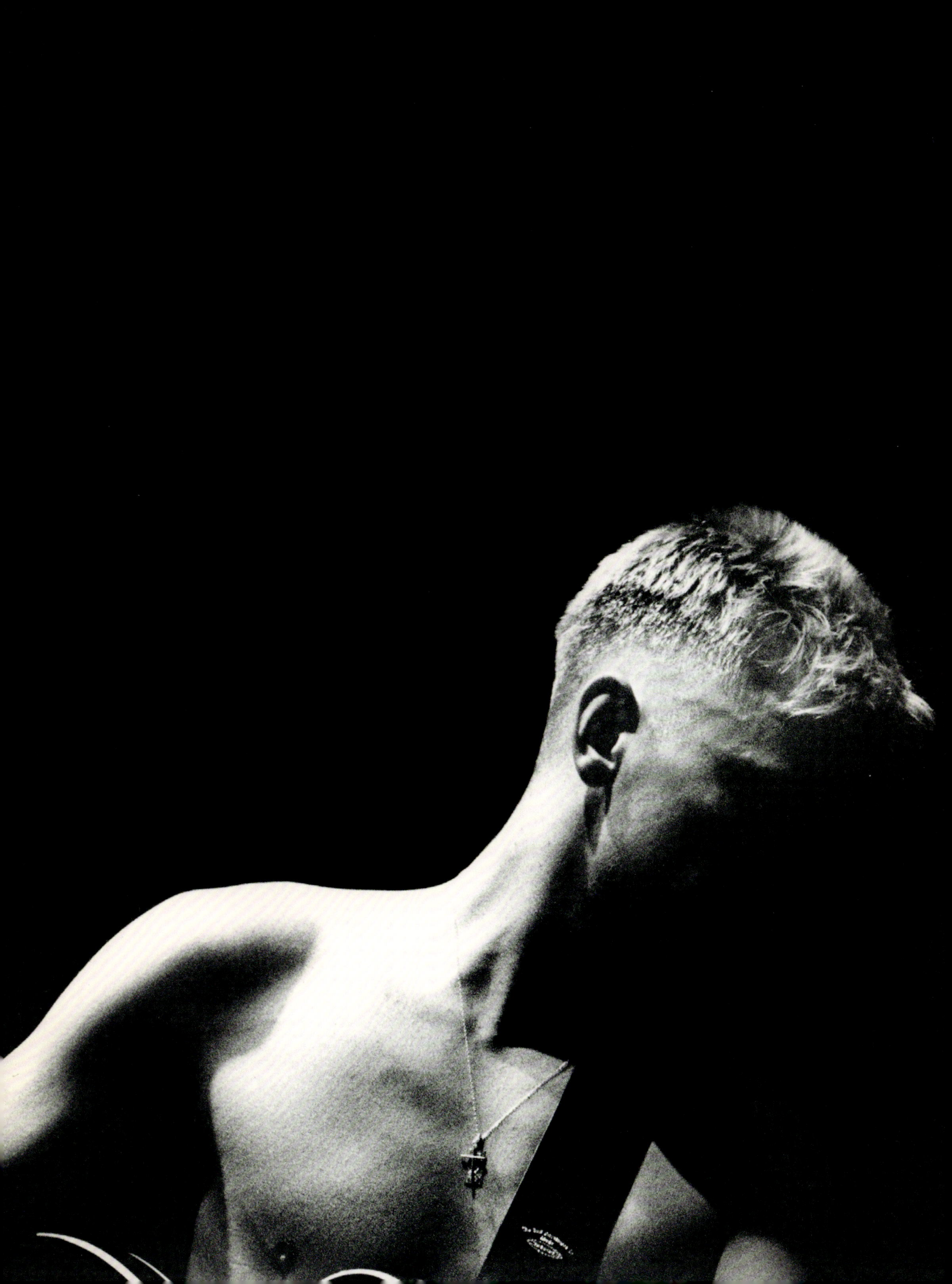

In March 1984, the miners of Great Britain, led by the widely disliked but stubborn Arthur Scargill, had gone on strike. They were seeking better conditions for an industry the government of Great Britain, led by the widely disliked but stubborn Margaret Thatcher, regarded as moribund. On May 14, New Order played a benefit for the striking miners. Their first overtly political statement (assuming the Nazi business was an unfortunate misunderstanding) was a roaring success and afterwards they met Tom Atencio. Once a marketing manager at Blackstreet/MCA, he was now the representative of Quincy Jones's Qwest Records, a Warner Bros label with one act – although that act was Frank Sinatra, so swings and roundabouts. They played two new songs "The Perfect Kiss" and "Face Up" and there was even an encore which featured "Blue Monday" and, astonishingly, Joy Division's "Decades", the first time a *Closer* song had been played live. More astonishingly still, their next show in Amsterdam three days later, finished with "Love Will Tear Us Apart".

Gillian and Bernard, Seaside Festival, De Panne, Belgium, 11 August, 1984.

"SOMEBODY ASKED ME IF I'D HOLD HIS DOG COLLAR AND DRAG HIM AROUND, IT WAS QUITE AN EYE-OPENER."

GILLIAN

The live dates ground on, but in August, Channel 4 aired *New Order Play At Home*, part of a documentary series where bands such as Siouxsie & The Banshees and Echo & The Bunnymen were given an hour of national television to do as they pleased. There is music ("Temptation" takes on a whole new life) mostly taken from a Haçienda show, but the real meat was elsewhere. A naked Tony Wilson was interviewed in a bathtub by a clothed Gillian; Richard Boon pointed out some of The Haçienda's inadequacies; Bernard interviewed Peter Saville; Stephen interviewed a gun-fondling Martin Hannett; Rob interviewed himself ("Good question, Rob"); the elusive Alan Erasmus took a motorbike ride with a T-shirted Hooky and a few Factory acts ganged up on Tony Wilson in an unsuccessful attempt to discover where the money was going.

Unsettlingly, underneath the rictus grins and faux bonhomie, everyone seemed to share the notion that Wilson was a charlatan, but they couldn't fathom how and why. That many of the interviews took place inside The Haçienda might have been a clue.

That summer saw New Order take part in the BBC's *Rock Around The Clock*, an all-day alternative rock extravaganza simultaneously broadcast on television and radio. They played live at the BBC's London studio, two days after a performance at St Austell Coliseum (demolished 2015), Cornwall. Hooky arrived first. He waited and waited. Then he waited some more. Having travelled the 270 miles on the day, in fearsome Saturday traffic during one of the UK's major tourist weekends, the others strolled in almost (but, lest we forget, not actually) too late. They were acutely hungover and collectively in a mood most foul. The atmosphere was poisonous, but the three latecomers looked different: Stephen ready for a day as a trainee accountant, Gillian in a pretty summer dress and Bernard, looking for all the world like an extra in Wham!'s "Club Tropicana" video: bleached blond hair, black vest, ankle socks, trainers and worryingly tight, white shorts. It seems trivial, but things would never be quite the same again.

In October, shortly after Factory bought a boat (it sank), album number three was beckoning and it was time to return to the studio or, in this case studios, since this time they recorded at Jam Studios in Tollington Park, a few miles north of Britannia Row. The band were tiring of their old haunt and it would primarily be used for mixing.

Although much of the material had been written at Cheetham Hill, they were still mostly writing lyrics by committee and the overall vision was still holding. Myriad factors served both to pull the band apart and bind them together. The disparity in working hours between Bernard and Hooky was again an issue and the latter would always claim he'd worked harder than the others. But they were all enthusiastic devotees of London's nightlife,

Hello Mainstream

not least the fetish club Skin 2. "Somebody asked me if I'd hold his dog collar and drag him around," remembered Gillian. "It was quite an eye-opener."

In December, with the album complete, New Order signed to Qwest in the United States. The deal saw Qwest securing the rights to Joy Division's releases, *Movement* and *Power, Corruption & Lies*, to which they would now add "Blue Monday". Seeing control slipping away, Rob was unhappy, despite having bonded with Quincy Jones over the producer's pool table in Malibu. Rob would never reconcile himself to Tom Atencio, but the band were delighted that one aspect of their career was being run professionally. Quincy Jones would visit Bernard's home. Still sends him a Christmas card each year, apparently…

Hooky's daughter Heather was born in March 1985. There was another difficult gig on April 9, when the band took so long to return for an encore at Birmingham Tower Ballroom, that the dissatisfied audience had vanished into the night. "I don't feel any compulsion in pandering to audiences, because most of them are real cunts," muttered Hooky. "They shout, they scream, they spit, they throw bottles. The world's full of these people, unfortunately." Before the month was out, though, they played emotional homecoming shows at the University of Salford ("Sister Ray" was given a once-over) and Macclesfield Leisure Centre, supported by Happy Mondays. This time the big occasions went perfectly.

Intra-band tensions were beginning to resurface. That same month, shortly before a trek to Hong Kong, Japan, Australia (where Hooky decided a ponytail was an acceptable way to style his mane) and New Zealand, Hooky claims his bass was exorcised from the non-album track "Shellshock", which they had recorded with Arthur Baker's sidekick John Robie, their first outside producer since Baker himself. "John gives you discipline and then I can put my own expression onto that discipline," purred Bernard.

On May 13, *Low-Life*, was released, at the same time, significantly, as "The Perfect Kiss" – the first New Order single to be taken from an album. The hand of Qwest was guiding them towards productive commercial decisions and they embarked upon a deliberate policy of demystification. After all, they were so anonymous that few had noticed it wasn't the real thing when Rob appeared in Hooky's absence on stage in Washington. The cover featured not only the band's name, but interchangeable images of actual band members, although Stephen was the front lead (he would make incognito visits to record shops, switching the pictures around). It was as if they wanted people, specifically American people, to buy their records. There was a certain sense of liberty.

The title was taken from the non-hyphenated "Low Life", a column in *The Spectator* magazine by England's most celebrated roué, Jeffrey Bernard, who had declared "I'm one of the few people who live what's called the low life."

There were no experiments such as "Ecstasy". There were no new musical directions. There were no self-sabotaging curveballs such as "Why don't you piss off?". There were no superior singles held back. However, there was fabulous songwriting. This was the first New Order album to sound like a unified, coherent statement. And there was the feeling that everyone was at the top of their game.

If any album can be judged, by its first ten seconds, it's *Low-Life*. "Love Vigilantes", the only song for which Bernard wrote all the lyrics, began with Stephen's whip-cracking drums before Bernard's melodica batters down the door. It's confident and assertive in a way they'd never dared be before. It would go on to incorporate the country music to which the Buzzcocks crew had introduced Joy Division. Stephen had always loved Flying Burrito Brothers and Gillian reckoned "Love Vigilantes" was an update on Kenny Rogers' cover of "Ruby Don't Take Your Love to Town". There was also pop, echoes of Mr. Bloe's "Groovin' With Mr.

Macclesfield Leisure Centre, Cheshire, 19 April, 1985. They played the venue that night.

Hello Mainstream 123

"IT'S LIKE A REBEL SONG, BUT VERY TONGUE-IN-CHEEK. IT'S LAUGHING AT REDNECKS. THE MORE RIDICULOUS MY LYRICS ARE, THE LESS SERIOUS THE SONG IS."

BERNARD

Bloe" and that strangely elegiac way Bernard could have with a vocal.

Bernard, of course, played down his creation: "It's like a rebel song, but very tongue-in-cheek. It's laughing at rednecks. The more ridiculous my lyrics are, the less serious the song is." In fact, this rare story-song finds Bernard's lyrical standby, a soldier, returning home, probably from Vietnam. He finds his wife sprawled on the floor holding a telegram saying he was dead. Whether he's a ghost or the telegram was mistaken is tantalisingly unclear, but New Order were newly focused and euphoric.

The single "The Perfect Kiss" was equally wondrous. There's a terrific lyric which takes in both masturbation and gangland crime, although Bernard did suggest it was based on a gun-toting but gregarious US fan. There were frogs and sheep to be heard (Stephen's idea) and while the single version cut the explanatory line "Now I know the perfect kiss is the kiss of death", the extended, kitchen-sink heroics version is a New Order zenith. There was more. Until now, even with the *Brideshead* man on board, New Order videos had been unashamedly perfunctory. That would change.

Michael Shamberg recruited Jonathan Demme to helm "The Perfect Kiss". Demme had recently directed Talking Heads' beguiling concert film *Stop Making Sense*, and, if not quite a concert, "The Perfect Kiss" was a performance. Over nearly eleven minutes, a succession of close-ups cast New Order as four individuals rather than a collective. Demme captured New Order's underbelly: glamorous Gillian's inquisitive awkwardness; cute Bernard's wariness; careful Stephen's shrugging compliance and – plectrum in mouth – hunky Hooky's swagger. It was tense, weirdly sexual for this most publicly unsexual of bands (although much of *Low-Life* was positively priapic) and more revealing than a slew of interviews.

That Jeffrey Bernard quote about living the low life began the electro-rock collision "This Time Of Night". Not a New Order maven, he hinted he might sue, so they turned his volume down. Surprisingly, it worked. There was a reference to Elvis Presley's "Wooden Heart", there were some now-rare Hooky backing vocals and there were some vague allusions to Skin 2.

Much loved by Gillian, the thrilling "Sunrise" began almost as if it was going to break into "Atmosphere". It was an aural apparition. Instead, there was that country twang again, the spaghetti western guitars pushed right to the front and it would be the most in-your-face and punky they had been since Joy Division. They weren't just an electro act, you see.

Recorded on speed apparently, the full, seventeen-minute version of "Elegia" would appear on 2002's *Retro* box set and it is New Order's finest instrumental by some distance. Drum-free according to Stephen, it's another moment where those spaghetti western guitars became less of a background influence and more the dominant force. The *Low-Life* version lasts for just under five minutes and it's a beautiful tribute to Ian. Later, it found its true home on screen: *Pretty In Pink*, *CSI*, *Stranger Things* and a host of other films and television shows. If "Ecstasy" was instrumental filler, "Elegia" was essential.

Bernard rushed most of the lyrics to "Sooner Than You Think" in a Zurich hotel room after a party – bless him for rhyming "reasonable" with "seasonable" – but the music was the first *Low-Life* backdrop to be completed. Bernard is at his cheekiest, but that backdrop, while very much of its time, is as warm and welcoming as any New Order excursion.

The chiming harpsichord introduction to *Low-Life*'s second single, "Sub-culture", promises something special and while Gillian thought the song "trite", it delivers, or at least it did until John Robie made a hash of the remix. The album version is shorter and superior. Once again Bernard takes us to Skin 2 and prays to the god of onan, but he still manages to sound like a little boy lost, or, at the very least, tied up.

Honed in a live setting before it went to

Hooky, Gillian, Stephen, Bernard: and the world's least accommodating sofa.

Hello Mainstream 125

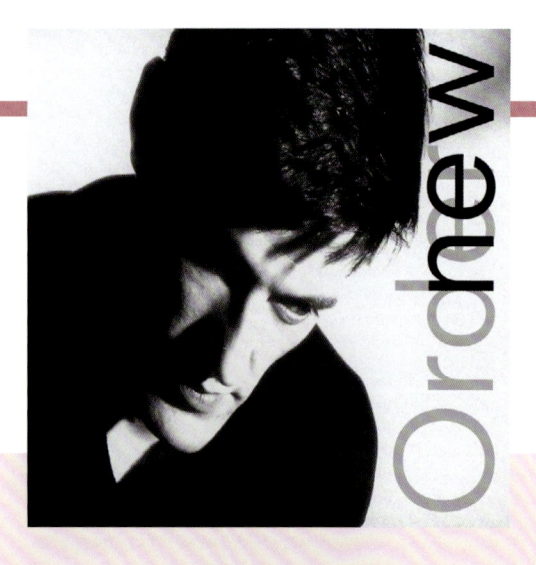

LOW-LIFE

TRACK LISTING

Love Vigilantes
The Perfect Kiss
This Time Of Night
Sunrise
Elegia
Sooner Than You Think
Sub-Culture
Face Up

Released 13 May 1985
Label Factory – FACT 100
Recorded at Jam and Britannia Row, London, England
Produced by New Order
Personnel
Bernard Sumner: vocals, guitars, melodica, synthesizers and programming
Peter Hook: 4- and 6-stringed bass and electronic percussion
Stephen Morris: drums, synthesizers and programming
Gillian Gilbert: synthesizers, guitars and programming
Cover Art Peter Saville Associates
Notes
The only sleeve with the band actually on the cover, designed again by Peter Saville. They were photographed individually by using a Polaroid film (the band never really believed those photos would end up on the cover). Cover comes wrapped in onion skin paper.

studio, the urgent "Face Up" was a curious ending. In the aftermath of *Low-Life*'s release, the band thought it their finest moment. Audiences were always less sure, although it did mention "In A Lonely Place". Bernard was as bitter as he'd ever been, but the tension between the weary "Oh I cannot bear the thought of you" and the hopeful sounds behind him made for something special. In fact, New Order had undoubtedly become special: they remained four individuals, but together, at one bound. they merged the best aspects of electro, rock, indie, pop, hardcore dance and even house music, which had yet to break out of its Chicago and New York heartlands.

Low-Life hurtled to number seven in the UK charts and ninety-four in the US, where their stock continued to rise as they fled the dance ghetto they'd accidentally marooned themselves in. *NME* argued that *Low-Life* was "New Order's *Closer*", but more accurately it was the final shedding of Joy Division. Ironically, the new-found distance would eventually leave the way open for them to include more Joy Division songs live. Steve Sutherland was more perceptive in *Melody Maker* when he argued "it's all so minimal it's mountainous."

As had happened with *Movement* and *Power, Corruption & Lies*, a new album meant a new level of acceptance. The dates got bigger, the money more serious, but some of the old problems remained. They had new cars – a Mercedes for Bernard; a Toyota Supra for Hooky; a Volvo for Stephen; a little Fiat 500 for Gillian – but much of the booty went to The Haçienda. Meanwhile, as their Boston fans would prove on August 2, audiences were still capable of rioting if there were no encores. Before that, though, there was a headline slot at the WOMAD on Mersea Island (the most easterly inhabited island in the UK – The New Seekers recorded "I'd Like To Teach The World To Sing" there). There they headlined the world music festival above fellow Mancunians, The Fall, and a host of unlikely bedfellows such as Toots & The Maytals, Nusrat Fateh Ali Khan,

Gillian on guitar at Manhattan Club, Leuven, Belgium, 17 December, 1985.

Above: *Bernard and Hooky, Manhattan Club, Leuven, the home of Stella Artois.*

Thomas Mapfumo and The Pogues, who were less than delighted when New Order admitted a donkey into their dressing room. Wisely, they did play "Blue Monday" and they did play an encore.

In October, John Robie's remix of "Sub-Culture" was unveiled. The feeling when it only reached number sixty-three in the British charts and didn't trouble the American ones was mostly relief. Peter Saville was so appalled he refused to design a sleeve for it (if only he hadn't liked "Blue Monday"...) and Hooky loathed the cheesy, girly backing vocals. The pair would never reconcile, especially after Robie shoved a vol-au-vent in Hooky's hirsute face. Still, Robie had achieved the remarkable feat of making a dance remix less danceable than the original.

The year did not end well. In December they were investigated by the tax authorities and, as they trekked around France, Holland and Belgium, Rob's behaviour was beginning to show cause for concern. Always fiercely territorial and every bit as hedonistic as his charges, it appeared that the financial situation, the Haçienda and the invasion of his territory by Qwest had dented his aura of invincibility. There was trouble ahead. Again.

"IT'S ALL SO MINIMAL IT'S MOUNTAINOUS."

STEVE SUTHERLAND, *MELODY MAKER*

Right: *Rob Gretton, 1 November, 1985. "Without him, they would never have broken through and they would have had to compromise much more."*

Hello Mainstream 129

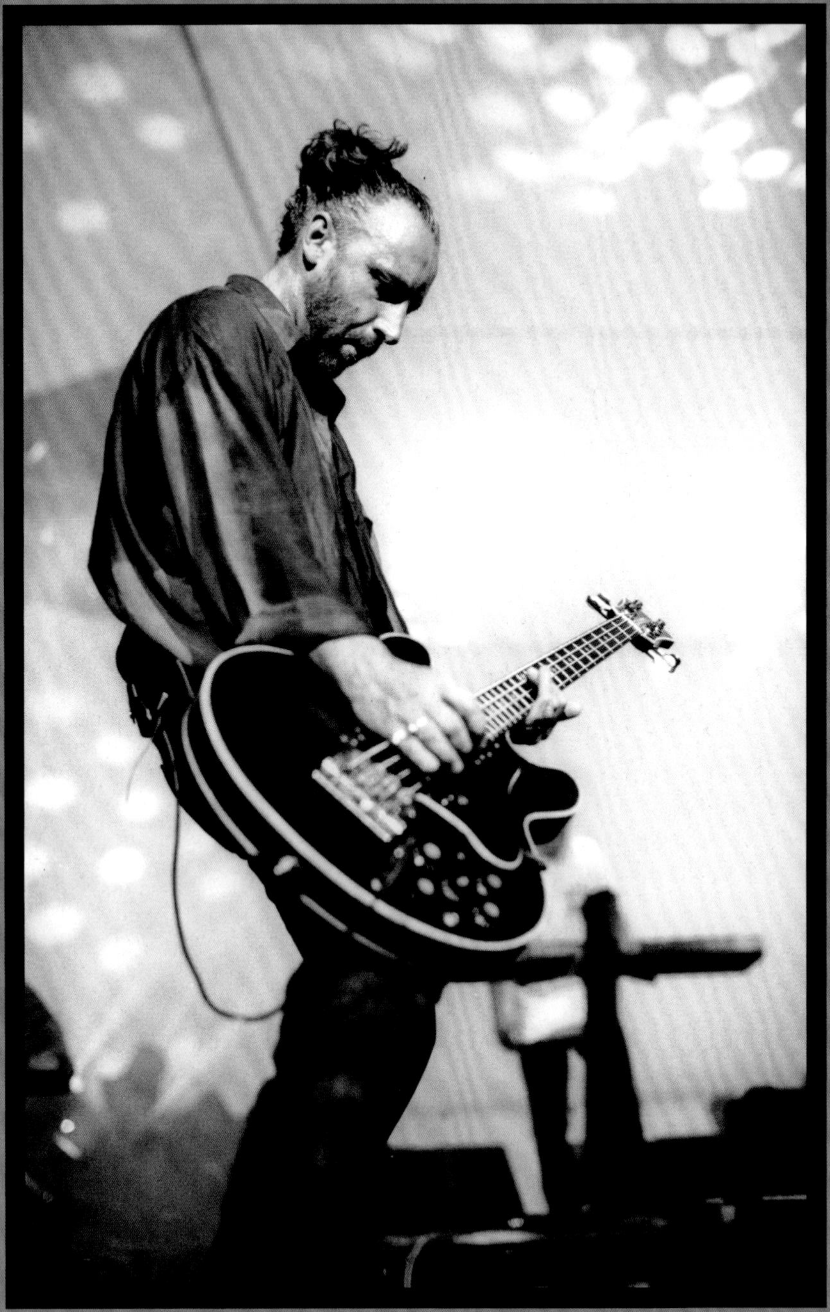

24-HOUR PARTY PEOPLE

24-HOUR PARTY PEOPLE

By early 1986, The Haçienda was selling the cheapest beer in Manchester, but according to Hooky, Rob was instead consuming ten grams of cocaine a day. The inevitable result was a cocaine-induced psychotic breakdown and Rob was committed to psychiatric care. The band toured Ireland without him.

In February, John Hughes' brat pack film *Pretty In Pink* was released. The adolescent melodrama took its title from a Psychedelic Furs song, but New Order were winners too. "Elegia" and the instrumental version of "Thieves Like Us" were in the film but not the soundtrack, while "Shellshock" made both, albeit featuring in the film very briefly. The great leap forwards was still to come, but it was another building block in the United States.

"Shellshock" was recorded with John Robie and released as a single in March. There were a slew of mixes, most of which suggested Robie's "Sub-Culture" misstep was a one-off and the almost ten minutes of the 12-inch extravaganza bubbled with invention. It flew out of the traps and into the clubs with an alacrity the lumpen "Confusion" had signally failed to muster.

Bernard had produced singles by Factory's Quando Quango in 1983 and Marcel King (once of Sweet Sensation, who had a British number one single with "Sad Sweet Dreamer" in 1974) plus EMI-signed Mancunians, Foreign Press. He also produced the first Happy Mondays single, "Freaky Dancin'". "He did a really decent job," said Happy Mondays singer Shaun Ryder, "he captured the looser, dancier feel we had live." Bernard's new charges were so feral that, as they recorded B-side "The Egg", Ryder and freaky dancer Mark "Bez" Berry liberated the remains of a Chinese meal Bernard had discarded in the bin and tucked in.

By April, New Order were back in the studio, making the fourth album. They returned to Jam

Left: Pretty In Pink, *starring Andrew McCarthy, Molly Ringwald and Jon Cryer, 1986.*

Right: *New Order in a kitchen, Dresden Road, London N19, September 1986.*

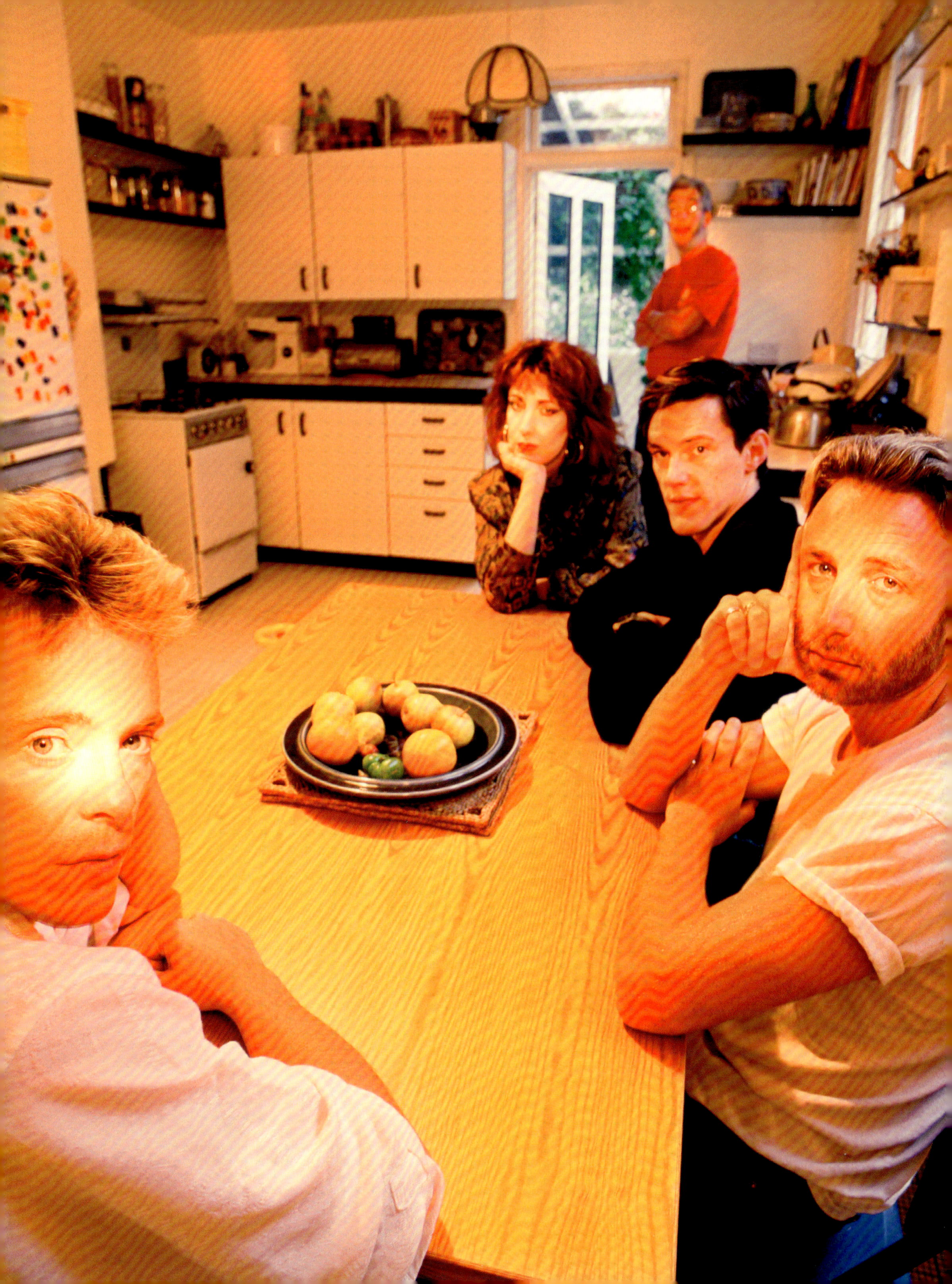

"WE WERE PARTYING SO MUCH IT GOT IN THE WAY OF THE RECORD. WE BECAME NOCTURNAL."

HOOKY

Left: *Stephen, Gillian, Bernard, Hooky: The Roxy, London, 1986. One of them collected ironic T-shirts...*

Orpheum Theatre, Boston, 6 December, 1986. They opened with "Blue Monday" that night...

in London – a flat near Hyde Park was rented – where most of the backing tracks were recorded, but they also racked up the bills at, early fans, U2's Windmill Lane studios in Dublin, before mixing at Amazon in Liverpool, where Echo & The Bunnymen were struggling to finish their self-titled, career-stalling fifth album.

During recording, the band began to embrace a more hedonistic lifestyle. "We were partying so much it got in the way of the record. We became nocturnal," admitted Hooky.

Rob was back, although he and his authority were irrevocably diminished. He did, though, instigate a new fitness kick and Hooky and Gillian were the most receptive. The recording sessions were typically stressful. Hooky and Bernard were in separate musical camps and again operating on separate schedules. It wasn't quite pioneer versus Luddite, but Bernard was obsessed with dance, while Hooky – scared and scarred by "Shellshock" – insisted on guitars. Bernard, of course, was late with his lyrics and the expensive Windmill Lane sessions overran. This time, those lyrics were mostly worth waiting for. The solution was simple but ultimately divisive: one side of the album would lean towards electro; the other towards rock, in the manner of other split-sided projects such as Brian Eno's *Before and After Science* and David Bowie's *Heroes*.

In August the Tony Wilson-directed, fate-temptingly titled live video, *Pumped Full Of Drugs*, bought some time. The show, May 1985's gig at Shinjuku Koseinenkin Hall wasn't

24-Hour Party People 135

BROTHERHOOD

TRACK LISTING

Paradise
Weirdo
As It Is When It Was
Broken Promise
Way Of Life
Bizarre Love Triangle
All Day Long
Angel Dust
Every Little Counts

Released 29 September 1986
Label Factory – FACT 150
Recorded at Jam, London, England; Windmill Lane, Dublin, Eire; Amazon, Liverpool, England
Produced by New Order
Personnel
Bernard Sumner: vocals, guitars, melodica, synthesizers and programming
Peter Hook: 4- and 6-stringed bass and electronic percussion
Stephen Morris: drums, synthesizers and programming
Gillian Gilbert: synthesizers, guitars and programming
Cover Art Peter Saville Associates
Notes
Another Peter Saville/Trevor Key design, representing a bar of zinc and its serial number. A few special editions were coated with titanium zinc. Certain editions, including the original Factory Records CD, the 1993 London Records re-release and the 2008 Collector's Edition, feature the 12" version of "State of the Nation" as a bonus track (although it is not listed as such). It is identical to the version found on Substance.

vintage and the mood – especially Bernard's – was downbeat, but there was a new song: "As It Is When It Was". The video's title came from Bernard jokingly introducing "This Time Of Night" as "Pumped Full Of Drugs", but life was imitating art.

Ruth Polsky died on September 7. The uber-networker was outside the New York's Limelight Club, queuing for a Certain General show (she was always on any guest list going, but this was an Aids benefit and she was determined to pay her way). A car ran a red light, hit a taxi and careered into her. Rob represented the band at her funeral. Hooky pleaded poverty, but, as we know, they had never been good at funerals. A fortnight later, the single "State Of The Nation", partly recorded in Japan, was released as a seeming taster for the album. A week after that came the album itself, Brotherhood, a title Gillian still regards as "too blokey."

Surprisingly Qwest had sanctioned the deployment of "State Of The Nation" as an extra track on the CD version of Brotherhood, rather than on the album proper. It was not as other New Order songs. Unusually, the title was a staple of the lyrics, but more unusual still, it was a protest song of sorts suggesting that the (unspecified) state of the (unspecified) nation "is causing deprivation". The B-side remix, titled "Shame Of The Nation", was their final John Robie collaboration and was recorded in Stockport. The package stumbled to number thirty in the UK.

Brotherhood's sleeve ended the demystification policy that had served Low-Life so well. It was a photograph of a sheet of metal. As Stephen would later admit of the overt split between two musical directions on his least favourite '80s album, "the experiment didn't quite work. I liked it better when it was mixed up."

The rock side came first. Even Hooky didn't go for "Paradise", a sort of Dolly Parton tribute, which sort of updates "Jolene". There was, he argued, too little bass and too many voices

Barney, Great Woods Center For The Performing Arts, Mansfield, Massachusetts, 18 August, 1987. They opened with "Bizarre Love Triangle" that night.

cascading on top of each other. He's wrong on both counts, the multiple voices take it to another level and it's his bass that makes it such a juggernaut of sound.

The rattling "Weirdo" was the first time since "Dreams Never End" that the guitars had soared like prime time Cure. The chorus is an earworm, Stephen drums with a metallic heaviness and Hooky binds everything together yet again: even he didn't take against this one.

Fresh from the *Pumped Up With Drugs* video, Ruth Polsky's favourite "As It Is When It Was" was tentatively recorded in Tokyo alongside "State Of The Nation". It found them taking another fork on the road. Hitherto, quiet New Order (and quiet Joy Division) had meant menace and despair. Here there was the novelty of acoustic guitar, a trademark but now increasingly rare yelp from Bernard and probably his best lyric yet, a reflection on Salford where "In those days when the sun was warm/I ran into the street where I was born" carries a genuine emotional kick. The bassline was pure "Love Will Tear Us Apart". "You can rip yourself off, even if you do it unconsciously," explained Hooky.

Its opening riff is cheekily cannibalised from "Isolation", but Bernard was bitter again on "Broken Promise". It raced along at such a frenetic pace that they would always struggle to recapture its magic live. Whether those lyrics were aimed at Hooky ("...you sit there looking

24-Hour Party People 137

> "I'M VERY PROUD OF IT, BUT I COULDN'T BE THAT HEAVY ALL THE TIME, I LIKE A LAUGH."
>
> BERNARD

Barney, Aragon Ballroom, Chicago, 26 November, 1986. They opened with "Shellshock" that night.

at me all day" prefigures one of Bernard's complaints about the bassist's behaviour) or, less likely, poor forgotten Sue, was never made clear, but anger galvanised Bernard. He was, possibly for the first time in his life, on fire. "It's trying to write a token rock track," argued Stephen dismissively. "We could have done better."

Stephen's drums drove "Way Of Life", but it's more than just a percussive rumble. Its guitar riff alludes gently to "Love Will Tear Us Apart"; the bassline is the one from "Age Of Consent" but backwards and there's a most uplifting chorus. Lyrically, though, Bernard is once again pointing fingers with venom – "When I look at you, I know you're lying" – and it was hard not to wonder if all was OK at home and at work.

One of New Order's last genuinely collaborative lyrics, "Bizarre Love Triangle" was what the members who weren't Hooky had been working towards all along. It was pop, dance and indie in one extraordinary package. It sounded great in clubs and on radio, but it was swathed in New Order strangeness and so perfectly structured it would be recast as a straight folk ballad by the Australians of Frente! or Cantopop by Sandy Lam or pop hip-hop by Black Eyed Peas and Jay-Z amongst many others. Unbelievably, it only reached fifty-six in the UK. "Our greatest miss," rued Stephen.

Bernard rarely dips into serious issues, but "All Day Long", a dark but subtle tale of child abuse with sampled strings, suggests he sells himself short. Naturally, being Bernard, he had to play down any notion of soul-baring: "I'm very proud of it, but I couldn't be that heavy all the time, I like a laugh." It's as beautiful and as dark as anything Joy Division put their name to. "A lovely song," noted Stephen, "it doesn't have any drumming."

Bernard had been broadening his horizons, hence the use of a muezzin's call to prayer on "Angel Dust", but it also had gunshots, distortion, furious guitarwork and the muscle-flexing sense that, for all their embrace of the commercial, New Order were still pirates at heart.

The deceptively simple "Every Little Counts" is a catchy singalong with undertones of Lou Reed's "Walk On The Wild Side" and, once again, Hot Chocolate whose first bassist, the unfortunately named Trinidadian Tony Wilson, was turning out to be a major influence. After early brooding, it explodes in a delicious keyboard interlude, before ending the whole album with a "A Day In The Life" style flourish. Yet again, Bernard is railing, but he brings a lightness of touch and even he can't help laughing when he declares "...you are a pig, you should be in a zoo" on the first verse. For the rest of the song, he struggles to keep himself together. "We could have done it again," admitted Bernard of the pig line. "But we thought 'Fuck it, it works as it is'." Quite right, too.

Brotherhood soared to nine in the UK and a deceptively unimpressive 117 in the US, where it was seen as cutting edge, but with tunes. It's *Low-Life*'s non-identical twin, although as Cath Carroll (who had been in a band alongside Tony Tabac and would soon sign to Factory as Miaow) noted in the *NME*, "it swings in bolder fashion." Steve Sutherland was back on the case for *Melody Maker*: "It's infuriatingly enigmatic, with passages of thundering majesty and lyrics of embarrassing openness." Neither rock nor dance won, but neither lost. That battle was about to be fought.

In October, Jonathan Demme's whipsmart Melanie Griffith vehicle *Something Wild* featured "Temptation", but Pete Shelley of the long-faded Buzzcocks had more to be pleased about when the soundtrack also featured Fine Young Cannibals' version of his "Ever Fallen In Love (With Someone You Shouldn't've)". It would become a global hit. His money worries were over.

According to Hooky, Smiths guitarist Johnny Marr sounded him out about forming a side-project in November, but the visit of *Smash Hits* to Los Angeles during the American tour reinvented New Order and Bernard in particular. But not in a good way.

As befitted its name, *Smash Hits* (closed 2006) was a pop-loving magazine for pop lovers, but it was also gloriously and cheekily irreverent. New Order had seemed to understand this when they'd dispatched Gillian to talk to them around "Temptation". She'd told the sales powerhouse that she and Stephen "go off videoing dead moles" and everyone was happy. They really should have known what to expect when Sylvia Patterson flew to Los Angeles in November. It wouldn't be questions about how deeply they mourned Ian.

Patterson was swiftly barred from the dressing room and left to hover, waiting to interview Bernard "with a face like a smacked arse", muttered ever-gallant Hooky. After the show, the bassist already had company, but Bernard – whose room at the Sunset Marquis hotel was next to Patterson's – was in full party mode when Rob insisted the interview take place in Bernard's room there and then.

As if auditioning for a Marx Brothers farce, Bernard bundled his two female companions into a wardrobe and threatened to break Patterson's legs if she mentioned any such shenanigans, hence the feature's subsequent headline, "Ask Us Anything Horrible and We'll Break Your Legs". As interviews go it was no Frost-Nixon.

The next morning, Patterson and her photographer bumped into the women. They'd taken Bernard's beige shorts which had $200 in their pocket. The photograph, featuring girls, shorts and dollars made the magazine. Although she tells the tale slightly differently, Patterson still has those shorts. Naturally, the fallout didn't help Bernard's home life, but for a decade or more, it also changed perceptions about New Order. They were now 24-hour party people. It wasn't an act.

On December 5 they played a full, thirteen-song set as a benefit for Ruth Polsky at the 1018 Club, New York. They encored with "Love Will Tear Us Apart" and for the first time as New Order, they played "Atmosphere". For once, they got mourning a death right.

Now a genuine global concern, they spent the first half of 1987 on the road. They covered the Lou Reed novelty "Ostrich" occasionally and there were intermittent airings of "Atmosphere" and "Love Will Tear Us Apart". The *Smash Hits* incident was a rare public lifting of the veil that surrounds successful pop groups, but as the audiences grew, so did the temptations. Resisting wasn't really on the agenda.

Still, there was time to re-record "Temptation" and "Confusion" for the forthcoming compilation which would be the sales monster they'd been threatening. The theory behind the re-recordings was to make the still regularly-played songs more akin to the live versions. "Confusion" was a wistful improvement; "Temptation" didn't need touching.

In June, they recorded "True Faith" and the planets aligned, but this time in a positive way. It was completed over ten days at Advision, London, where Buzzcocks had recorded the original "Ever Fallen In Love (With Someone You Shouldn't've)". Tom Atencio wanted a pop hit from a pop producer, so, at his suggestion, they recruited outsider Stephen Hague to oversee them. According to Hooky, Hague preferred the track without bass until Tom Atencio stepped in. A large tax bill had convinced Bernard of the idea's merits, although, as ever, he was tardy with the lyrics. Bernard was locked in a room with a bottle of Pernod at the band's phoneless flat on Cleveland Terrace, near Paddington, and told to emerge only when he had something coherent. He eventually did, although Qwest would censor him, believing the original line, "Now that we've grown up together/They're all taking drugs with me" might not find favour with Midwest American radio stations.

Stephen Hague was an American former session musician (he'd worked with Gordon Lightfoot and Dolly Parton) who now specialised in producing British bands. He took on New Order after fashioning Pet Shop Boys' debut, *Please*, and a Pete Shelley solo album, *Heaven and the Sea*, both of which were firmly

Shaun Ryder, Happy Mondays, Haçienda. "The E spread like a tidal wave across the Haçi from our alcove…"

in the electro camp. "For 'True Faith', the band came with elements of the groove, a basic bass/snare-drum pattern they had kicked around," Hague recalled in an interview in 2005. "There was also a rough version of the programmed bass part, along with a couple of chord changes for the verse and chorus. There was no song written yet, just a direction."

There were no drums either, just a hi-hat and cymbals which Stephen muffled with a pillow. Bernard and Stephen Hague sang backing vocals. Hague encouraged the band to record separately, but was transfixed by their approach: "...the amazing thing was no matter how much they might consume in terms of alcohol or any other substances, their moods remained very stable. No one would get sloppy, pissed off or say anything stupid. To be honest, I found it a little spooky."

Always destined to be part of a single to promote the upcoming compilation, "True Faith" was meant to be the B-side to the gorgeous "1963", Bernard's curious, historically inaccurate look at the JFK assassination. When Qwest heard the finished results, they flipped the songs. That's how labels are supposed to work.

That summer, according to Shaun Ryder, Ecstasy came to The Haçienda. After discovering the drug in Amsterdam, Ryder and his cronies were its first Manchester dealers. The introduction of Ecstasy and its acid house

"THE AMAZING THING WAS NO MATTER HOW MUCH THEY MIGHT CONSUME IN TERMS OF ALCOHOL OR ANY OTHER SUBSTANCES, THEIR MOODS REMAINED VERY STABLE."

STEPHEN HAGUE

> "DURING THE ACID HOUSE PHASE, I WAS PERHAPS PARTICIPATING IN A LITTLE TOO MUCH FUN. I ACTUALLY WORE SOME DUNGAREES, HALF DONE UP. NOT A GOOD LOOK."
>
> BERNARD

soundtrack would herald Dave Haslam's phase two – the successful phase – of The Haçienda. "Mike Pickering says he could see the E spread like a tidal wave across the Haçi from our alcove," smiled Ryder. Bernard later confessed, "During the Acid House phase, I was perhaps participating in a little too much fun. I actually wore some dungarees, half done up. Not a good look."

Later in June, there were festivals to generate revenue. They headlined Glastonbury, where "True Faith" made its debut. "I loved playing there," cooed Hooky. "My three highlights are the three times we played Glastonbury." The following week, there was the Aarhus Festival. If New Order played a worse show, nobody can remember it, although in fairness *they* don't actually remember this one.

They were scheduled after Miles Davis, not a man famed for his time keeping or the brevity of his sets. On and on the jazz giant went. The sponsors foolishly plied New Order with crates of the local extra-strength (7.2%) Elephant Lager. When the band finally went on stage after midnight, they could barely stand. Gillian fell into her keyboards and was out of tune for the entire shambles.

"I never drink beer, but this tasted so nice," she explained. "I didn't realise how strong it was. All I can remember is Hooky glaring at me, Miles Davis watching from the side of the stage absolutely pissing himself and me coming off stage, thinking: 'Have we been on yet?'"

"The police were called at the end," reckoned Stephen. "We were wanted for crimes against music."

In July, shortly before a co-headlining tour of the US with Echo & The Bunnymen, "True Faith" reached number four in the UK and thirty-two in the US. This was the game-changing song they'd been seeking, and they'd been building towards it since "Blue Monday". Hooky was disappointed in how low his bass was mixed. "He was absolutely right," admitted Stephen Hague. "I didn't have experience of mixing bass as a lead instrument." The video, directed by Philippe Decouflé, who would choreograph the 1992 Albertville Winter Olympics' opening and closing ceremonies, added to the jubilant feel, although not for nothing did Hooky title a chapter of one of his books "My Knee Was In The Video". Bernard explained that the song "was about drug dependency. I don't touch smack, but I tried to imagine what it's like to be a smackhead" – so it was fitting that Decouflé created a surreal, cut-up world which meant little but looked mesmerising. The song won a 1988 Brit Award for Best Video.

"True Faith" might have been the game-changing song, but *Substance* was the New Order album America had been waiting for – the heavyweight behemoth that would set them up for the next twenty-five years and beyond.

The notions which spawned a career résumé were silly, inspired and cynical in equal measures. Tony Wilson had a car which included the new-fangled technical wizardry that was a CD player. He rather fancied listening to New Order's singles as he drove, but the overwhelming bulk of those singles weren't featured on albums, so why not fill the gap in the market by corralling them on one career-spanning package? Greatest hits albums don't always work in America, Qwest had haphazardly padded out previous albums with singles, but the gap for a collection was unquestionably there. Factory's finances were also imploding, even before the deadweight of The Haçienda, since no other act on their roster sold records. To salvage his label, Tony Wilson suggested a special deal for *Substance*. Instead of the usual 50/50 split, why not make it 25/75 in Factory's favour? This would mean that

Echo & The Bunnymen's Ian McCulloch guests at the Festival of the 10th Summer.

Factory would then be able to pay New Order the money they owed from previous albums. This money had been spent on assorted vanity artists such as The Wake, Anna Domino and The Royal Family and the Poor, and assorted vanity projects such as Alan Erasmus's ludicrous trip to Moscow – an idiotic attempt to move Factory into classical music. Catastrophically for New Order, Rob acquiesced.

The track listing was logical in selection, and breathtaking in quality. Unlike with Joy Division's *Still*, nobody could feel short-changed. All singles bar "Procession" and "Murder" were on the first disc, but both were on the second disc of B-sides, which in turn omitted only "Dub-Vulture" (a remix of "Sub-culture") and "Bizarre Dub Triangle" (a remix of "Bizarre Love Triangle"). "Ceremony" was the version featuring Gillian. "Temptation" and "Confusion" were the recent re-recordings and every A-side was the 12-inch version other than "The Perfect Kiss", "Shellshock" and, of course, "Sub-Culture". The traditional Factory mis-title saw "Cries and Whispers" mistaken for "Mesh".

Released in August 1987, the biggest seller of their career would be a UK number one (at last) and would reach number thirty-six in the US, where it would sell over a million on its way to platinum status. Len Brown of the *NME* announced it was "a counter-revolution against glumness" and New Order ascended to another plane of existence.

The subsequent US tour reflected that new status. For the first time, band and crew were billeted in separate hotels and Bernard decided he would now talk with one journalist, per country, per year. The show at Irvine Meadows, CA should have been a career highlight – a celebration of how far they had come, where they were and where they could go. For the first and last time they elected to play the first disc of *Substance* in order, before encoring with "Atmosphere" and "Love Will Tear Us Apart". They were on top of the world. What could possibly go wrong? As it was New Order, something could…

Before the show, Bernard told the others he wanted to work with different people. In fact, he had been collaborating during the summer with erstwhile Smiths guitarist Johnny Marr, a friend since the pair had met at the Quando Quango sessions in 1983. Bernard later said, "We had been driven to distraction by both the love and hate for our mother groups. The intensity had burnt us out. Something had definitely gone wrong and working together provided

NEW ORDER
—
SUBSTANCE 1987

Opposite: *Hooky, Pier 84, New York City, 25 August, 1987.*

"IF WE'RE NOT RECORDING, I DON'T DO ANYTHING. I JUST LIE IN BED AND THINK A LOT."

BERNARD

144   Decades: Joy Division + New Order

recuperation." It wasn't the end of the world, or of New Order, it just felt like it.

In December, there was the release of another single and it didn't come from *Substance*. Michael Shamberg had secured another film commission, this time for Beth B's dreadful televangelism satire *Salvation!*. Not for the first time, there was a misunderstanding. The band assumed she wanted filmic snippets. She did, but she required a proper song too. When the misunderstanding was cleared up, deadlines beckoned and "Touched By The Hand Of God" was allegedly written and recorded in a day and sent off to Arthur Baker for a remix. Michael Shamberg recruited future Oscar winner Kathryn Bigelow to direct the video, which saw the band bewigged and spoofing the amp-smashing, hair metal acts of the day, weaved around a nonsensical narrative starring Bill Paxton. When a car crash scene was axed, MTV loved it and it reached number twenty in the US and topped the US dance charts.

The year of their greatest triumph ended with a mini-victory when they were asked to write the theme to *Best & Marsh*, a soccer show featuring superstar players George Best and Rodney Marsh. Tony Wilson presented... Of *course* he presented.

1988 should have been a vintage year. New Order had released a universally loved album and the live shows were better than ever – despite a certain reluctance to travel from Bernard, who was fast becoming a studio bunny, the exact opposite of Hooky. Instead, they were sowing the seeds of their own destruction. "I'm a complete and utter lazy bastard," admitted Bernard. "If we're not recording, I don't do anything. I just lie in bed and think a lot." He read a little too – be it D.M. Thomas's *The White Hotel*, Irving Stone's fictional Vincent Van Gogh biography, *Lust For Life*, or assorted history tomes – but it took him six months to finish a book. When the money began to roll in, he'd install an indoor pool underneath a retractable floor where he could play with his remote-controlled boats.

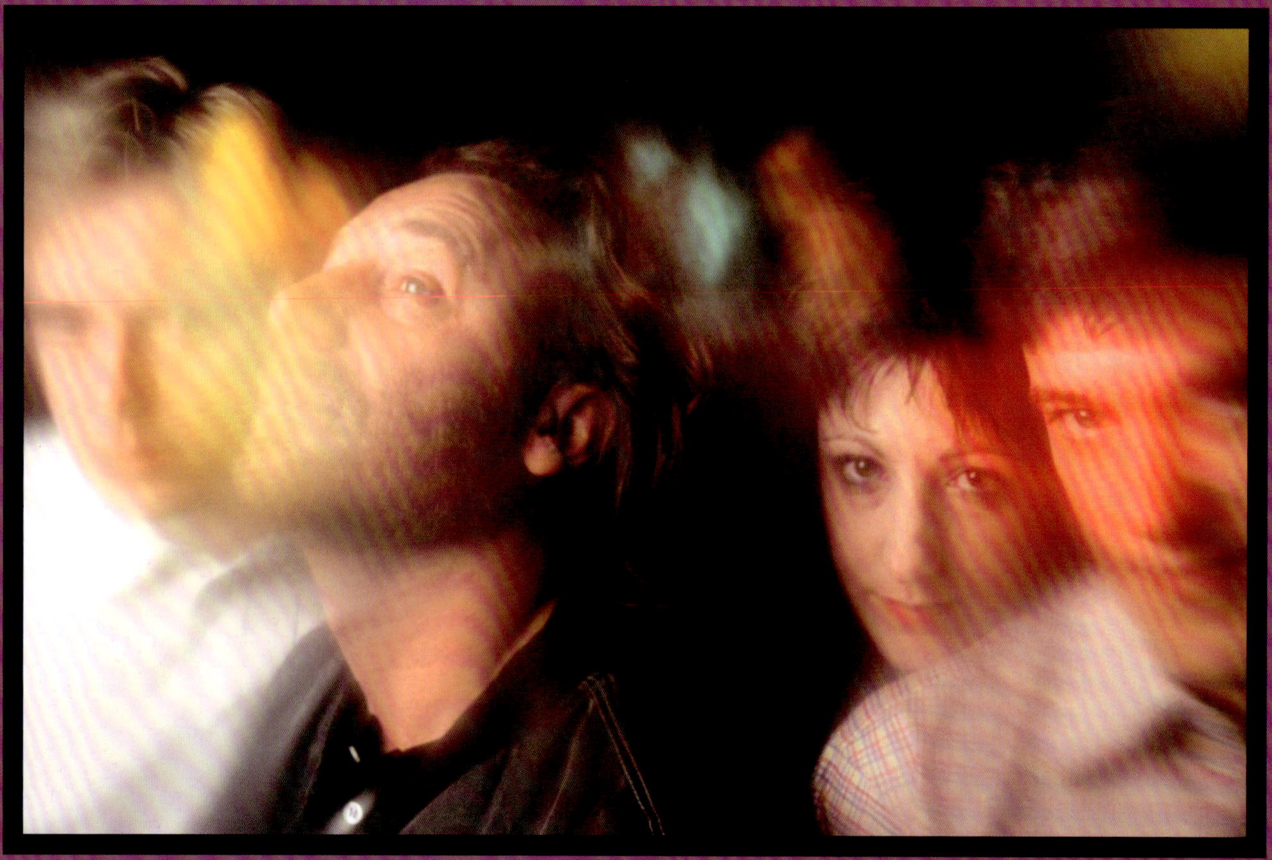

Y VIVA ESPAÑA

Y VIVA ESPAÑA

Such is the ongoing acrimony, it's difficult to precisely pinpoint where and when the relationship between the two schoolfriends began to break down. Hooky resented Bernard's increasing dominance, his work with Johnny Marr and the gradual eroding of his bass. "The worst person I've ever been in a band with was Bernard," he told *Uncut* in 2010. "If he didn't like a track, he wouldn't play on it. He was the most unhelpful person, whereas Ian was eager to please. Any situation was better without Bernard." There was more, there was always more with Hooky. "Poor old Bernard has no idea how many rooms full of people have celebrated his departure over the years. He was a moody, tight-fisted bastard who made our lives a misery." Yet, even Hooky had to admit, "But of all of us, he did the most work."

Bernard accepted he wasn't always the easiest of workmates, telling Mick Middles, "I'm not really icy: I just don't like idiots. If I don't want to do something, I just will not do it: that makes me difficult to work with."

Bernard began to see Hooky as a boor and a bore, an obstruction to the progress which could only be achieved in the studio rather than on the road. "Hooky saw some kind of imagined competition inside the band," he expanded. "Any perceived rivalry existed nowhere except inside his head. This burning resentment was tiresome, palpable and pointless."

The tensions would drip, drip and drip, until they became a flood. Of course, they were both right and they were both wrong.

Quincy Jones himself became involved in remixing "Blue Monday" and the band did overdubs for his version. The spur was a $250,000 offer from the soft drink Sunkist who wished to use it in an advertisement with ghastly new lyrics: "When you're drinking in the sunshine/Sunkist is the one". Bernard was expected to sing. Needless to say, Rob nixed the idea, but the mock-up they did for 1993's *New Order Story* spawned the myth that a commercial had actually appeared.

Barney, Stephen, Hooky, 1989.

"HOOKY SAW SOME KIND OF IMAGINED COMPETITION INSIDE THE BAND, ANY PERCEIVED RIVALRY EXISTED NOWHERE EXCEPT INSIDE HIS HEAD."

BERNARD

Opposite: *Johnny Marr: New Order's Yoko Ono?*

February saw the release of the *Salvation!* soundtrack. "Touched By The Hand Of God" was featured alongside, at Beth B's request, instrumental versions of "Salvation", "Let's Go" (to which they would return), "Sputnik" and "Skullcrusher" (which had already featured live with lyrics). Hooky wasn't at the Brits when "True Faith" won its Best Video award, but Bernard was less than gracious in his speech, taking pointless umbrage at Andrew Lloyd Webber lauding the '50s television producer Jack Good.

Just after the film, *Bright Lights, Big City*, starring Michael J. Fox premiered with "True Faith" on the soundtrack, the perfectly adequate Quincy Jones reboot, "Blue Monday 1988", bought a little time. It made the top three in the UK and number sixty-eight in the US. Before Christmas 1987, Stephen and Gillian had told Portuguese television the band were writing new songs and an album would be released before Christmas 1988. True, they were writing, but Bernard was becoming frustrated with what he saw as Hooky's Luddite streak and had half an eye on a solo album.

They rehearsed at Cheetham Hill, but the tensions brought only sterility. They came up with a radical solution. In a decision that was ill-thought-out even by Factory and New Order's standards, they decided to record in Ibiza. In 1988, the Balearic Island where Sid Vicious had lived as a tot was sunny and beautiful, but it was also a centre for hardcore clubbing and drugging – exactly the sort of environment New Order didn't need. Allegedly oblivious to the cultural shift the island had taken, Hooky had read about an Ibiza studio called Mediterranean and he and Terry Mason had undertaken a reconnaissance trip. The pendulum of blame was swinging his way. "I felt for the next record we should get out of the way. Where better than the peace and quiet of Ibiza? I couldn't have got it more wrong."

Green shagpile carpet adorned the walls of the Mediterranean. It was pretty basic and not just for a band who did so much of their most innovative work in studios. However, it did have a swimming pool and 24-hour bar, courtesy of one Herman the German (Herman wasn't German). Their new best friend became Pedro, a one-armed drug dealer who supplied them with industrial quantities of Ecstasy. Night after night they went to Ibiza old town, then the club Amnesia, soaking in the Balearic beat. They'd stay until 8.30 a.m., before finishing at Manhattan in San Antonio just before lunch. Then they'd drive home. Unsurprisingly, there were actual car crashes in addition to the metaphorical one that was happening around them. Tony Wilson and Hooky's partner Iris (he was having an affair with Jane Roberts, his guitar tech, at the time) dropped in and there was an endless succession of visits from a plethora of home city ne'er-do-wells, including Happy Mondays, who, as we know, were already enjoying The Haçienda's renaissance.

"Our intentions were bad," smiled Bernard. New Order partied until they disgusted even

"WE JOINED A BAND TO GET AWAY FROM HAVING TO ANSWER TO BOSSES. LIKE THE MONDAYS, WE DON'T GIVE A FUCK WHAT PEOPLE THINK."

BERNARD

themselves when a lake of vomit appeared on the pool table after an evening visit from a coachload of Club 18-30 holidaymakers. After three wasted – in every sense – months, they returned home with one completed-ish tune, "Fine Time", two song portions and – since the sun-averse Stephen had worked quite hard (relatively) – a smattering of useable drum tracks. Bernard dryly noted, "We'd earned the right to make an album in a sunny place, but with all the island's distractions we didn't get as much of it done as we'd have liked."

In 1992, Factory would replicate the Ibiza fiasco when they sent Happy Mondays to Barbados to record *Yes, Please!*, their wretched fourth album, the one which bankrupted the label. Soon New Order were on their way to Peter Gabriel's Real World studios in Box, Wiltshire. A cost of £10,000 a week should have concentrated their minds and their powers, but there were still frequent trips to London's club scene and they were distracted by outside projects.

Bernard was now openly working with Johnny Marr. Hooky had formed a band called Revenge – named after George Michael's leather jacket on the "Faith" video, rather than on his feelings towards Bernard, although Hooky was, shall we say, aware of the ambiguity. Meanwhile Stephen and Gillian were crafting the soundtrack to the BBC's *Making Out*, which starred old friend Margi Clarke.

Amidst the rubble, there was a Joy Division revival. They were proving to be the band whom death could not kill. Five years after the first "Love Will Tear Us Apart" reissue, "Atmosphere" was resurrected. It reached a disappointing thirty-four in the British charts, but it served as an appetiser for the unimaginatively titled compilation, *Substance*, which meant New Order's *Substance* would have to be retitled *Substance 1987*. It was a top ten British hit and reached 146 in the US. Comprising of seventeen non-album tracks (twenty when it was remastered in 2015), it meant *Unknown Pleasures* and *Closer* finally had a proper companion.

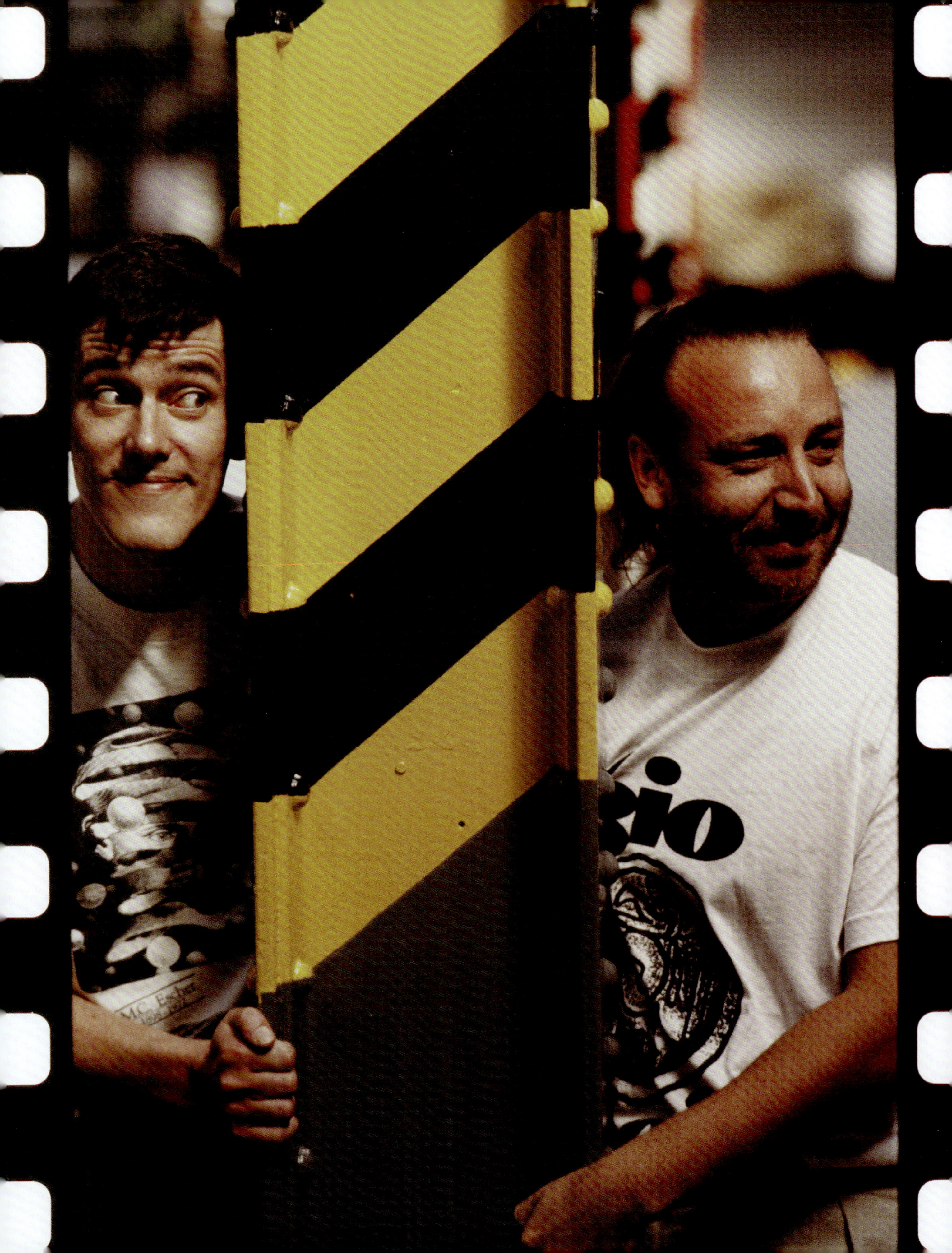
M.C. Escher

The New Order album was finally finished and Real World foolishly agreed to a party to celebrate. Rob invited a coachload of Haçienda regulars and some locals, while Mike Pickering DJ'd. Hooky had lost the musical battle – later admitting "There was an epic power struggle between sequencers and me. I still wanted us to be a rock band" – but not yet the war. Meanwhile, Bernard would provocatively tell *NME*: "90% of rock is archaic, whereas the same proportion of dance music is wonderful." The musical and cultural landscape had changed too. Happy Mondays were no more Bernard's Chinese meal bin-dippers – they were a major force, especially in Manchester where their druggy, dancey approach had seized the moment. Bernard tried to leap aboard their bandwagon, telling *NME*: "We joined a band to get away from having to answer to bosses. Like the Mondays, we don't give a fuck what people think." Even Hooky was getting in on the act too, co-producing "Elephant Stone" by The Stone Roses, who were about to be at the vanguard of the revolution.

"Bizarre Love Triangle" featured on the *Married To The Mob* soundtrack, but in November, the first fruit of the new era dropped. Making their Ibiza stay even more pointless, Bernard rerecorded his vocals to "Fine Time", and got it right, only for them to be wiped. Written after a monumental night out at Amnesia, the single itself throbbed with Hooky's bass and Gillian's keyboard washes. It was a real statement of dance-inclined intent and, in case anybody had any doubts, the image on the sleeve was raining pills. It climbed to eleven in the UK and five remixes by dance pioneer Steve 'Silk' Hurley swamped the 12-inch (one of which included Bernard's faux sex noises in a daft attempt to emulate Donna Summer's "Love To Love You Baby"), alongside the majestic near-instrumental "Don't Do It" – think a less rushed

Stephen and Hooky, The Haçienda, Manchester, 25 July, 1990. There may have been a band playing behind the post.

TECHNIQUE

TRACK LISTING

Fine Time
All The Way
Love Less
Round & Round
Guilty Partner

Run
Mr. Disco
Vanishing Point
Dream Attack

Released 30 January 1989
Label Factory – FACT 275
Recorded at Mediterranean, Ibiza, Spain; Real World, Box, England
Produced by New Order
Personnel
Bernard Sumner: vocals, guitars, melodica, synthesizers and programming
Peter Hook: 4- and 6-stringed bass and electronic percussion
Stephen Morris: drums, synthesizers and programming
Gillian Gilbert: synthesizers, guitars and programming
Cover Art Peter Saville Associates
Notes
The cover is another Peter Saville/Trevor Key design, using a garden ornament cherub statue. The first New Order album to reach number one in the UK charts and their last album on Factory Records.

Y Viva España 153

> "WE COULD QUITE POSSIBLY END UP AS AWFUL AS U2. NO, NOT AS AWFUL, BUT WE COULD BE AS BIG, IF WE WERE PREPARED TO SWEAT IT."
>
> **BERNARD**

"Murder" – which began with a harpsichord, sampled heavily and glided to effortless victory.

When "Fine Time" was released, the band were in Brazil, playing their first live dates of 1988. There, the extra-curricular activities were excessive even by New Order's standards. They returned to play a homecoming show at Manchester's G-Mex and, although their son Jack – after Jack Woodhead – would be born nine months later, Hooky and long-suffering Iris parted company. "We stayed together for ten years," lamented Hooky. "Saying that, I was away for eight and a half of them."

Technique, the fifth New Order album, was released in January 1989. For the first time, all the lyrics were Bernard's and they were at one with the zeitgeist. The Ibiza jolly may have been a disaster, but it suddenly seemed prescient. "We had no idea Ibiza was going to take off," admitted Bernard. His marriage was finally ending – he and Sue divorced later in the year – and although he had taken extensive steps to comfort himself, his latest lyrics reflected his disillusion.

Following "Fine Time", the flab-free, anthemic "All The Way" was all choppy Cure-esque guitars and Bernard's self-justification, but it was as conventionally rock as "Technique" would ever be.

If not quite as countrified as "Love Vigilantes", "Love Less" had a merry sounding twang, but the lyrics saw Bernard finger pointing again, this time at his domestic arrangements: "I worked hard to give you all the things that you need". Three tracks in and, on balance, they were a guitar band.

"Round & Round" flew with an electro flourish, a beautiful melancholic chorus and lyrics which slowly evolved to become fixated on Tony Wilson's financial acumen: "You waste your time like my money". Possibly oblivious to the criticism, the subject himself pushed for it to be a single. Here, at least, he was right.

A fragment from Ibiza found its way onto "Guilty Partner": Bernard strumming his acoustic under a tree in the sun. The track oozed bass. It wasn't a peak, but it did show how the rock and dance factions could work in tandem without either being compromised.

John Denver's publishers were fascinated to hear "Run". So fascinated in fact, that, noting its similarity to "Leaving On A Jet Plane", they sued. The case was settled out of court and Denver's subsequent writing credit is evidence of his victory. Bernard is hostile again, but there's a busy instrumental tsunami behind him and John Denver's fairy dust enhanced rather than diminished. Hooky claims he still can't see the similarity. Bless.

New Order song titles rarely made it to the actual song lyrics and "Mr. Disco" is no exception, although how any of them let something so naffly named through remains a mystery. It deserved better. It begins like Simple Minds' "Waterfront", namechecking Ibiza, Benidorm and Majorca after twisting and turning around a vibrant dancefloor middle eight. There are no cows, but there are, probably, cowbells.

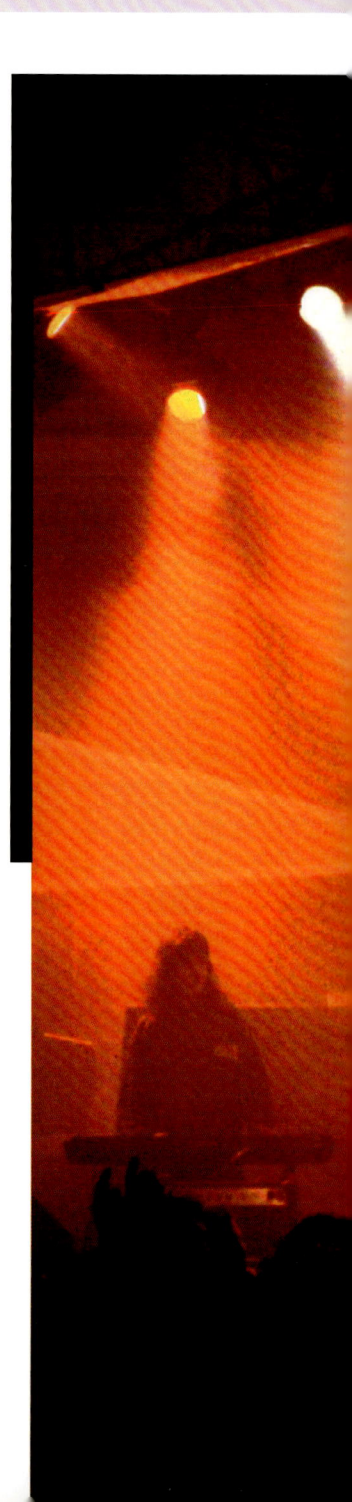

The band wanted the melancholic "Vanishing Point" to be a single. On balance, Factory were right to deny them, but it's still *Technique*'s most crucial track, merging imperious instrumental beauty with Bernard pointing out that his life "ain't no holiday", while Hooky brought textures and cutting edge vibrancy: it was his *Technique* track of choice.

Technique closed with the summery, guitar-led, electronica-drenched "Dream Attack". Bernard is less nihilistic than elsewhere on the album and there's a sense of optimism and the sunny uplands of a bright new future. A future that wasn't to be.

Technique divides opinion. It was a product of its time, its creation and intra-band relations. That, despite everything, it was strong, coherent and so frequently inspired is a tribute to how New Order never quite lost sight of the bigger picture, although Hooky was still up for a fight: "When most bands take vocals off, it's diabolical. With us it's wonderful."

Touring Technique, *1989.*

So at one with the times that it sailed to number one in the UK and thirty-two in the US where, as befitted the arena act they now were, it sold over half a million. "We just wanted to travel the world and have fun. As a by-product of having fun, we became successful," argued Bernard. As one breathless review said, it was "...so effortlessly great, so beguilingly heroic, so vibrant and thrilling that one wishes one could weep." More objectively, it was another peak, albeit a peak which led to the subsequent trough. Again, Bernard saw the future: "We could quite possibly end up as awful as U2. No, not as awful, but we could be as big, if we were prepared to sweat it. Personally, I'm not. Even getting a record out now has become this big operation. Anyway, I don't follow music, I'm usually out of me box when I listen to tapes people give me."

During January's two-date tour of France, Hooky was on the brink. Not only was he living apart from pregnant Iris, but during a show at Le Transbordeur in Villeurbanne, he played the wrong bassline to every song. Equally worryingly, nobody seemed to notice.

In February, the Stephen Hague-produced version of "Round & Round" was released as a single. He made it punchier, less bass-y, less drum-y. It reached a disappointing twenty-four in the UK and a more than respectable sixty-four in the US. "Best & Marsh" made the B-side, alongside the instrumental version of "Vanishing Point" which had become the theme to *Making Out*. It was rushed, "a little half-baked" admitted Bernard, but it alerted more hip members of the Football Association, the governing body of English soccer, to the fact (the false fact admittedly) that here was a band who know the sport.

To Bernard's dismay, it was time for another American tour, a massive jaunt which took in almost forty dates from April to July. It would, the assumption went, consolidate their hard-earned status. "We're mega cockrock in the States now," trilled a delighted Hooky. "And we could

Barney, Lake Compounce, Bristol, CT, 11 July, 1989.

have been years ago if we hadn't done so many New Order things, like playing small clubs."

There were lavishly catered aftershow parties with strobe lights and DJs, which were followed by excursions around the local clubs, climaxing with hotel room adventures. A show in Detroit was rescheduled when Bernard's stomach lining rebelled and he regularly did not attend soundchecks. After the tour, they were mentally and physically broken and, for the first time, they began to publicly hint at internal disharmony. "There has been tension in the group, that is true," confessed Bernard to *NME*. "We did the tour to see if we could handle a mega-tour. To be frank, we couldn't. By the end of it, we were sick of New Order: thirty-six nights of 20,000 seaters made me ill. I was forced by doctors to give up drink for two weeks, that was like asking Bob Marley to give up his dope. I just thought 'I don't want to be here, why am I doing this?' I'd rather be on the dole than go on tour again."

On 15 July, in a moment which couldn't have been more Factory, 50,000 tour programs arrived. The tour finished four days later and 49,000 tour programs were shipped back to the UK and pulped. There wasn't just one party after the final show at Meadowlands, East Rutherford, NJ, there were three. Bernard, Hooky and Stephen and Gillian, held separate ones in separate rooms. None of them made an appearance at the others'.

It was time for a break, but there was just one more contractual commitment to fulfil: a headline slot at the Reading Festival. Since it involved seeing each other again, nobody was thrilled, but everyone was on their best behaviour and a quintuple closing whammy of singles was the perfect way to call a halt. "We didn't want to play Reading," admitted Bernard. "But we were contracted to do so. I'm glad we did." For the first time in New Order history there was nothing on the horizon: no songwriting sessions, no studios and no dates. They would not play a concert for four years.

Gillian, New York, October 1989.

> "WE DID THE TOUR TO SEE IF WE COULD HANDLE A MEGA-TOUR. TO BE FRANK, WE COULDN'T. BY THE END OF IT, WE WERE SICK OF NEW ORDER."
>
> **BERNARD**

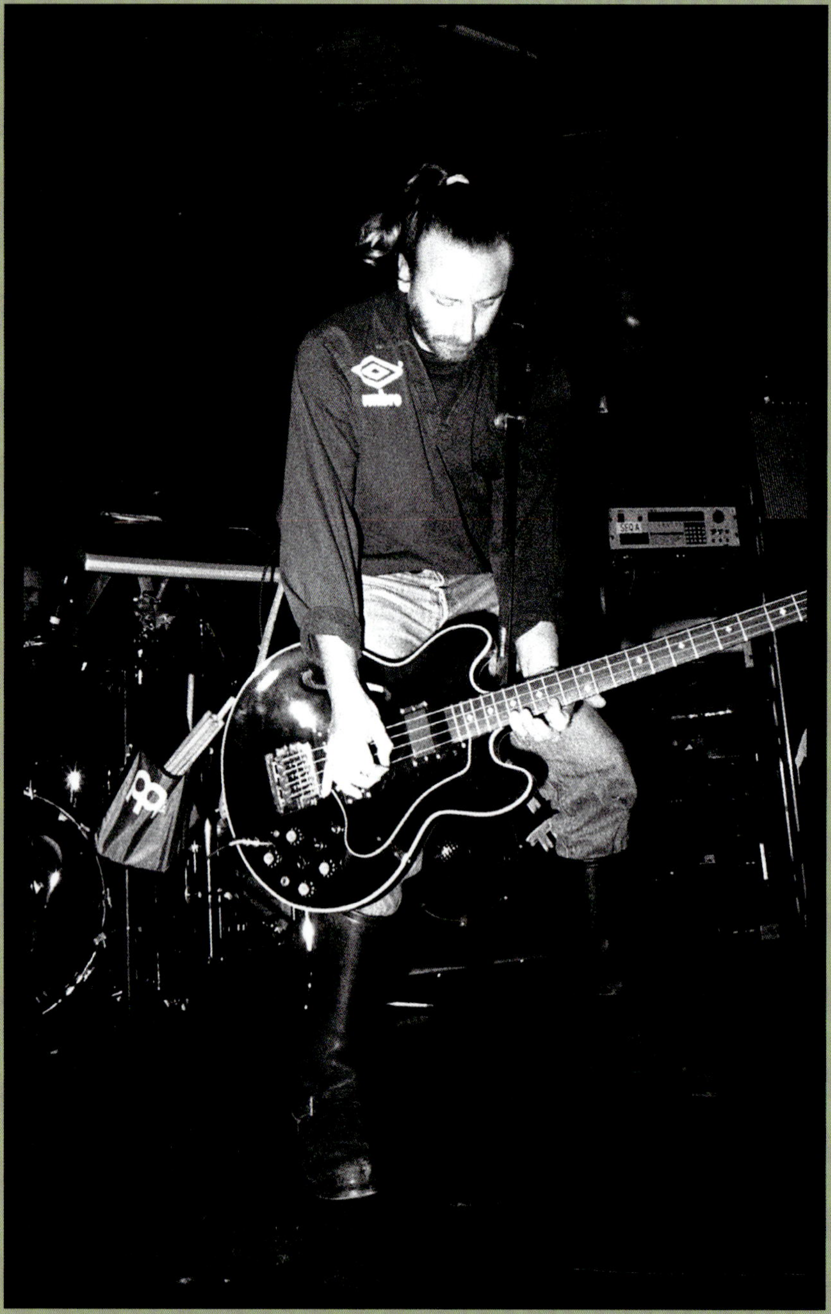

SINGLE LIVES

SINGLE LIVES

Right: *Revenge (from left): Dave Hicks, Hooky, Chris (CJ) Jones.*

Below: *Bernard and Johnny Marr, the Electronic years: Sunset Strip, Los Angeles, August 1990.*

The solo projects were beginning to take flight. Bernard's exploratory collaboration with Johnny Marr was christened Electronic and they planned to tour. For Revenge, Hooky recruited guitarist Dave Hicks, from Lavolta Lakota, a band he'd been doing the live sound for, plus keyboardist Chris 'CJ' Jones, engineer at the toe-curlingly named Suite 16, the studio Hooky co-owned, where there was a picture of Ian on the wall. Meanwhile, the other two would become The Other Two.

All three acts would initially sign to Factory, but the label's financial troubles were becoming public knowledge against a backdrop of excess, such as a £25,000 boardroom table which hung from the ceiling. With the decline of Ecstasy, gangs began to circle the Haçienda. EMI and CBS sniffed around New Order, but they weren't ready to cut the umbilical cord. Anyway, CBS's man blew his label's case when he declared that the Paul King solo album was the best he'd ever worked on.

For the rest of 1989, there were dribbles of New Order business to attend to. There was almost a collaboration with revered film director Michael Powell. Michael Shamberg had made contact, with a view to Powell making a New Order video. Instead, Powell attempted to recruit them for *The Sands Of Dee*, a short film based around Charles Kingsley's poem starring Tilda Swinton, for which he would use "Age Of Consent". Alas, New Order baulked when

160 Decades: Joy Division + New Order

> "WE HAD A LOT OF ENERGY IN THE '80S. IT JUST WASN'T OUR OWN, IF YOU KNOW WHAT I MEAN. IT WAS THE KIND OF ENERGY THAT YOU CAN BUY."
>
> BERNARD

Powell requested £100,000 funding, diaries clashed and the director died before the film could be made. The seven-track New Order video, Substance appeared in September, as did Hooky's son, Jack Bates, and the single "Run2", a weedy remix of "Run" by R.E.M. producer Scott Litt with a cover inspired by Bold washing powder. It stumbled to forty-nine in the British charts. The feeble B-side, "MTO" sampled "Fine Time".

At this time, Tony Wilson met David Bloomfield, the Football Association PR who'd enjoyed the "Best & Marsh" theme. There was a World Cup being held in Italy in 1990. England had qualified and the team needed a song.

Meanwhile, in November 1989, Revenge were first out of the solo blocks with their distinctly earthbound "7 Reasons" single. It sounded a little like Martha's "Light Years From Love". It wasn't a disaster, but it didn't chart and it was no "Getting Away With It", the following month's gorgeous first single from Electronic. Wheeling out the big guns, Bernard and Johnny Marr recruited Pet Shop Boy, Neil Tennant, to sing alongside Bernard. Tennant's bandmate Chris Lowe helped out, Anne Dudley arranged the strings and, as he had for "7 Reasons", Peter Saville designed the sleeve. Reaching number twelve in the UK and thirty-eight in the US, it sold over half a million copies. One-nil to Bernard.

What did they want? Clearly anything that didn't involve working with each other. Hooky's idea that Bernard was a nascent dictator seems flawed, not least since Johnny Marr was no sideman. Likewise Hooky's theory that Bernard didn't want to tour wasn't quite right: the rest of Bernard's career would suggest he simply didn't want to tour with Hooky. Perhaps Hooky just wanted a meat'n'potatoes rock band who recorded quickly, toured heavily and got on. He didn't seem to be reaching for the stars.

The '80s had begun tragically, but the decade had eventually been good to New Order, through a combination of gifts they never

Above: *Pet Shop Boys Chris Lowe and Neil Tennant, MTV Video Music Awards, Los Angeles, 1986.*

Opposite: *Hooky, your page 163 fella…*

expected to have, a little luck and the ability to push on and discover new musical vistas. As Bernard cryptically put it – although not nearly cryptically enough – "We had a lot of energy in the '80s. It just wasn't our own, if you know what I mean. It was the kind of energy that you can buy."

In January 1990, Revenge made their live debut at, of all places Skin2, in, of all cities London. Equally as surreal, that month the gang startled even themselves by getting back together. Since winning the World Cup in 1966, the England soccer team had failed to distinguish themselves, both on the pitch and in the recording studio. The impossibly chirpy "Back Home" was a number one in 1970, but Smokie's Chris Norman; an unspeakable version of "He's Got The Whole World In His Hands" retitled "We've Got The Whole World At Our Feet" and even guaranteed hitmakers Stock Aitken Waterman had failed to score with successive choirs of footballers who couldn't sing. Recruiting New Order was a sign things would be very different in 1990.

Rob, the only soccer maven in the camp, wasn't bothered. Surprisingly, the band were, especially Bernard. Since he himself wasn't a soccer fan, Bernard recruited Keith Allen, actor, irritant and father of future pop star Lily, to write lyrics, from which some (including the original title "E For England"), but not all, drug references would be exorcised. Bernard also hired Kenneth Wolstenholme, the BBC's commentator at the 1966 Final to rerecord his iconic phrase "they think it's all over… it is now" and he asked Stephen Hague to produce, after the left-field first choice, Swans drummer Roli Mosimann, hadn't worked out. Gillian and Stephen's theme for the television show *Reportage* formed the backing track and after recording at Real World, they were ready to go in March. All they needed was some singing footballers to come to Jimmy Page's Sol Studio, chosen because of its proximity to Bisham Abbey, where the team trained.

162 Decades: Joy Division + New Order

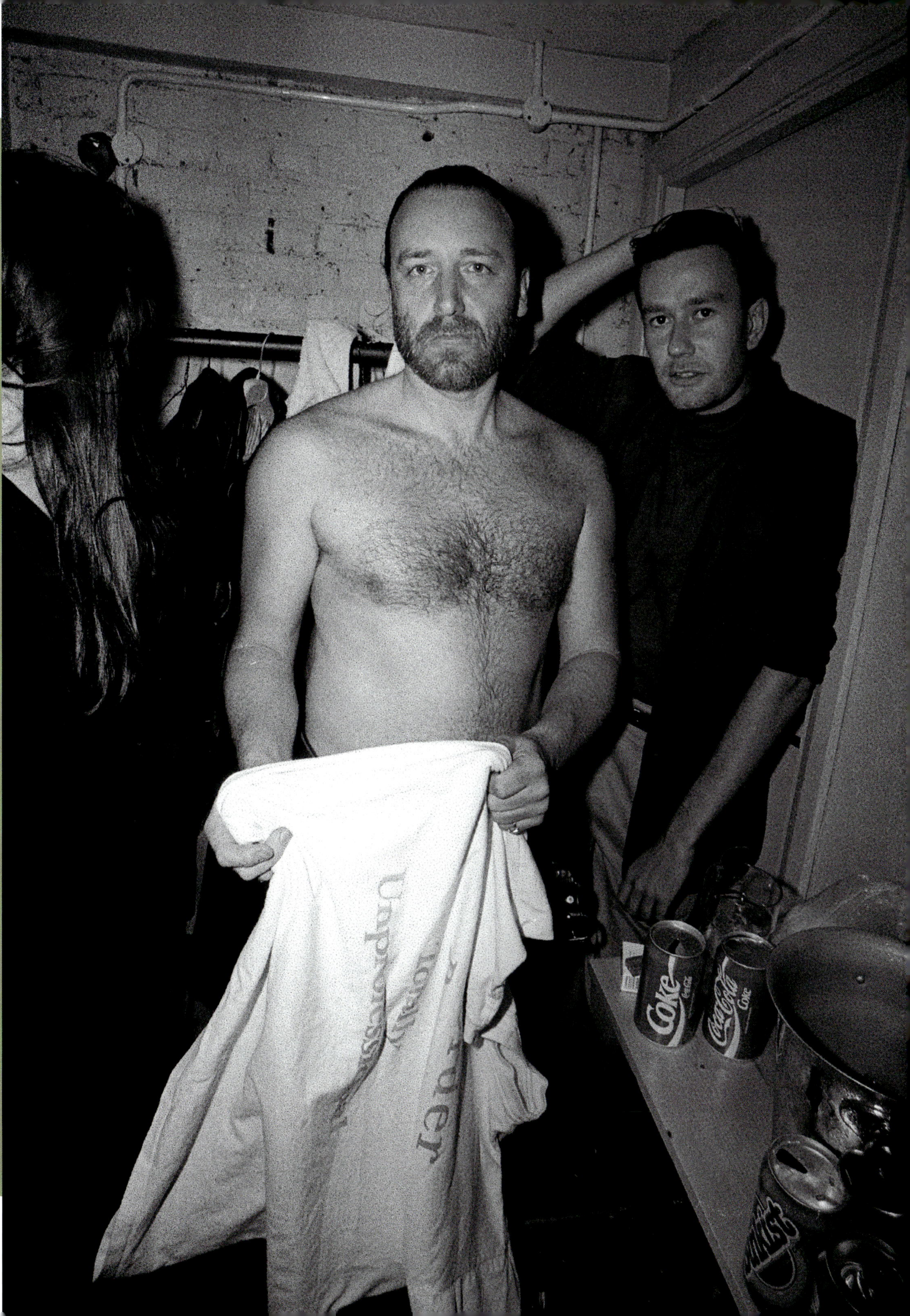
Coke
Coca-Cola

Bernard Sumner and his Elvis suit, the "World In Motion" video, 5 May, 1990.

Six players turned up: John Barnes, Paul Gascoigne, Des Walker, Peter Beardsley, Steve McMahon and Chris Waddle. They demanded to be paid their £2,000 fee in cash and since they had to open a Top Man store in Middlesbrough (just the 250 miles from Bisham Abbey), time was finite. Being greeted by an overly refreshed Hooky and a Bernard hungover from singing "Spanish Heart" at an 808 State show the previous evening (they would record it for the 808 State album, *ex:el*) didn't augur well, not least since the players were far from enthusiastic although, as Barnes generously noted, "If it was going to be the same old crap, why bother, but this was actually alright."

Budding alcoholic Gascoigne drank three bottles of champagne in fifteen minutes and, on being told there was a rap in the song, the future hitmaker (his version of "Fog On The Tyne" would reach number two in the UK) had a go. But for all Gascoigne's undoubted charisma, nobody could understand his Geordie accent, so Walker and Barnes competed. "Des was rubbish," remembered Barnes, "but I'd been rapping since I was seventeen and I used to be into bands like The Sugarhill Gang, so I thought it was quite straightforward." The footballers, other than Barnes, didn't actually make the finished record, which was probably for the best. They fled after an hour with their envelope.

For the video Hooky visited Bisham Abbey to film with the entire squad, who were preparing for a friendly with Brazil. Barnes, though, was injured so his sections were filmed at Melwood, the training ground of his club team, Liverpool (sold to developers in 2020). Fresh from working at Clear, Johnny Marr's home-studio, Bernard turned up in an Elvis outfit, which but for one brief shot, was rejected by director Philip Shotton, who'd worked on *Reportage*.

Released in May and backed by the Mosimann-helmed "The B-Side", "World In Motion", the first and only New Order UK number one and their last single on Factory,

164   Decades: Joy Division + New Order

soundtracked a new, Ecstasy-fuelled era in British culture, one where soccer would consolidate its position as the national sport and shed much of its hooligan aura. The band who made the song didn't really exist anymore, although later in the year both Joy Division and New Order would have old John Peel sessions turned into albums. This new cultural landscape of which "World In Motion" was such a crucial part helped The Haçienda turn a profit of £160,663.

Despite the chart topping New Order single, 1990 was a year of solo projects. In May, Revenge released their only album, the ludicrously expensive *One True Passion* and there would be a couple of singles, "Pineapple Face" and "Slave". They would tour the UK, the US and Brazil. It was all perfectly serviceable, but from the earliest of days, it was clear Revenge were destined to plod.

Meanwhile, Bernard and Johnny Marr were beavering away on the Electronic album, although their version of Donovan's "Colours" with Shaun Ryder would never see the light of day. As "Getting Away With it" receded into the distance, they were unsure which direction to take. After they supported Depeche Mode for two nights at the 60,000 capacity Dodger Stadium, in Los Angeles (unlike New Order, they stuck to the same set for both nights), with Pet Shop Boys as guests (their first live appearance in the US), the album planned for August was redrawn. Bernard's new Electronic schedule ensured that a New Order regrouping, loosely scheduled for November, wouldn't happen, although Stephen and Gillian had spurned offers of soundtrack work to make the reunion.

Des Walker and John Barnes recording "World in Motion".

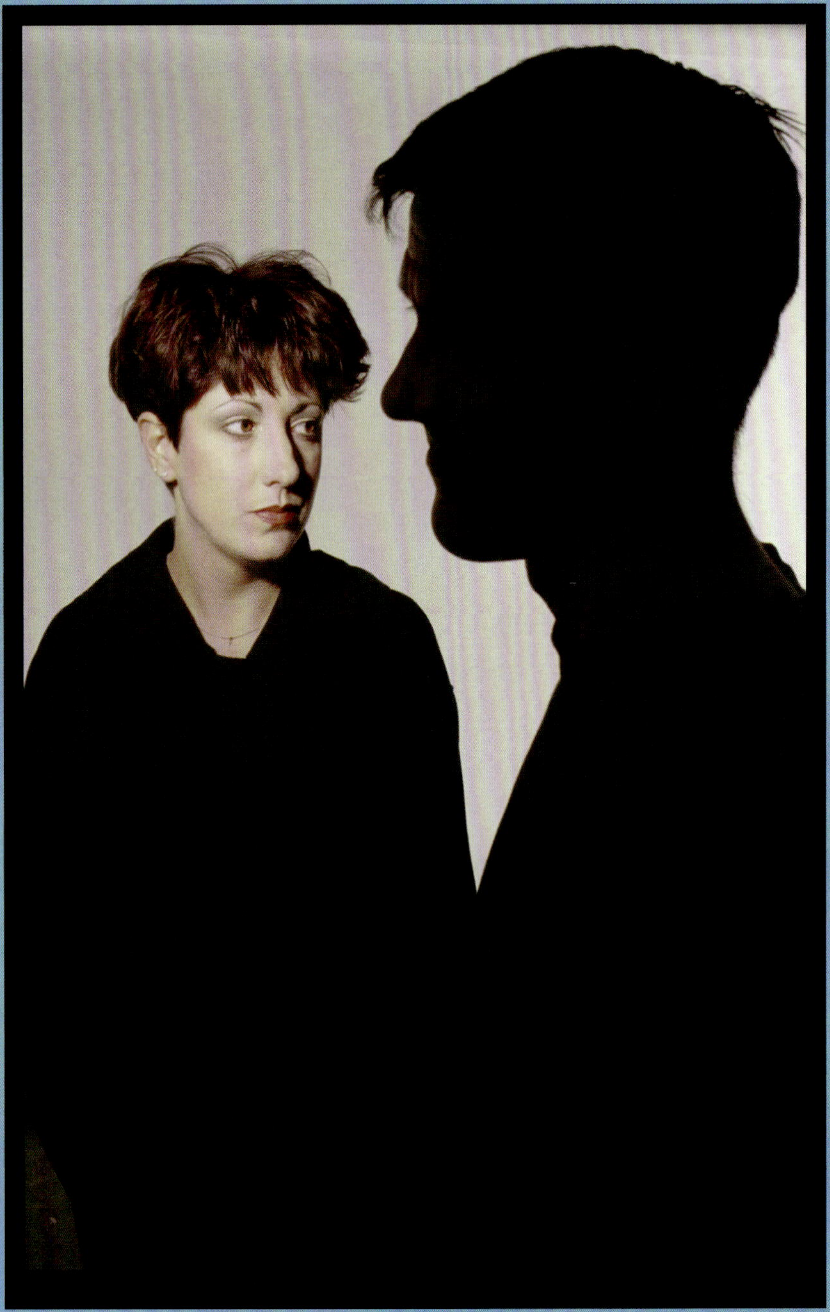

JOYLESS DIVISION

JOYLESS DIVISION

If 1990 had been the year of New Order resting, recuperating and taking a step back, 1991 was the rudest of awakenings.

It began well enough when Electronic made their British debut at The Haçienda. on January 9. To celebrate the renewal of the club's licence, there were glasses of champagne at the door and Neil Tennant, who had enjoyed many a Haçienda night with Bernard and Johnny Marr, turned up to anoint it "probably the best nightclub in the world." The sound was dreadful of course.

Then things turned really dark. The profit-making, Ecstasy-fuelled and friendly Haçienda was suddenly invaded by a hardcore gang culture and Dave Haslam's third and final phase began. The losses began spiralling again and, after a gun was pulled on a bouncer, The Haçienda was temporarily closed on January 30. "If we hadn't shut it down immediately, somebody would have been killed," reasoned Bernard.

State of the art security was introduced, pushing security costs to over £6,000 a week, but with both Factory ("leaking money like an elephant with cystitis," as Hooky poetically put it) and The Haçienda facing financial meltdown, one thing was becoming clear: whatever the questions were, only a new album by some if its directors could provide some of the answers.

On April 18, three days after Electronic's "Get The Message" single was released, forty-two-year-old Martin Hannett died of a heart attack after what Shaun Ryder claims was a "massive bender which lasted for days" with Ryder's cousins. Years later, Hooky paid wise tribute in *Rolling Stone*: "He gave us the gift of longevity. He saw something in our music that Bernard and I, the most outspoken members, fought. We wanted to sound like The Clash and Sex Pistols. He saw something more."

The Haçienda reopened on May 10. On 1 June, a bouncer was stabbed. In between, Electronic finally released their eponymous debut album. Against a backdrop that saw Bernard having heart palpitations during the recording and those trips to The Haçienda every Friday, they'd plumped for stately electro and it just about worked. It sold a million copies and reached number two in Britain and 109 in the US. "Bloody good for a band nobody had heard of," noted Bernard, disingenuously. "Getting Away With It" was excluded from the first British pressing, but there was another Pet Shop Boys collaboration, "The Patience of A Saint", while "Gangster" had been mooted for the non-existent Bernard solo album and Bernard rapped on "Idiot Country", his take on rave culture. Rob had initially looked after them, but he was soon usurped by Johnny Marr's manager, Marcus Russell.

Time and money were pressing. With Bernard free at last, New Order met at Stephen and Gillian's house in August to face some unpalatable truths, chiefly that they didn't have any option but to make a new album.

*Electronic, Wembley Hall,
12 December, 1991.*

Joyless Division 169

The Haçienda dancefloor. Bez from Happy Mondays, second left.

"IT WAS A VERY UNPLEASANT RECORD TO MAKE."

STEPHEN

First there were schedules to be cleared. Electronic closed work on their first album with a single in September, the unremarkable "Feel Every Beat". The Revenge EP, *Gun World Porn*, kept them ticking over. There was BBC Radio 1 *Live In Concert*, a New Order album comprising most of the Glastonbury 1987 set where "True Faith" made its debut. Peter Saville designed the sleeve and it went to thirty-three in the British charts, selling an impressive 60,000 copies.

In March, as Happy Mondays went to Barbados to make *Yes, Please!*, New Order went to Real World to record their sixth album in an atmosphere polar bears might have regarded as being on the chilly side. Belgian dance innovator, Pascal Gabriel, had been briefly trialled as producer (he would be credited with whatever "pre-production" is on "Regret" and "Young Offender") and they thought about doing it themselves. Eventually, they returned to who they knew: Stephen Hague. "We needed help," admitted Stephen months later. "If we hadn't got him in, we'd still be doing it and probably not speaking to each other." In the end, Hague was half-producer, half-babysitter. "Instead of me asking Hooky to turn down the bass, Stephen [Hague] would ask him to do it," remembered Bernard.

170 Decades: Joy Division + New Order

The recording dragged on and on. Although he had approved the initial template, Bernard regarded the others' contributions as not being up to the required standard. He worked with engineer Owen Morris, rewriting almost everything, while rueing the democracy which saw each member being paid equally. He asked for 50% of the publishing. Rob was still on 20% and the others shared the rest, an arrangement further complicated when Stephen Hague demanded a writer's cut. After producer and bassist agreed that Hooky had been let down by the finished "True Faith", Stephen Hague recorded Hooky separately. On its release, Hooky still believed the record was more Electronic than New Order. "It was," mused Stephen with characteristic understatement, "a very unpleasant record to make." They had a bar installed at Real World.

Elsewhere, a local Manchester band called Oasis introduced their newest member, Noel Gallagher, when they supported Revenge in Oldham in April. Electronic left the sinking Factory ship in June, shortly before their non-album single "Disappointed" was released. Another Neil Tennant collaboration, it was recorded for the soundtrack to the part-animated *Cool World* film and Stephen Hague remixed it into the British top ten. New Order were almost involved in the film *The Crow*, which featured a character called Sergeant Albrecht. Director Alex Proyas asked them to re-record "Love Will Tear Us Apart" for £50,000. Bernard declined, citing the ongoing recordings. In the end, Nine Inch Nails covered "Dead Souls" on the soundtrack.

In September, Happy Mondays' hopeless *Yes, Please!* didn't even make the UK top twenty. In October, The Other Two were go. Sung by Gillian, "Tasty Fish" was a sweet-natured slab of synthpop which peaked just outside the British top forty. An album was finished, but in November, Factory was finally and officially bankrupt. "We lost so much money, all down the drain to support stupid Factory quirks and buildings," sighed Stephen. "I never want anything to do with Factory again."

Factory owed £2 million, including £150,000 each to Joy Division, New Order and Electronic. On the other hand, Revenge and The Other Two owed significant sums to Factory. Its property empire was in negative equity, the New Order album was delayed and, with Happy Mondays a busted flush, once again nobody else on the label sold records. Worse still, the deals Factory had made with its cash cows, Joy Division and New Order, were on a handshake basis – Tony Wilson's "freedom to fuck off" clause – and either party could walk away at any time. Factory didn't own the catalogs, so it had nothing to sell, as potential purchasers London Records discovered to their delight.

Inspiral Carpets roadie Noel Gallagher, Haçienda, 1989. Subsequent whereabouts unknown.

JOYLESS DIVISION

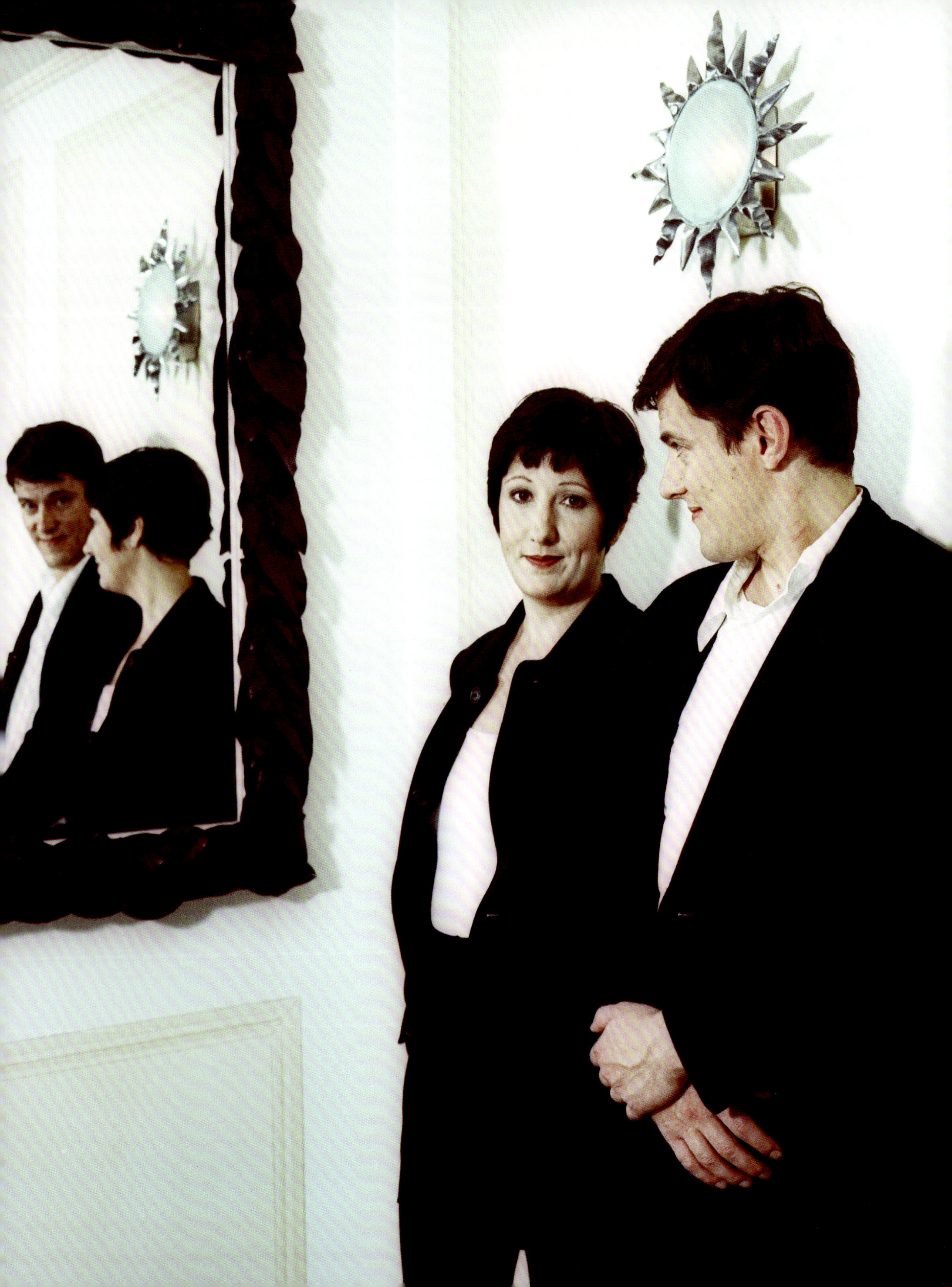

"SOMETIMES I LOOK AT BERNARD AND EVEN THOUGH HE THINKS HE CAN MAYBE DO WITHOUT NEW ORDER, IT'S BLOODY OBVIOUS HE CAN'T."

HOOKY

A deal was sealed the week before Christmas. Debbie Curtis, Rob and Bernard travelled to London to sign to London Records. Hooky was on an aeroplane; Stephen and Gillian were in the Seychelles and New Order were on a major label (they remained on the Warner Bros label Qwest in the US), all those years after Ian would have loved to have signed to RCA. "Signing to a major was actually a relief," admitted Bernard.

As Hooky found himself more and more in thrall to drugs and drink, Revenge stuttered to a halt in January 1993. Tony Wilson passed on Oasis, but on April 12, New Order returned, performing their latest single "Regret", on *Top Of The Pops*, via satellite from the *Baywatch* set on Venice Beach, CA. David Hasselhoff was there, although never in the same shot as the band. Bikini-clad women were having a conversation on a telephone and the members of New Order looked so overdressed for the Californian heat they might as well have worn handkerchiefs on their heads. Still, they were back, the genuine collaboration that was the strident but melancholic "Regret" was worth the wait and the cowboys-at-sunset sleeve was beautiful.

The official music video was a split-screen delight but, now a major label was in charge, there was a stylist and a £200,000 bill. Backed with a succession of spring-heeled remixes and the instrumental Republic out-take, "Vicious Circle", "Regret" flew to number four in Britain – they'd never reach such heights again – and twenty-eight in the US,

Gillian and Stephen as The Other Two, London, 1993.

their best placing. Things looked good, but as we all know from bitter personal experience, looks can be deceptive.

The sixth album, *Republic*, finally arrived in May, so late that its original reason for existing – saving Factory – was no longer relevant. They made little effort to conceal the inner tensions now. "I don't know if we'll carry on," Hooky confided to *NME* with an undercurrent of desperation. "Sometimes I look at Bernard and even though he thinks he can maybe do without New Order, it's bloody obvious he can't."

Peter Saville had moved to Los Angeles where he'd found work with advertising agency Frankfurt Balkind. The move wouldn't last, but he was inspired by California for Republic's sleeve, which contrasted tranquillity and destruction in a succession of vividly retouched images. It was his best, most thought-provoking work in years. Alas, the album wasn't New Order's best, most thought-provoking work in years. Bernard had found new love with Sarah Dalton and their son Dylan had been born in 1992, so his omnipresent bitterness surely now had nothing to do with his home life.

"Regret" was an auspicious start and "World", the second single, wasn't too far behind, with its insistent "that's the price of love" refrain, courtesy of Dee Lewis, backing vocalist for a succession of A-listers including Peter Gabriel and Pet Shop Boys. It was smooth, mellow and assured, but it lacked heart, as did so much of *Republic*.

JOYLESS DIVISION 173

The possibly bass-free "Ruined In A Day" certainly made flesh Hooky's worries about them making an Electronic album and letting Keith Allen make the video wasn't one of their better ideas. The single version predictably misfired, reaching number twenty-two in the UK, although the sinuous Sly & Robbie remixes added trumpets. *Republic* was an album of drifting and nothing drifted more than "Ruined In A Day". New Order had never sounded tired before. They did now.

"Spooky", *Republic*'s unnecessary fourth single – how things had changed on that front – benefited from a lively Fluke remix. There was more bass, Bernard's best singing on the album and the tentative reintroduction of the electro and rock blend. When Gillian's keyboards take over around the three-minute mark, it's beautiful too.

The oomph-free, sub-Electronic, mono-paced "Everyone Everywhere" had a gentle, unassuming chorus and some nifty acoustic guitar, but little in the way of inspiration.

Pascal Gabriel's work found its way onto the bitter "Young Offender", but it offers no definitive answer to the question of how *Republic* might have sounded with him on board rather than Stephen Hague. More Balearic? Perhaps. More assertive? Surely. More inspired? Hmmm.

Despite Dee Lewis's best efforts and something approaching a bass groove, the plodding "Liar" is so pedestrian Bernard gives up towards the end in favour of some half-hearted "doo-doo-doo" scatting. Rob may have blanched when he heard the lines "I'm growing tired of waiting/ For you to say goodbye" and "Were you abandoned in your youth?/ Because if not, you will be soon". As might Hooky.

Calling a track "Chemical" was tempting fate, but as a confused, disengaged song it didn't tempt enough fate. It rattled along merrily

For many, 1992 was Revenge's Paddington Bear year.

enough but, and not for the first time on *Republic*, Stephen's drums sounded flat. Maybe that's what Pascal Gabriel would have brought: better drums.

The tale of a devastating 1692 earthquake in Port Royal, Jamaica, "Times Change" finds Bernard comparing himself to Christ and rapping, even before some stentorian keyboards and melodica join in. No wonder it's the moment *Republic* begins its gentle upswing. It's the album's first and last sighting of bonkers, out-there New Order. How we'd missed them.

That upswing continued with "Special", where the band at last sounded like four leaders competing against each other once more. Bernard was at his most biting and bitter and nobody could misinterpret "I'm sick of trying/ I mean that it's over".

The closing "Avalanche" was mostly Stephen and Gillian's work and it's her singing "faith" repeatedly which takes a gorgeous near-instrumental to an even better place. It sounded like the end of something – probably the band – but it was a gracious, heart-tugging way to finish.

So that was that; an album which cost £430,000 and had only been created to save an already doomed Factory Records. *NME* gushed it was "near triumphant" as if willing it to be so, but Simon Price was smarter in *Melody Maker*, lamenting it has "few of the extremes of euphoria and elegia which characterised *Low-Life* and *Brotherhood*." While it was far from a disaster, it was a musical failure in part. Now, they had to tour the thing.

The album was a British number one and charted at a career-best eleven in the US, so London Records and Qwest pressed for dates. Hooky was desperate to go; Stephen and Gillian were as ambivalent as ever, but Bernard was reluctant, noting, "I didn't want to drink myself to death." Eventually even he had to bend to the will of the majority and since *Republic* was mostly his baby, he had more riding on its success than the others. They played four European festivals before heading back to the

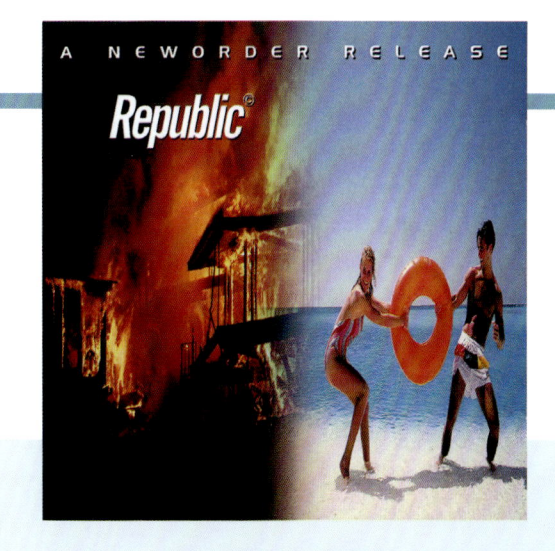

REPUBLIC

TRACK LISTING

Regret
World
Ruined In A Day
Spooky
Everyone Everywhere
Young Offender

Liar
Chemical
Times Change
Special
Avalanche

Released 3 May 1993
Label London – 828 413.1
Recorded at Real World, Box, England; RAK, London, England
Produced by Stephen Hague & New Order
Personnel
Bernard Sumner: vocals, guitars, synthesizers and programming
Peter Hook: 4-and 6-stringed bass, programming
Stephen Morris: drums, synthesizers and programming
Gillian Gilbert: synthesizers, guitars and programming; vocal on "Avalanche"
Cover Art Peter Saville & Pentagram
Notes
Republic became New Order's second consecutive album to top the UK Albums Chart and was nominated for the 1993 Mercury Music Prize.

United States. Having agreed to take part under duress, Bernard was now firmly in charge, so they managed just nine dates over three weeks, playing the same set each night.

There was just one remaining contractual obligation and, as it had been after the *Technique* tour, it was the Reading Festival. They played the same set as they had at the America shows and that was that.

To coincide with Reading, the ITV network broadcast *The New Order Story*, which would be made commercially available later in the year. Narrator Jenny Seagrove's comically misjudged narration belonged in a low-budget porn movie, there was a faux game show hosted by Keith Allen, real if bumbling interviews, table talk at The Haçienda, plus cameos from Quincy Jones, ("New Order was always different, as human beings, as musicians"), Bono and Neil Tennant. There was an awful lot of Tony Wilson, whom Bernard refers to as "a bleeding parasite ... bloodsucker"; a besuited Hooky surrounded by women in party outfits and the Sunkist mock-up. Everything, in fact, except for their feelings about each other.

In August the song now titled "World (The Price Of Love)" reached an impressive number thirteen in the UK and ninety-two in the US, their last chart placing. "Spooky" reached twenty-two in Britain in December.

Hooky was at a dangerous loose end. Bernard was back with Johnny Marr. Gillian and Stephen were engaged to be married and she bought him a tank to celebrate. The Other Two's delayed album was released by London Records in November. Co-produced by Stephen Hague, whose studio clutter was regularly tidied by his clients, *The Other Two & You* was very much of the Saint Etienne dreamy, indie-dance school. It spawned the single "Selfish" and was pleasant without being essential. They had looked for outside vocalists after Stephen Hague suggested Stephen Morris take singing lessons. Kim Wilde and Alison Moyet were mooted, but the answer was closer to home and Gillian took over. "Why bother making a record on our own?" Stephen asked in *NME*. "Because no one else turned up."

New Order ebbed away further in 1994. Stephen and Gillian were married, a move which surprised no one. So too was Hooky – a move which surprised everyone – in Las Vegas by an Elvis impersonator, three months after meeting volatile comedienne Caroline Aherne. She was an extraordinary talent whether as part of *The Fast Show*; as the little old lady Dorothy Merton on her spoof chat show, *The Mrs Merton Show* ("What first attracted you to

Gillian at Reading Festival, 1993, the last New Order show for five years.

Monaco, The Lomax, Liverpool, 12 September, 1997.

the millionaire Paul Daniels?" she famously asked the magician's much younger wife Debbie McGee) or later when she co-wrote *The Royle Family*. She bought Hooky a Harley-Davidson for his fortieth birthday.

Hooky flirted with Killing Joke – there were rehearsals at Suite 16 and some of the work would appear on Killing Joke's contributions to the *Freispiel* soundtrack – but when *The Mrs Merton Show* began airing, he became house band leader for £30,000 a season, alongside Dave Potts, another Suite 16 engineer who had been part of Revenge. The two were working on what would become Monaco.

It wasn't all good news: Bernard, Stephen and Gillian pulled out of funding The Haçienda and Iris did a love cheat exposé on Hooky with the *Sunday Mirror*: "Jane (Roberts) was his roadie, but I discovered she was twiddling with more than his amplifier." Still, in November, Hooky played the first of a few dates with Durutti Column, having guested on their 1993 track, "The Next Time". Durutti Column had signed to Factory Too, Tony Wilson's doomed attempt to re-float the brand. They even wrote a Hooky tribute, "Hooky's Tune".

The material recorded for RCA, plus a 1977 demo (and bizarrely "As You Said", a track recorded shortly before Ian's death) resurfaced for commercial release. It was a footnote, but not a disgraceful one and a reminder of what Martin Hannett had brought to the table. More pressingly, "True Faith" rose into the British top ten once again, via a passable remix by the Perfecto team of Steve Osborne and Paul Oakenfold.

The single was a taster for *The Best Of New Order*, which would reach number four in the UK. With London Records keen to milk their investment, the shoddy UK version contained nothing from before "Thieves Like Us". It did include new remixes of "True Faith", "1963",

JOYLESS DIVISION 177

"Bizarre Love Triangle" and "Round & Round" alongside "Blue Monday '88". The US version went as far back as "Dreams Never End", but ignored *Brotherhood*. It was no *Substance*, but the eighteen-track video version was a joy.

1995 was another year of barrel-scraping. In January, the Arthur Baker remix of "1963" went to number twenty-one in the UK to finish the *Best Of* campaign and with no sign of New Order activity, an increasingly lost Rob told Manchester journalist Mick Middles, "Maybe the band will get together and record again someday. Maybe they won't. Maybe it isn't as much fun as it used to be. Perhaps they never had that much in common."

London Records were beginning to understand that they'd been sold a very expensive pup. The Deborah Curtis memoir *Touching From A Distance* renewed interest in Joy Division, even as it punctured holes in Ian's halo. Bernard, Hooky, Stephen and Tony Wilson spoke to her: Rob refused. Desperate to see some return on their investment, London seized the moment, whipping out "Love Will Tear Us Apart" for the third time. Obligingly it reached number nineteen, as it had second time around in 1983. It was a precursor to yet another Joy Division compilation, *Permanent*, which included a new mix of "Love Will Tear Us Apart", the original B-side version of "Love Will Tear Us Apart" and assorted usual suspects, including album tracks. That perfectly preserved Joy Division catalogue was becoming a burden to those who now owned

> "MAYBE THE BAND WILL GET TOGETHER AND RECORD AGAIN SOMEDAY. MAYBE THEY WON'T. MAYBE IT ISN'T AS MUCH FUN AS IT USED TO BE."
>
> ROB

Barney, in a room of his own, Manchester.

it, but *Permanent* reached number sixteen in the British charts.

"Blue Monday" was also released for the third time. Now titled "Blue Monday '95" and remixed by German duo Hardfloor, it spluttered to seventeen in the British charts. There was another desperate album to flog titled *(the rest of) New Order* and, as David Bennun thundered in *Melody Maker*, "well might it cower behind parentheses and lower-case letters." Even so, it went to number five in the British charts and included remixes of nine singles and "Age Of Consent". For lucky early purchasers there was an entire CD of "Blue Monday" remixes. Without exception, the new versions traduced the original and what once was a groundbreaking strength of New Order – fabulous remixes of great originals – was now a reputation-shrivelling weakness.

1996 was another near write-off. London left Joy Division and New Order alone, but Hooky's tempestuous marriage fell apart. Later in the year, though, he would meet Rebecca Jones, who would offer the stability he'd missed since Iris Bates, and Monaco would begin working in earnest.

Delayed by *Republic* and Johnny Marr's work with The The, the second Electronic album, *Raise The Pressure* (its title taken from Jon Savage's excellent book, *England's Dreaming*) was released in July. Preceded by one single "Forbidden City" and followed by another, "Second Nature", it would reach number eight in the UK and a disappointing 143 in the US. Recording was more sedate, fatherhood had matured both Bernard and Johnny Marr and Bernard was experimenting with Prozac.

"I'd not made an album straight since 1977," he explained. "I felt that was dependency." This time around, their chief collaborator was Kraftwerk's Karl Bartos, rather than the tentatively mooted Nile Rodgers of Chic. They all worked in Dusseldorf before the German came to Manchester. Bartos brought problems. Firstly, he was a minor Kraftwerker and the genius of that group clearly lay elsewhere. Secondly, rather than bringing the spirit of Kraftwerk, he'd discovered the Beatles. They culled thirty songs down to thirteen but, as Bernard admitted, it was "a messy, difficult album." They didn't tour it. In fact, Electronic wouldn't play live again.

Rob's lifestyle was beginning to catch up with him but, beset by heart and thyroid problems, he began to campaign for a New Order tour. It would have to wait. Bernard provided vocals for "This Time I'm Not Wrong" a surprisingly guitar-driven number seventy-eight single for

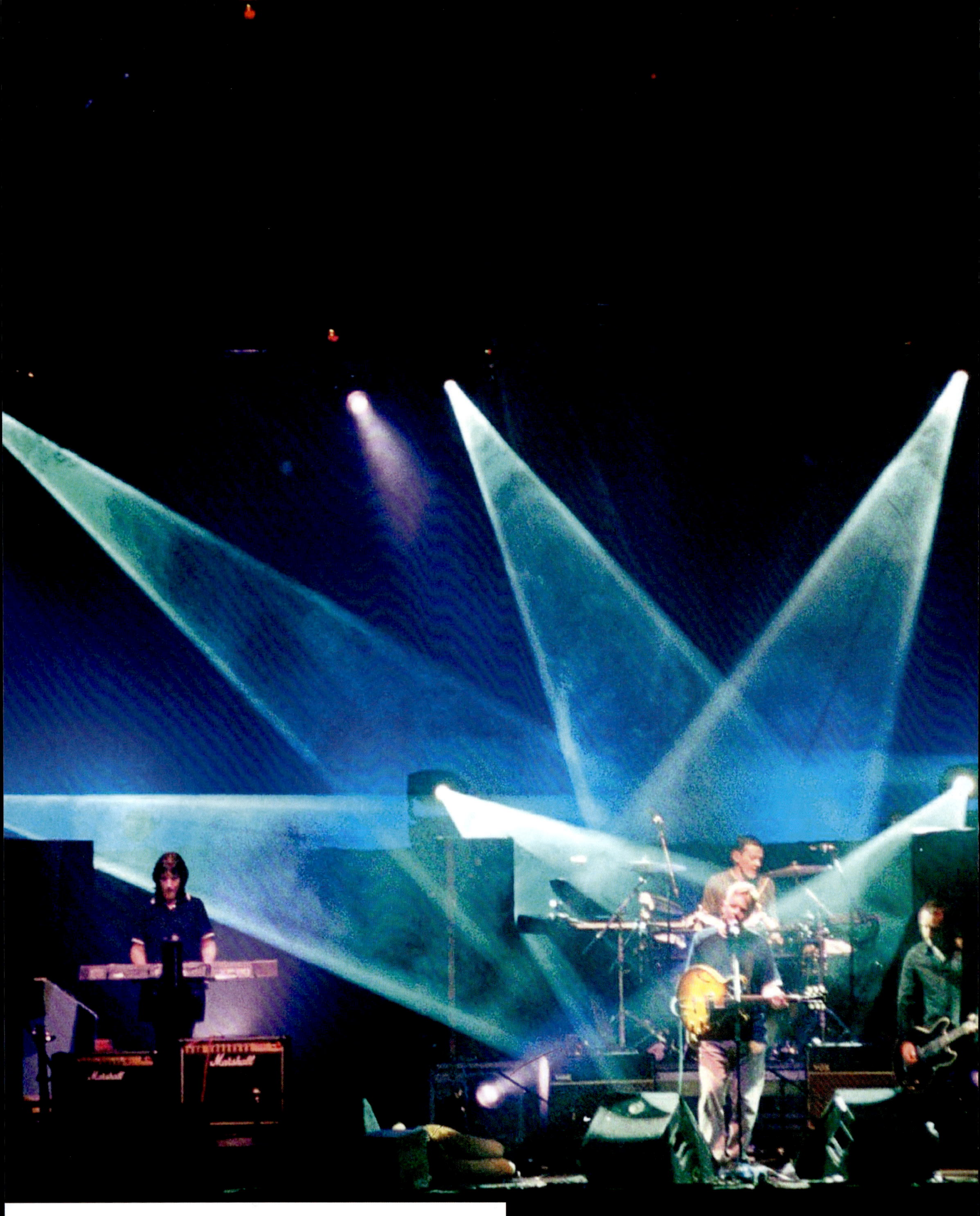

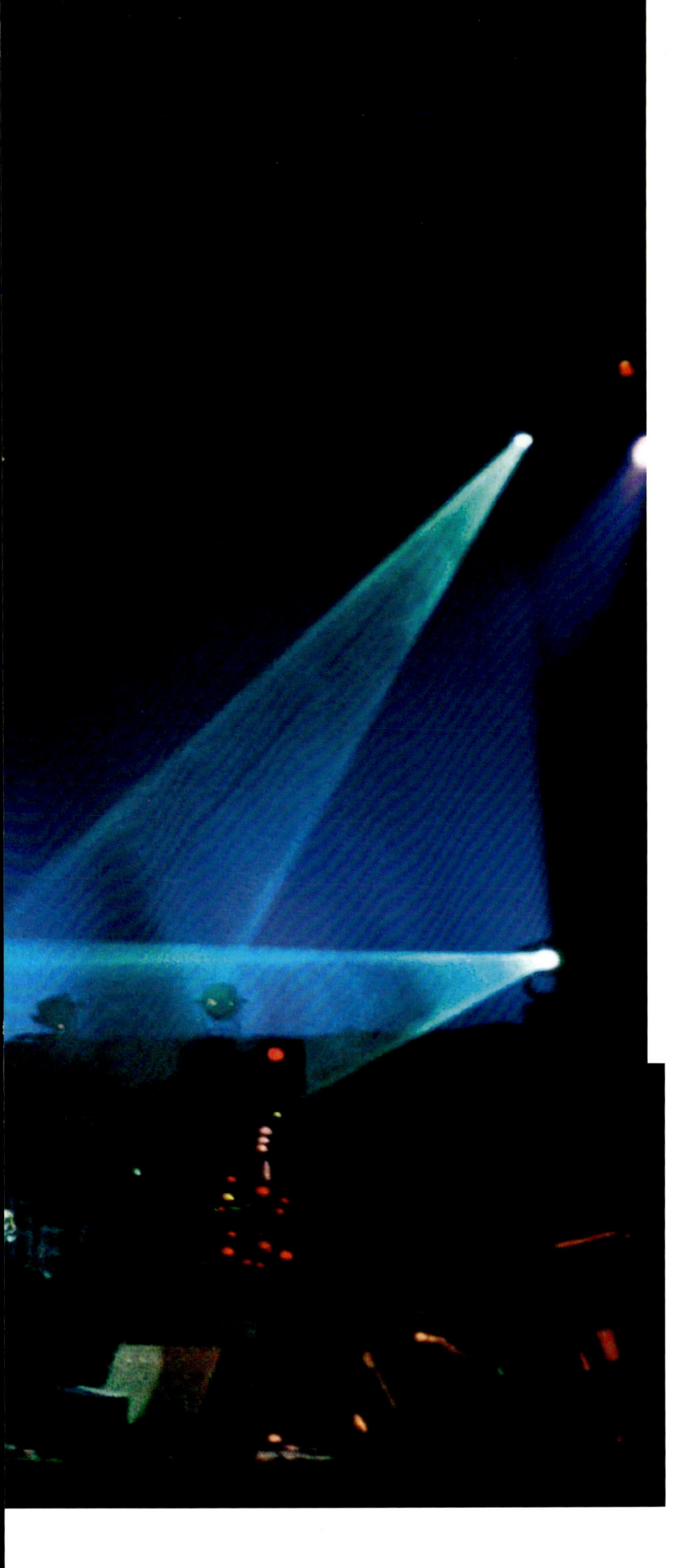

fellow Mancunians Sub Sub, who recorded for Rob's occasionally successful label, Rob's Records. They would later change their name to Doves and achieve significant UK success.

Managed by Steve Harrison who also oversaw The Charlatans' career and whose aunt had lived next door to Ian, Hooky's Monaco had secured a major label deal with Polydor. The first single, "What Do You Want From Me?", his dissection of the Caroline Aherne relationship, was a number eleven hit and remains the best work by any band member outside the mothership, possibly because of how much it sounded like vintage New Order. Released in June 1997, the excellent album, *Music For Pleasure* sold half a million and also went to number eleven in Britain. Nothing on it could touch that first single, although follow ups, "Sweet Lips" (a number eighteen in the UK) and "Shine" (only charting at number fifty-five in the UK), weren't too far behind. "Under The Stars" – an extra track on the US edition – was a tribute to Ruth Polsky. Bernard wasn't the only one who could thrive without the others.

Finally, on June 28, shortly after Hooky stopped paying what he claimed was £7,000 a month towards it, The Haçienda closed for good. A visiting party of magistrates on the licensing committee had seen some of the violence first-hand. "It was too far ahead of its time," lamented Bernard, curiously.

The magazine *Touch* released New Order's long forgotten, twenty-two-minute "Prime 586" as a single titled "Video 586". Strictly for completists, it only reached number eighty-six in the UK. Then, just in time for Christmas 1997, came *Heart and Soul*, a four CD Joy Division box set, which made it to seventy in the UK. It comprised almost all the studio output, bar the version of "Love Will Tear Us Apart" on the original's B-side and the version of "Walked In Line" which made *Still*. Alas, several tracks on the last two discs of rarities and live tracks weren't of releasable quality and the packaging

Let's get the old gang together again: Reading, 1998.

fell apart after minimal use: Factory lived on in London.

In February, with Hooky three months into his marriage with Becky, Rob finally convened the band meeting he'd so desperately sought. Grudges old and new (Stephen argued he'd written most of *Republic*; Bernard admitted to dumping it) were aired, but Bernard, of all people, suggested some concerts.

So it came to pass that on July 16, New Order, re-formed if not reformed, played the 3,500-capacity Manchester Apollo. The guest list was a thousand strong. There was a surprise airing for "Paradise", a bunch of singles, and not only did they play "Atmosphere" and "Love Will Tear Us Apart", but "Isolation" and "Heart and Soul" too. There were more shows: the Reading Festival yet again where Monaco appeared the same day; an airing of "Temptation" at the ceremony which announced the 2002 Manchester Commonwealth Games; a show at the larger Manchester Arena and a New Year's Eve show at London's Alexandra Palace where Hooky kissed Bernard, Noel Gallagher watched from the sidelines and Happy Mondays dancer Bez guested on "Fine Time" and "Blue Monday". They would not play again for three years.

Around the New Order shows, Monaco contributed "You Should Be Dancing" to the confused Bee Gees tribute album *Gotta Get A Message To You*, which also featured Robbie Williams and The Orb, Boyzone, Steps and Lightning Seeds. More seriously, Hooky's daughter Jessica was born in October with the lung virus, bronchiolitis. The tot would pull through, but after Alexandra Palace, Hooky drove straight back to the Manchester hospital where Jessica was recovering. And just to show that "Blue Monday" can never die, Orgy's stupendous, drum-tastic version was the most played song on American radio in 1998.

1999 promised much but delivered little. There was another meeting at Stephen and Gillian's farmhouse, this time to agree to the making of a new album. Hooky and Bernard were even socialising again.

First, though, there were other commitments to negotiate. In April, Electronic released their third and final album, the more guitar-orientated *Twisted Tenderness*. It reached nine in the UK but, having been dropped by their American label, it would not surface in the US until 2000 and even then it would not trouble the charts. "Vivid" was a top twenty UK single, but the project had run its course and recruiting Arthur Baker as producer was a step back rather than forwards.

The same month, The Other Two finally unveiled their second album, *Super Highways*, which would be followed by the single version of the title track. With Gillian still far from confident about her vocals, they brought in Melanie Williams, guest vocalist on Sub Sub's hit "Ain't No Love (Ain't No Use)", to co-write and sing. The results were a gentle advance on *The Other Two & You*. It didn't chart and they wouldn't release another album.

On May 15, Rob Gretton died of a heart attack aged just forty-six. At the end he was addicted chiefly to Caramac chocolate bars and relieved his charges were reunited. "He could be a vindictive bastard, but I had the greatest respect for him," said Hooky, ungenerously. Rob had been the first to spot that Warsaw might be great and the one who pushed for increased keyboards and for Gillian's introduction. Moreover, he was New Order's conscience until the end. Without him they would never have broken through, and they would have had to compromise much more to maintain control over their releases. But equally, without Rob, their business would have been run more professionally. They would surely have not committed so much for so long to The Haçienda and Rob's insularity prevented them being bigger in the United States, quicker. By the time of his death, Rob's moment had passed, but nobody ever questioned his status as the fifth member of Joy Division and New Order.

And in June that year, there was *Preston 28 February 1980*, a pointless album which did nothing to enhance Joy Division's reputation as one of the great live bands.

Rob Gretton, during the July–August 1993 North American tour.

"HE COULD BE A VINDICTIVE BASTARD,
BUT I HAD THE GREATEST RESPECT FOR HIM."

HOOKY

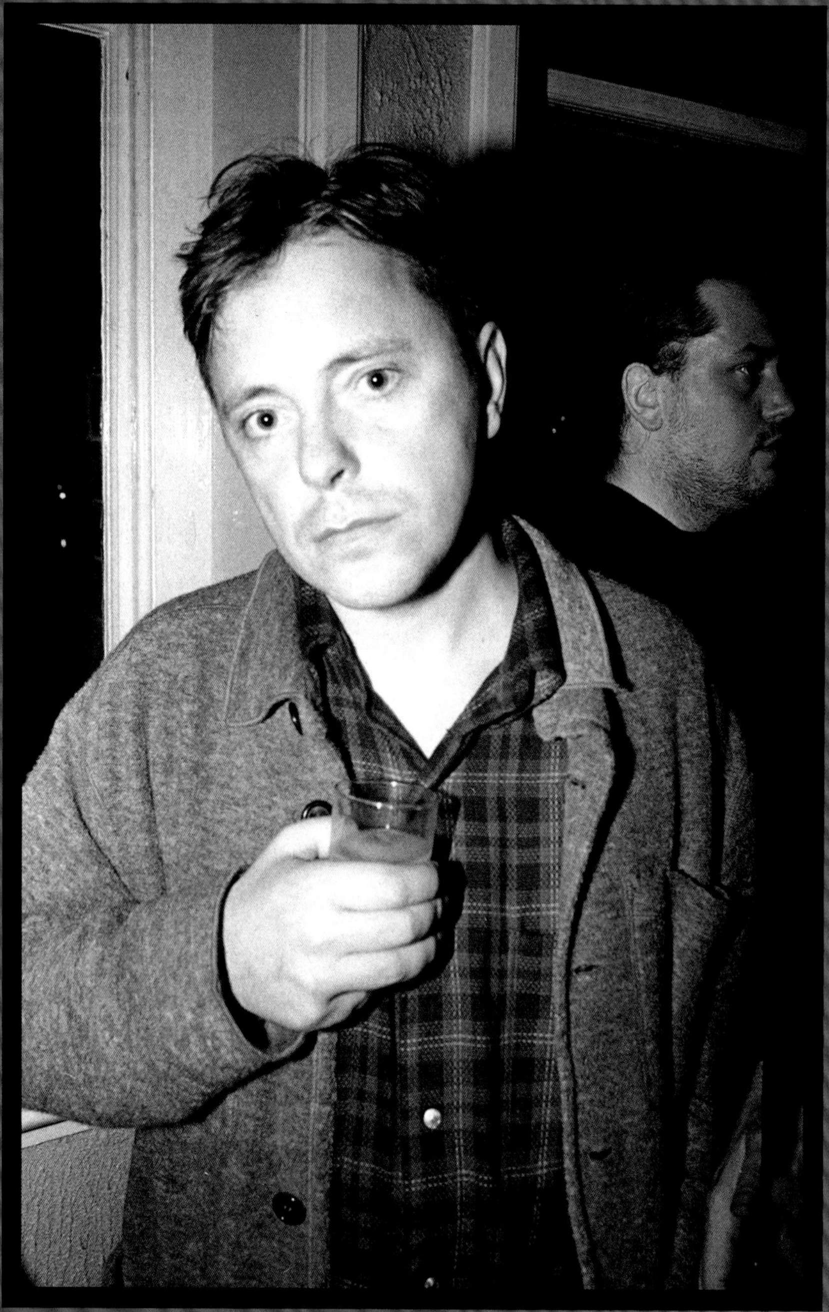

ONE LAST PUSH

ONE LAST PUSH

The new century began disastrously for Hooky. His mother, Irene, died on January 2 and soon Monaco were – unfairly, all things considered – dumped by Polydor after the label heard the second album. Still, in February, the soundtrack to the film of Alex Garland's novel *The Beach*, featured a new New Order song, the appositely titled "Brutal", which had been recorded the previous September with producer Rollo Armstrong of Faithless. Bernard was on fine form, as was Hooky, but Armstrong wasn't the man for them and even when Perfecto's Steve Osborne was brought in to rescue, it wasn't quite fast enough. It featured only briefly in the film and wouldn't make the next album, but it secured more New Order work for Osborne.

With the band recording at Real World and getting on as well as they could, June saw a pointless reissue of the 1987 Glastonbury show. Joy Division's *The Complete BBC Recordings* followed in August, collecting the John Peel sessions, the *Something Else* performances and an interview with Ian and Stephen. Meanwhile, the first New Order John Peel sessions from 1981 and '82, initially released in 1990 as *The Peel Sessions*, were sloppily reissued as *The John Peel Sessions*, presumably in the hope nobody would notice they were the same product.

The self-titled Monaco album Polydor had spurned was picked up by the Papillon label, who promptly failed to promote it properly. At the same time, the relationship between Dave Potts and Hooky was souring rapidly. There would not be another Monaco album and they played their final show on 31 August at London's Scala. Hooky had bigger fish to fry.

The seventh New Order album – but their first in eight wearying years – was ready in early 2001, although it wouldn't be released until August. It cost £505,000 – it would have been more had they paid Jerry Lee Lewis the $50,000 he demanded to play piano on one track. They called it *Get Ready*. As Hooky confessed to the *Guardian*: "That was probably the happiest I've been with these fuckers. At the time I could have murdered him for saying it, but Sumner was right all along: we needed time to find ourselves."

More importantly, Gillian and Stephen now had two daughters, Tilly and Grace. The youngest, Grace, hadn't been well and in March when she was diagnosed with transverse myelitis, an inflammation of the spinal cord which affects the entire nervous system, Gillian walked away from the band. They agreed Stephen should stay. Once again, Hooky excelled himself: "No more having the world thinking that someone brought something of value to New Order when they didn't. You should never have a couple in a band."

April saw the Joy Division live album, *Les Bains Douches: 18 December 1979* (The Shower Baths), which featured a 1979 Paris concert padded out by selections from two 1980 Dutch shows and New Order's *316* video which

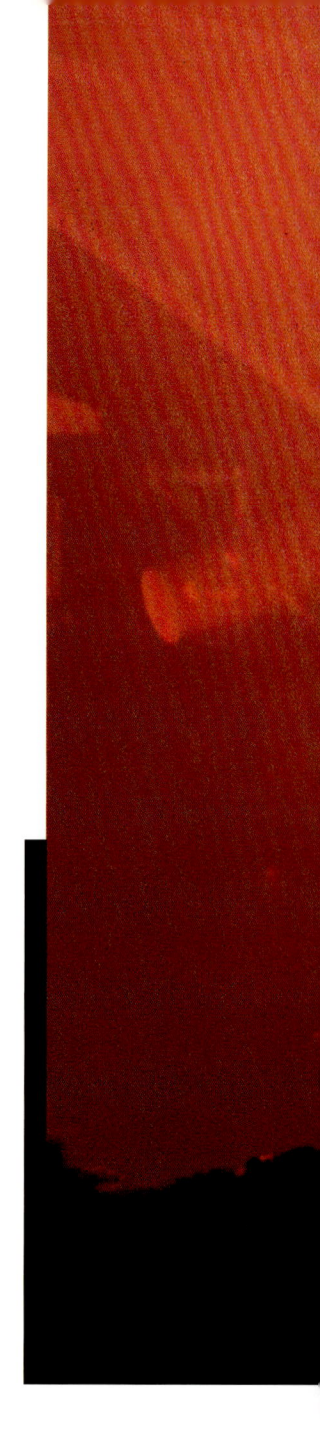

New Order, the arena act. The days of diffident live shows were long gone.

"THAT WAS PROBABLY THE HAPPIEST I'VE BEEN WITH THESE FUCKERS. AT THE TIME I COULD HAVE MURDERED HIM FOR SAYING IT, BUT SUMNER WAS RIGHT ALL ALONG: WE NEEDED TIME TO FIND OURSELVES."

HOOKY

unnecessarily bound the Taras Shevchenko concert and the Reading Festival 1998 together.

Hooky's drinking reached some kind of peak during *Get Ready*'s final mixing at Trevor Horn's Sarm West studio, but, more reassuringly, even before the release, there would be live dates. The others had covered for Gillian in the studio, but Bernard suggested a live replacement, Phil Cunningham, once of Johnny Marr-produced, indie also-rans Marion and an Electronic collaborator.

The first show was at the 1,200 capacity Liverpool Olympia on July 18. They opened – *opened* – with "Atmosphere". They played "Your Silent Face" for the first time in over a decade, and there were five new songs. Phil Cunningham wasn't the only debutant. Who was that on guitar? Why, it was Smashing Pumpkins leader Billy Corgan, a guest on *Get Ready*. Heavens.

"They mentioned they were doing some dates and asked if I'd like to be in the band," Corgan, who regarded Joy Division as his Beatles, remembered. In 2018, Corgan would invite Jack Bates to join Smashing Pumpkins as touring bassist. "Playing with New Order was one of my greatest musical experiences. The most exciting part was when they played Joy Division: I got goosebumps."

For these dates, they flew first class rather than business; the hotels were elite and the schedule light. The ensemble played dates in Japan, the US and, for reasons still not clear, they supported Robbie Williams in Cologne, much to the bewilderment of his audience, not all of whom were born when "Blue Monday" was first released.

Then, following the single "Crystal", came *Get Ready*. The album was dedicated to Rob Gretton and was mostly the work of Bernard and Hooky, with extensive production and mixing contributions from Steve Osborne. The Peter Saville-designed cover featured the German actress Nicolette "Coco" Krebitz. As *Q* magazine (closed 2020) said, "New Order have made better albums," but the dance experiments were

> "PLAYING WITH NEW ORDER WAS ONE OF MY GREATEST MUSICAL EXPERIENCES. THE MOST EXCITING PART WAS WHEN THEY PLAYED JOY DIVISION: I GOT GOOSEBUMPS."
>
> BILLY CORGAN

Opposite: Billy Corgan performs with New Order at Shoreline Amphitheater, Mountain View, California, 31 July, 2001.

GET READY

TRACK LISTING

Crystal
60 Miles An Hour
Turn My Way
Vicious Streak
Primitive Notion

Slow Jam
Rock The Shack
Someone Like You
Close Range
Run Wild

Released 27 August 2001
Label London – 8573896211
Recorded at Real World, Box, England; Sarm Hook End, London, England; Rockfield, Rockfield, Wales
Produced by Steve Osborne, New Order, Flood, Bernard Sumner
Personnel
Bernard Sumner: vocals, guitars, melodica, synthesizers and programming
Peter Hook: 4- and 6-stringed bass and electronic percussion
Stephen Morris: drums, synthesizers and programming
Gillian Gilbert: synthesizers, guitars and programming
Additional Pete Davis: programming (tracks 1–6, 8–10); Simon Hale: string arrangements, conducting (track 10); Dawn Zee: backing vocals (tracks 1, 9, 10); Billy Corgan: special guest vocals (track 3); Bobby Gillespie: guest vocals (track 7); Andrew Innes: guitar (track 7)
Cover Art Peter Saville: cover art direction; Jürgen Teller: photography; Howard Wakefield: design; Sam Roberts: design
Notes
The album was dedicated to Rob Gretton, the manager of Joy Division and New Order, who died in 1999. The cover model is German actress Nicolette Krebitz.

One Last Push

over. From now – but only for a while – they would be a guitar band.

The guitar-driven "Crystal" reached number eight in the UK and its quirky, jagged, Arthur Baker-produced B-side "Behind Closed Doors", on which Bernard claims he listens to The Corrs at home, would be an extra track in some countries. The "Crystal" which opened *Get Ready* was longer and more luxurious than the single version. Bernard is at his most forceful. Backing singer Dawn Zee of Manchester house act Jersey Street, does a stellar turn and there's a sense of urgency not always obvious on *Republic*. There was also a version with Bernard singing over backbeats by Corvin Dalek, a salient reminder that Bernard almost gave the track to the Hungarian DJ until wiser heads prevailed.

"60 Miles An Hour" would be the second single and it reached number twenty-eight. The keyboard's surge towards the end separated it from the herd, but the almost garage thrash was another new direction. This was an album to be played live.

Billy Corgan guested on "Turn My Way", where his introductory backing vocals set the

New Order and Bobby Gillespie. Shack probably rocked.

190 Decades: Joy Division + New Order

scene for one of New Order's more psychedelic turns. In the event, he was underused, but it's irresistibly catchy.

Bernard hadn't quite shed his electronica fetish and the meandering "Vicious Streak" was the closest New Order came to replicating *Republic*. It's far too long, although its "I keep hanging on" refrain was a masterstroke until the dreary extended exit.

Stephen's whiplash drums and Hooky's earthquake bass catapulted "Primitive Notion" towards essential. There were even elements of "Temptation" and it's as messy – delightfully messy – as New Order had ever been.

Calling a song "Slow Jam" boded nothing but ill. So it proved, and in New Order's world, a lazy song title tends to be matched by a lazy song. Bernard was singing about the ocean again (albeit after having drunk beer), but ultimately it was sunk by its Oasis-style clunkiness.

There were more guests on "Rock the Shack": Primal Scream singer Bobby Gillespie (who had been at the Liverpool Olympia show but had refused to sing) and their guitarist, Andrew Innes. The pair add little, but the thrashy, trashy feel evokes Primal Scream's dull *XTRMNTR* album.

"Someone Like You" takes one minute and forty-two seconds to get to the vocal. Bernard's at sea once more, but it was given a series of hefty remixes as a chart-avoiding single released in December. Despite Stephen's absence, it's a forgotten gem and it's full of mischief. It was Bernard's best guitar-work in too long.

Get Ready wasn't overly burdened with catchy choruses, but the one on "Close Range" came close. Dawn Zee was stellar again and, unusually, the guitars sounded properly mixed.

Its title and its closing statement "I'm gonna live to get high" notwithstanding, "Run Wild" was a closing, strings-laden lullaby and Bernard's return to his melodica is joy piled upon joy. It sounds nothing like its *Get Ready* siblings, but Bernard is at his most lovelorn. Dawn Zee's performance is, again, stellar and it offers a real balm at the end of a torrid album.

Get Ready went to number six in the UK and forty-one in the US, but the bottom line was

24 Hour Party People film poster. It's always good to know what Moby thinks…

Steve Coogan and Tony Wilson at the 24 Hour Party People premiere, Chelsea West Theater, New York.

that, while *Republic* sold three million copies, it sold just 300,000. The reasons were manifold, although *NME* detected "a sense of idiot joy. Being in New Order never sounded half as much fun as it does here." *Get Ready* wasn't a zeitgeist album like so many of its predecessors. The rise of Oasis and the fall of The Haçienda meant New Order no longer symbolised Manchester. Many disappointed purchasers of *Republic* had not returned. Ultimately, *Get Ready* had great moments and great ideas, but very few great songs.

2001 finished with *Fractured Box*: the Joy Division live albums from Preston and Paris in one needless package. In January and February 2002, when they reconvened for several Big Day Out festivals in Australia, something was different. They were co-headlining with The Prodigy and they were playing "Transmission", but The Prodigy were better.

In February, Kylie Minogue played the Brits, mashing up her hit "Can't Get You Out Of My Head" with "Blue Monday" and two very different worlds entwined seamlessly as "Can't Get Blue Monday Out Of My Head". She'd go on to record it too – only to toss it off as a B-side. The rest of 2002's concert schedule was a jaunt around the lucrative European festival circuit – they played "She's Lost Control" – finishing in July in Manchester, their last date for three years.

As ever, there were distractions, most notably Michael Winterbottom's *24 Hour Party People*, the light-hearted, fictionalised account of Factory's rise. Steve Coogan starred as Tony Wilson ("I run Factory Records; I think"). Ian and New Order were played with reasonable accuracy (John Simm, who played Bernard, actually appeared on stage with the band at Finsbury Park in June during "Digital") and there were cameos from Tony Wilson (of course), Mike Pickering, Dave Haslam and Keith Allen – but not New Order. "People ask was it really like that?" chuckled Bernard. "No, it was much more extreme." New Order dominated the soundtrack with familiar material. There was a marvellous take on "New Dawn Fades" by New Order with Moby and New Order's new track, "Here To Stay".

The Haçienda was demolished. Crosby Homes kept the name and turned the site into 154 apartments and seven penthouse flats. The Haçienda Apartments' sales slogan was "now the party's over, you can come home."

Bernard had met The Chemical Brothers when he sang their 1999 single, "Out Of Control" alongside Primal Scream's Bobby Gillespie. "He's such a funny man, so interesting, passionate and charming," said Chemical Brother, Ed Simons. "He is a very avuncular presence in our lives." They returned the favour by producing the fierce "Here To Stay", which, despite Bernard arguing there was too much bass, was a surprise top twenty UK hit. The B-side, "Player In The League", was a *Get Ready* out-take and sounded like it.

In soccer news, England had qualified for another World Cup. "World In Motion" was remixed to little effect and exhumed as "World In Motion 2002". It didn't chart. The propulsive B-side "Such A Good Thing" was a *Get Ready* out-take, but it didn't sound like it at all, being a brilliantly sung, bass-led anthem. In a parallel, but better, world it would have been the all-conquering single *Get Ready* lacked.

In July, Joy Division and New Order appeared on record together for the first time, albeit via more re-hashings. *Before & After* merged Joy Division's *The Complete BBC Sessions* with New Order's *BBC Radio One Live In Concert* for the US market.

With New Order off the road, London Records set to work. *International* was a chronological fourteen-track compilation from "Ceremony" to "Here To Stay" for non-UK territories. There was an extra remix disc for France which included "Let's Go" and a three-track DVD for the US.

The Chemical Brothers: Tom Rowlands (left) & Ed Simons.

> "PEOPLE ASK WAS IT REALLY LIKE THAT?" NO, IT WAS MUCH MORE EXTREME."
>
> BERNARD

"Confusion" was hauled out yet again to reach a dismal sixty-four in the UK charts. The DVD *511*, featuring the John Simm Finsbury Park show, was released in December. More intriguingly, so was the four-disc New Order box (five for early purchasers), *Retro*. Each of the themed discs was curated by outsiders: *Pop* by writer Miranda Sawyer; *Fan* by journalist John McCready, *Club* by Mike Pickering and *Live* by Bobby Gillespie. The first two discs were fabulous; the second two rather less so and the whole project fell between several stools.

It was time to make another album. This time things would not go quite so smoothly and the project would take two years. Gillian was still out of action, so Phil Cunningham made his recording debut. Recording at Real World and Jane Seymour's house/recording studios, St Catherine's Court in Bath, the band would craft backing tracks, before Bernard would depart to write lyrics and vocal melodies on his own. It wasn't an ideal situation and Hooky's increasingly erratic behaviour added a different kind of tension.

They ripped through producers. Malmo man Tore Johansson fell foul of Hooky. Steve Osborne was defenestrated not once but twice. The final results would be helmed by veteran innovator John Leckie, indie favourite Stephen Street or Electronic engineer Jim Spencer. And since New Order were no longer frequenting clubs anymore (men in their late forties really *shouldn't* be frequenting clubs anymore), Stuart Price, fresh from being the musical director on Madonna's *Drowned World* tour, was recruited to add a dance edge, alongside programmers and future Emmy winner Mac Quayle.

New Order surfaced in April with a version of Jimmy Cliff's "Vietnam" for *Help*, a compilation in aid of the War Child charity which also featured fellow A-listers David Bowie, George Michael and Paul McCartney. Dawn Zee was featured and needless to say, her contribution was brilliant. In June, under the New Order name, Stephen, Hooky and Phil Cunningham contributed the thirty-minute soundtrack to

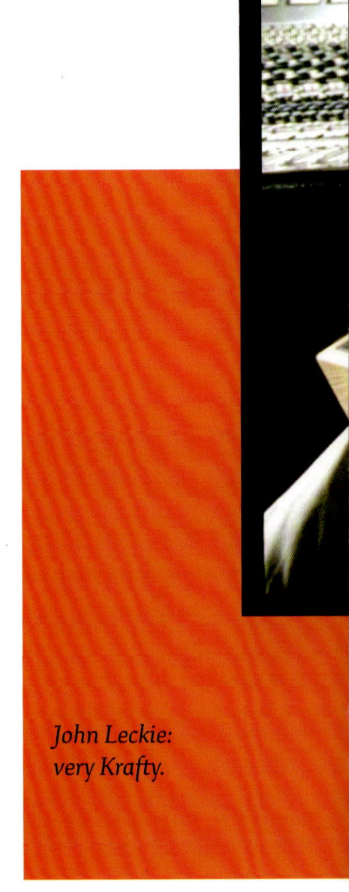

John Leckie: very Krafty.

a Peter Saville retrospective exhibition. The recording was released by London Records in a limited edition of 3,000 copies. By the time the whole band began mixing the album at Olympic Studios in London, Hooky's no-longer-concealed alcoholism had spiralled even further out of control.

Despite imbibing a decanter of sherry a day, Hooky started a new career as a DJ in the summer and he began to mix albums of Haçienda classics. For $20,000 apiece, he and Bernard appeared on bass and backing vocals respectively on "The Real Thing", a track buried on Gwen Stefani's *Love. Angel. Music. Baby.*

The New Order album took up all of 2004, but time had moved so quickly that even Revenge's *One True Passion* was remastered and reissued with an extra disc in the meantime. April's *In Session* gathered together New Order's Radio 1 sessions from 1998 and 2001.

Ana "Ana Matronic" Lynch from Scissor Sisters arrived to add backing vocals for "Jetstream" as material was repeatedly remixed to make it more radio-friendly. By November, the album was finally finished and Hooky was finally in rehab. He was out in time for Christmas and he spent New Year's Eve sober and DJing with Bernard at Brighton's Zap Club.

In 2005, a live Revenge album, *No Pain No Gain* appeared and then, on February 17, New Order picked up a Godlike Genius Award at the *NME* Awards and played live once more. The Hammersmith Palais crowd were treated to just four songs: the new single "Krafty" (which reached number eight in the UK), "Love Will Tear Us Apart", "Blue Monday" and, strangely, "Crystal". Since the audience were sozzled industry types it wasn't a proper gig, but New Order sounded just fine.

As much as £700,000 later, the eighth album, *Waiting For The Sirens' Call* (the only New Order album with a title track) was released in March. To celebrate, they played a show for French television. Peter Saville's lazy sleeve was a rushed effort, but the Japanese version had some "Krafty" remixes, including one in Japanese, while the US edition featured an extra Mac Quayle remix of "Guilt Is A Useless Emotion".

It began reasonably enough with "Who's Joe?" (produced by Jim Spencer). Bernard was at his most vocally compassionate, the guitar solo towards the end was left-field, but it never quite took off.

Despite its nods to R.E.M.'s "The One I Love", "Hey Now What You Doing" (produced by Stephen Street) is more of the same and, yes, there's a left-field guitar solo towards the end. The chorus was more whistle-able though.

A tale of infidelity, the title track (which was produced by Jim Spencer and reached number twenty-one in the UK) finds Bernard on the ocean again. Phil Cunningham's keyboards bring new textures, Stephen's drumming is at its clattering best and Hooky is rather lost in the mix. It's still the album's finest moment.

Scissor Sister Ana Matronic: for her, a writing credit on "Jetstream".

NEW order
WAITING FOR THE SIRENS' CALL

No

WAITING FOR THE SIRENS' CALL

TRACK LISTING

Who's Joe?
Hey Now What You Doing
Waiting For The Sirens' Call
Krafty
I Told You So
Morning Night And Day

Dracula's Castle
Jetstream
Guilt Is A Useless Emotion
Turn
Working Overtime

Released 28 March 2005
Label London – 25646 2202 2
Recorded at Real World, Box, England; St Catherine's Court, Bath, England
Produced by Jim Spencer (tracks: 1, 3, 5), John Leckie (tracks: 4, 7), New Order, Stephen Street (tracks: 2, 6, 10, 11), Stuart Price (tracks: 8, 9)
Personnel
Bernard Sumner: vocals, guitars, synthesizers and programming
Peter Hook: 4- and 6-stringed bass
Stephen Morris: drums, synthesizers and programming
Phil Cunningham: synthesizers and programming, guitars
Cover Art Peter Saville: art direction, photography; Anna Blessman: photography; Howard Wakefield and Peter Saville Associates: design
Notes
Waiting For The Sirens' Call marks Phil Cunningham's recording and co-writing debut with New Order; although he had been playing live with the band since the *Get Ready* tour of 2001–2002. It is the first New Order album recorded without Gillian Gilbert who left the band in 2001 to look after her family.

"PROBABLY HALF THE KIDS DIDN'T KNOW WHO WE WERE. IT WAS STILL BRILLIANT. WE CAME TO MAKE PEOPLE FEEL SPECIAL, BUT THEY MADE US FEEL SPECIAL."

BERNARD

"Krafty" (produced by John Leckie) was almost a New Order parody. A number eight hit, it would be their last top ten single and acknowledged Kraftwerk in its title alone. That at least ten remixes would eventually be available, suggests nobody was quite sure which way to take it.

There's a sneaky little flirtation with reggae on "I Told You So" (produced by Jim Spencer) which shimmers confidently, despite a lyric eulogising getting high. Dawn Zee is unleashed towards the end and the whole package takes the album up a notch.

Bernard's laddish tale of a drunken night out with attendant hangover, ill-behoved a forty-nine-year-old millionaire, but "Morning Night and Day" (produced by Stephen Street) was Hooky's finest moment on the album and the deranged instrumental coda showed New Order still had magnificence in them.

Like "Slow Jam", "Dracula's Castle" (produced by John Leckie) struggles to transcend its title. Lyrically shallow, musically pedestrian and with an instrumental break that sounds like it's played on stylophone, it's a career low. It didn't work live either.

Ana Matronic's work on "Jetstream" earned her a writer's credit. As a single it reached number twenty in the UK, but, again, the deluge of remixes indicated confusion as to what should be the definitive version. She does a fair job, but, with producer Stuart Price desperately seeking Madonna, she has precious little to work with.

If the two previous tracks formed the least appetising double whammy of New Order's oeuvre, "Guilt Is A Useless Emotion" (again produced by Stuart Price) was a slight upturn, not least since its interlude echoed Farley "Jackmaster" Funk's "Love Can't Turn Around". Dawn Zee was back for the second time and she's joined by Beatrice Hatherley, who would later write for Kylie Minogue.

With its acoustic bent and sparse arrangement, the love song "Turn" (produced by Stephen Street) harkens to the New Order of *Low-Life* and *Brotherhood* with a 21st-century twist. It might have been the way for the whole album to go if they'd been able to shed the stodge elsewhere.

Rather than a lullaby, *Waiting For The Sirens' Call* ended with the "Lust For Life"-influenced, tambourine-drenched rocker "Working Overtime" (produced by Stephen Street). The track provides proof, perhaps, that "Lust for Life"-influenced, tambourine drenched rock was not the band's strong point.

Too many producers had spoiled the broth. The band were unsure where they wanted to go – Bernard was firmly in charge but he'd swapped musical horses again – and they were sometimes settling for second best. Frankly, £700,000 for the album seemed excessive, but the songs which made *Waiting For The Sirens' Call* weren't the end of this story, for they had completed almost another album's worth of material.

As with *Get Ready*, they had made an album to play live. At the end of April, beginning with a lengthy show in Oakland, CA, they were back and a slew of bands who had grown up to their music were beginning to make inroads: The Killers, Franz Ferdinand, Interpol ("a Joy Division tribute band," according to Stephen), Secret Machines, LCD Soundsystem, The Bravery, Delphic and more. A few US dates, where Hooky's sobriety jarred with Bernard and Phil Cunningham's lack of it were followed by the European festival circuit again (including Glastonbury, where they were second on Saturday night's bill to Coldplay), before a Bernard-inspired November show at Oakwood, a Salford school for children with special educational needs. As Bernard admitted afterwards: "Probably half the kids didn't know who we were. It was still brilliant. We came to make people feel special, but they made us feel special. Creativity wasn't big when me and Hooky were at school in Salford." Later, some of the road crew returned to Oakwood to give talks to the children about jobs in the music industry.

Hooky, Coachella, Empire Polo Fields, Indio, California, 1 May, 2005.

In the meantime, the New Order machine still needed to be fed. April's *Best Remixes* was download only, but by September London had released *A Collection*, an expertly curated collection of videos on DVD and October saw *Singles*, an impressive, exhaustive compendium which included the non-single "Turn". *Singles* went to number fourteen in the UK.

They wouldn't tour again until – yes – the European festival circuit beckoned in 2006, but they did play an eight-song Joy Division set at Manchester Arena for a cancer benefit in January. They'd do the same again as an introduction to a proper New Order show at Wembley in October. According to Hooky, Bernard put a stop to it, saying it was a "bit miserable that stuff," although the difference in audience response to song six "Atmosphere" and song seven, "Waiting For The Sirens' Call" may have been a factor. Never again would New Order play a Joy Division set.

James Nice's excellent *Shadowplayers* documentary told Factory's tale in May and in July, filming began on *Control*, the bleak, fictionalised biography of Ian, directed by Anton Corbijn, a Dutch photographer who'd regularly worked with the group and who directed the 1988 video for "Atmosphere". Debbie Curtis and Tony Wilson were involved and New Order was tasked with the incidental music, some of which would find its way onto the soundtrack. "It was very accurate," acknowledged Bernard. "It's what's been going on in my head all these years."

Barney, Wireless Festival, Hyde Park, London, 24 June, 2005.

One Last Push 201

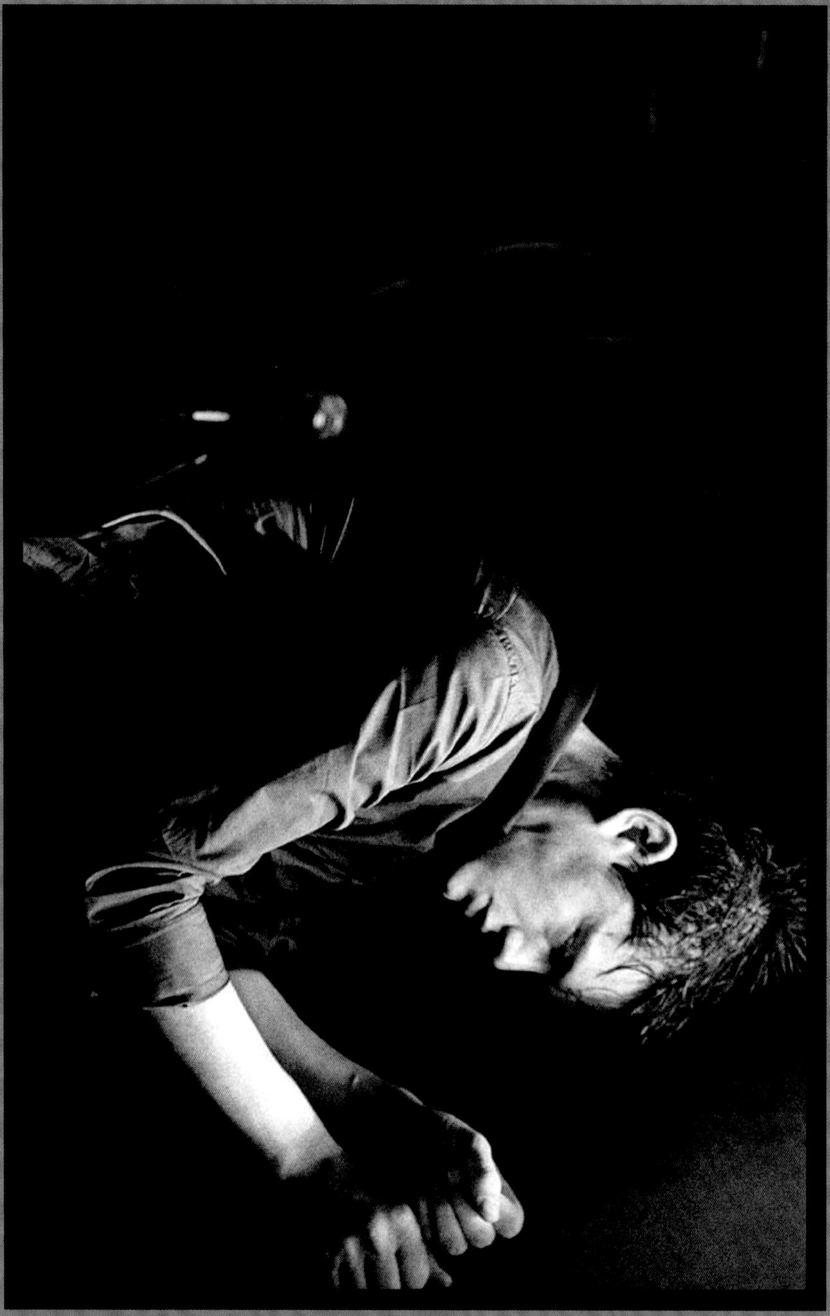

HOOK, SLUNG

HOOK, SLUNG

In November they were off to perform in Brazil and Argentina, before finishing the year with a London date. South America would be where Hooky and Bernard's relationship came to a permanent end. Years of backbiting, opposing musical directions and jostling for leadership culminated in the tour from hell where Hooky would stand in front of Bernard on stage writing petulant slogans on his amps. On their return, they had passed the point of no return.

Could the final breach have been averted? Surely. Did Hooky and Bernard want to avert it? Surely not. There was calm before the storm. Hooky began to assemble Freebass, which would feature three bassists: him, Andy Rourke, late of The Smiths and Gary "Mani" Mounfield of Primal Scream, but previously of Stone Roses.

Then, the week before the *Control* premiere in Cannes, Hooky was interviewed by Clint Boon of Manchester band Inspiral Carpets for the minor radio station XFM. Hooky was asked to review "Wish Upon A Dog Star" by Perry Farrell's band Satellite Party. He responded, "I spoke to Perry and he asked me to play bass, as he'd heard about New Order splitting up. Yeah, me and Bernard aren't working together."

A statement was rushed out: "As far as everyone is concerned, New Order will be going to Cannes next week as a band, to promote *Control*. This is probably just Hooky messing about. Everyone knows what he's like."

Hooky wasn't messing about and Bernard was furious. Cannes was warm, but the atmosphere was Arctic. Stephen and Bernard did interviews together, but there was only one question worth asking and it wasn't to do with *Control*…

Control itself was an artistic and commercial success. Sam Riley portrayed Ian and Ian's demons with ruthless sensitivity and, as Bernard carefully noted, it "generally captured the Ian we knew very effectively," before adding, "he would have stopped performing and become a writer."

There were bad-tempered business meetings and, in July, New Order released another statement: "After thirty years in a band together, we are very disappointed Hooky announced

Right: *Clint Boon of Inspiral Carpets and Hooky at XFM's Winter Wonderland, Manchester Apollo, 11 December, 2007. "Anything to say, Hooky?" "Yes…"*

Below: Control *movie poster.*

204 Decades: Joy Division + New Order

unilaterally that New Order have split up. We would have hoped he could have approached us personally. He does not speak for all the band. Therefore we can only assume he no longer wants to be a part of New Order."

That was that. Bernard married Sarah Dalton that month. Tony Wilson was there, but on August 10, having already lost a kidney to renal cancer, he died of a heart attack aged just fifty-seven. Peter Saville designed the invitations to the funeral – which Hooky and Stephen attended – and Tony's gravestone. His coffin was given a Factory catalogue number, FAC501.

When Factory collapsed, Tony Wilson faded from the New Order tale. But for all his lack of business sense and the hubris of his lunatic infatuation with The Haçienda, he gave Joy Division and New Order the freedom to fly and he gave them Martin Hannett. Without

> "AFTER THIRTY YEARS IN A BAND TOGETHER, WE ARE VERY DISAPPOINTED HOOKY ANNOUNCED UNILATERALLY THAT NEW ORDER HAVE SPLIT UP."
>
> **NEW ORDER**

A floral tribute to Tony Wilson outside the Haçienda Apartments, 20 August, 2007.

him, the members would have been financially richer – but musically much, much poorer.

New Order reluctantly disbanded. Gillian was diagnosed with breast cancer and Stephen needed to take time out to nurse her. Bernard sang on "Miracle Cure", a single by German electronic duo Blank & Jones and trudged on, forming Bad Lieutenant – named after the film starring Harvey Keitel as a cocaine-snorting cop – with Phil Cunningham and Jake Evans of Mancunian indie act Rambo & Leroy.

Post-*Control*, there was a slew of Joy Division product over the rest of 2007 and 2008. *Unknown Pleasures* (with a live disc of a 1979 Manchester show), *Closer* and *Still* were remastered and reissued. *Under Review* was a seventy-minute documentary bedevilled by poor sound quality. Another documentary, the Grant Gee-directed *Joy Division*, was made with Tom Atencio's blessing. It was much more rewarding and touched upon *The Joy Division Film*, 1979's Malcolm Whitehead-directed, seventeen-minute collage of live material, Adolf Hitler and Captain Beefheart which remains unreleased.

On record, the misleadingly titled Martin Hannett's *Personal Mixes* was mostly unlistenable studio flim-flam, but *Let The Movie Begin* had been released in Belgium in 2005: it was a mixture of interviews, live recordings and some of the RCA sessions. *The Best Of Joy Division* was a standard compilation with the added incentive of *The Complete BBC Sessions*.

There was less output from the New Order stable, but 2008's *Live In Glasgow* DVD was a recording of a 2006 show which included "These Days" and a fascinating second disc compiled from assorted live performances.

Better still, the first five New Order albums were reissued, each with a bonus disc of singles, 12-inch mixes and further delights. As if channelling Factory, the reissues released by Rhino (primarily a re-release label) were problematic or, as they put it, had "minor audio problems." When the dust settled, though, after the re-releases were re-released again in 2009, they would be the most superior and complete versions of each album, even when the single album box sets began to emerge in 2019.

With the New Order name still a source of dispute, *Never Cry Another Tear*, the only Bad Lieutenant album, was released in October 2009. The core trio were fleshed out by

Stephen, who, with Gillian on the way to recovery, co-wrote and drummed on two tracks and programmed another. Blur's Alex James contributed occasional bass and songwriting. Meanwhile, Tom Chapman, who'd been raised in France before moving to Manchester to try his musical luck after hearing The Smiths, contributed bass and songwriting to "Running Out Of Luck" after passing an audition for the live band by playing "Love Will Tear Us Apart". "I was encouraged to do what I do as bass player."

The album itself took its cue from *Get Ready* and *Waiting For The Sirens' Call*. There wasn't a bad note on it, but there weren't many magical ones and it stalled at number ninety in the British charts, a lowly position, although one which eluded the singles "Twist Of Fate" and "Sink Or Swim". It felt like the other side projects: New Order but with something missing. Bernard was treading water, but he gamely took Bad Lieutenant on tour, covering The Chemical Brothers' "Out Of Control", Electronic's "Tighten Up", "Crystal", "Waiting For The Sirens' Call", "Temptation", an acoustic "Bizarre Love Triangle", "Ceremony", "Regret", "Transmission" and "Love Will Tear Us Apart", but sadly not "In The Ghetto", Bad Lieutenant's contribution to *Key To Change*, an album for homeless charity, Centrepoint.

Whether Bernard enjoyed supporting Pet Shop Boys or going back to smaller venues remains unclear, but you don't have to be the unlikely lovechild of Miss Marple and Hercule Poirot to detect his feelings. Scheduled US dates supporting Pixies were scrapped owing to unspecified visa complications. They tried again in April 2010 with a San Francisco

Bad Lieutenant's Barney and Jake Evans, Liverpool Masque, 21 March, 2010.

Above: *Stephen and Tom Chapman rehearsing in Manchester, 22 September, 2011.*

headline and a Coachella sot, only to be thwarted by the Icelandic volcano eruption which closed UK airspace. After that, they never quite recovered.

After several years of toil, the Freebass album, *It's a Beautiful Life*, limped out in September 2010, by which time the band were no more. Their New Order-tinged dub was no disgrace, but three basses proved to be two too many.

That February, Peter Hook & The Light had made their debut at the opening night of Manchester's Factory (a venue co-owned by Hooky), featuring Gary "Mani" Mounfield, singer Rowetta, lately of Happy Mondays, and cannabis enthusiast Howard Marks. They played Freebass, Monaco, Joy Division and New Order material. An idea was born, but Joy Division had been gone so long that vinyl was back in fashion, hence *+- Singles 1978–80*, a box of ten 7-inch singles remastered by Stephen, plus a couple of CDs.

Hooky's idea was simple enough. If New Order weren't going to re-imagine their history, he was. And so he began a new career, one where he would seek to play every Joy Division and New Order song, album by album. With his son Jack Bates on bass (not wholly a chip off the old block: the academically gifted scion spoke French, Spanish, Italian, Catalan and Portuguese) and later Monaco's Dave Potts after that relationship had been patched up, Hooky would tour the world. Naturally, the others were appalled. Naturally, Hooky was unrepentant. He got to sing ("Getting a singer was impossible: keyboard warriors managed to scare off the three candidates I had. It took me a year to feel confident doing it") and he was in charge.

In February 2011, Hooky's Haçienda label released Peter Hook & The Light's *1102/2011*, an EP of "Atmosphere", "New Dawn Fades" and the unfinished, never previously recorded "Pictures In My Mind", which Rowetta sang.

More fun was *Total: From Joy Division To New Order*, June's compilation of five Joy Division songs and thirteen New Order ones including the previously unreleased "Hellbent". It would sell over 100,000 copies. "It is true that the record company are always thinking of new ways to flog New Order to people," shrugged Stephen. Naturally both sides were keen to give their side of the break-up. "The truth is Bernard's a twat and always has been," declared Hooky. "We're a bunch of fat old men arguing and it's pathetic."

Right: *Peter Hook & The Light perform at Concorde 2, Brighton, 9 November, 2013.*

208   Decades: Joy Division + New Order

> "THE TRUTH IS BERNARD'S A TWAT AND ALWAYS HAS BEEN. WE'RE A BUNCH OF FAT OLD MEN ARGUING AND IT'S PATHETIC."
>
> HOOKY

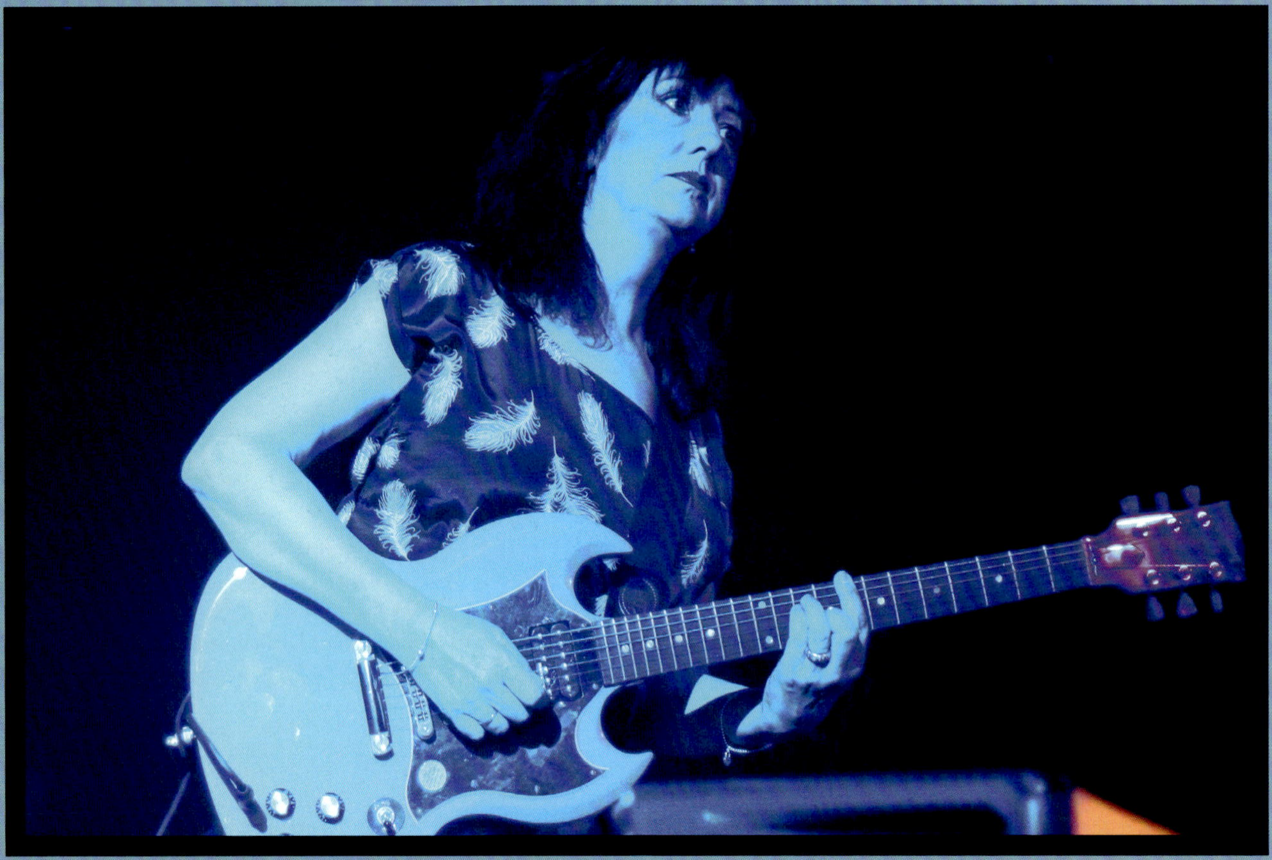

EVERYBODY'S HAPPY NOWADAYS

EVERYBODY'S HAPPY NOWADAYS

Whether they were spurred by spite, by Bad Lieutenant's failure or by genuine creative impulses, Bernard had been refreshed by sailing across the Atlantic Ocean and New Order returned. Tom Chapman was recruited permanently, and a fully recovered Gillian's lobbying to rejoin had been successful. "It was a bit weird at first, I had to get to know everyone," she confessed. On October 11 and 12, the quintet played their first shows without Hooky, at their old stomping ground Ancienne Belgique in Brussels and then the Paris Bataclan, both to pay medical costs for Michael Shamberg, who'd been suffering with a dreadful mitochondrial disease. "Age Of Consent", "Elegia" and "586" were revisited, but "Love Will Tear Us Apart" was the sole Joy Division contribution.

"We found out that Peter Hook was touring *Unknown Pleasures* through the press and it sucks to be honest," explained Bernard. "He seems to be doing it for the money. It was disrespectful to the rest of us, but I must admit that once he started doing it, we thought 'What are we doing holding back with New Order?' So, in a way – if you'll excuse the pun – he showed us the light. I don't know if we'd have carried on if he hadn't done those shows, but he opened the gateways of hell."

Hooky maintained New Order without him was like Sooty without Sweep or U2 without The Edge, their lead guitarist. "It's sad if you were really close friends, but we weren't really," reasoned Bernard as the band swept through South America, before finishing the year at East London's art deco Troxy. Hooky wasn't impressed with his replacement Tom Chapman, improbably claiming, "He's miming to my bass on tape, he's the Milli Vanilli of bass."

After January's rush release of New Order's *Live At The London Troxy*, less than a month after the actual show, 2012 was more of the same. Peter Hook & The Light spent it taking *Unknown Pleasures* and *Closer* to a world which had never seen anyone play most of the latter album's songs. Rather than "why?", perhaps the question might have been "why on earth not?".

Starting in February in Auckland, New Order hit the festival circuit with a keenness that reconfirmed that Bernard's problem wasn't touring as such, just touring with Hooky. They

Above: *Newly bespectacled Stephen, Fox Theater, Oakland, CA, 5 October, 2012. The first date of the North American tour and the first time they played "Close Range" in a decade.*

212 Decades: Joy Division + New Order

Right: *Barney and Tom Chapman, Tempodrom, Berlin, 21 June, 2012. They played "Thieves Like Us" for the first time in 24 years.*

"THEY MIGHT BE USING THE NAME NEW ORDER, BUT THEY'RE NOT NEW ORDER."

HOOKY

played Poland for the first time, at the Open'er Festival on an air force base in the port of Gydnia. "The whole place had these concrete, cold war aircraft hangars beautifully lit; plus we had the best sushi we've ever had. Who knew you could get that in Poland?" mused Stephen.

They also played Festival No6 at Portmeirion, where The Prisoner was filmed and where they slipped in "Isolation", but disappointingly not The Prisoner-influenced "The Village". "We took our girls and rode around in golf carts because it's so hilly," remembered Stephen. "We all got loaded on the spirit of [Prisoner star] Patrick McGoohan and dressed up in costume. If the place is right and everyone is in a good mood, the fact you haven't had a soundcheck doesn't matter, because the audience is part of it and you feed off each other. It was perfect, I've been back every year since."

Hooky's candid memoir Unknown Pleasures: Inside Joy Division set out to debunk the myth and just about succeeded in re-casting them as three oiks, plus a singer in need of the serious help he would never find. Before the book, the notion they never read Ian's lyrics seemed unlikely. After it, it was risible to suggest they'd have bothered.

New Order finished the year with an extensive tour of the US and Canada and by the last date, they were playing "Shadowplay". There was, though, something missing, apart from Hooky. They were missing some new music. The short-term answer had been there since Waiting For The Sirens' Call in 2005, an album made without Gillian, but with Hooky. They had that clutch of songs left over. At the time, the idea had been to record three more for a 2006 release, but since they couldn't be in the same room together, that didn't happen.

Instead, they found seven lost sirens and a remix of the far-from-lost "I Told You So" to pad out the running time to thirty-nine minutes. They called it Lost Sirens and it was released in January 2013. They went to great pains to point out that Lost Sirens wasn't offcuts that weren't good enough to make the parent album, although they never actually explained why they hadn't made said parent album. Bernard called it a "non-completed album".

To everyone's credit, Hooky wasn't toned down on Lost Sirens. Indeed, there's more of him than on Republic. He's certainly all over the opening "I'll Stay With You" (produced by Stephen Street), a glorious anthem which in any other circumstances would have been a statement of intent and renewal. Instead, it's an obituary – the last stand of the old gang.

Bernard ruminates on fame ("With perfect hair and clothes/It's just another day in a life of a superstar") in the upbeat "Sugarcane" (produced by Tore Johansson). This track could have been essential, but Johansson lets it slip out of his grasp by toning down Hooky and rendering limp what, in more assured hands, would have been tumescent.

There's real beauty in "Recoil" (produced by Jim Spencer), where Phil Cunningham's keyboards are as laid-back and balm-inducting as anything by Robert Miles. Bernard is melancholic once again and there's space and a real warmth not always found in late period New Order.

There's plenty going on in "Californian Grass" (produced by Stephen Street), from the buzzsaw guitar, to Bernard's vocals which are deep and dark on the verses and light and airy on the chorus. It's packed with ideas, but it doesn't hang together properly and the lyrics, whether about drugs or turf, don't work at all. Perhaps this was what Bernard meant by "non-completed".

"Hellbent" (produced by Stephen Street) had already appeared on Total of course. It always seemed like an odd choice for a singles compilation and here in its natural setting it's still nothing out of the ordinary, but it is slightly Cure-ish.

The faux cod-funk of "Shake It Up" (produced by Mac Quayle) is the album's obvious nadir and another awful title for an awful song. If there is compelling evidence that Lost Sirens is just some stuff that wasn't good enough for

New Order's most beautifully situated show? Jodrell Bank, 7 July, 2013.

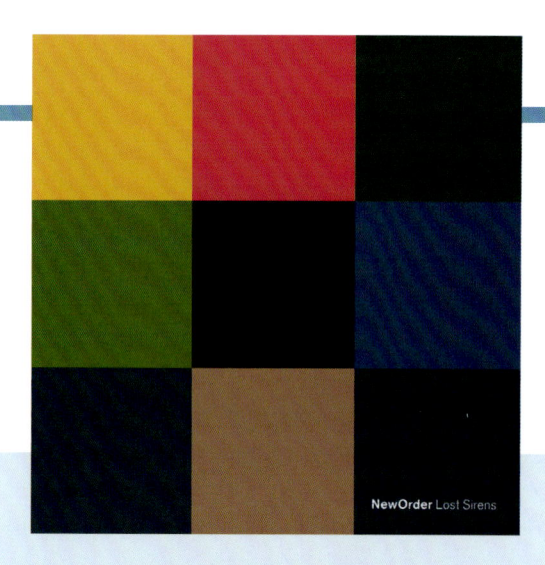

LOST SIRENS

TRACK LISTING

I'll Stay With You
Sugarcane
Recoil
Californian Grass
Hellbent
Shake It Up
I've Got A Feeling
I Told You So (Crazy World Mix)

Released 11 January 2013
Label Rhino – 2564653448
Recorded at Real World, Box, England
Produced by New Order, Stephen Street: production, mixing (tracks 1, 4, 5, 7); Cenzo Townshend: mixing (tracks 1, 2, 4–7); Tore Johansson: production (track 2); Jim Spencer: production (track 3), mixing (tracks 3, 8); Mac Quayle: production (track 6); Stuart Price: production (track 8)
Personnel
Bernard Sumner: vocals, guitars, synthesizers and programming
Peter Hook: 4- and 6-stringed bass
Stephen Morris: drums, synthesizers and programming
Phil Cunningham: synthesizers and programming, guitars
Cover Art Studio Parris, Wakefield
Notes
The tracks featured on the album were recorded during the production of 2005's *Waiting For The Sirens' Call*, but they never made it to the final release. It is the final album featuring bassist Peter Hook, who left the band in 2007 (almost 6 years before the album's release), and the only album by New Order to date ever produced from archival recordings.

Waiting For The Sirens' Call, it's here. Surely it was never intended for proper release.

"I've Got A Feeling" (produced by Stephen Street) is infinitely better. A big chorus, an ever-building tension and some good, old-fashioned weirdness.

And finally, "I Told You So" (produced by Stuart Price) was revisited, mostly to fill space of course, but it's space well filled. It's a more mysterious version than Jim Spencer's on *Waiting For The Sirens' Call*. There's more threat, much more Velvet Underground influence and some big drums which echoed like Joy Division. It concluded a curate's egg of a venture with more élan than it perhaps warranted.

Nobody quite knew what to make of *Lost Sirens*, although *NME*'s declaration that "it all feels a bit superfluous" was mean-spirited. Both band and audience had moved on since it was recorded and the London Records deal had expired, so Rhino put it out. It trundled gently to number twenty-three in the British charts. It's a cliché of course, but the best of *Waiting For The Sirens' Call* and *Lost Sirens* would have made a great album.

Live At Bestival 2012 was released in July with profits going to the Isle of Wight Youth Trust. Both factions continued to tour, but it wasn't practical to flog *Lost Sirens* on the road and "I'll Stay With You" was soon dropped from the set. New Order played Russia and Jodrell Bank, the scientific exploration site near Macclesfield, but talk of a new album was quietly shelved. Again, there was a distinct sense that they were water treading.

They eased themselves into 2014, on March 11 Bernard, Phil Cunningham and Tom Chapman played a short set at New York's Carnegie Hall for Tibet. Iggy Pop sang "Californian Grass" (its live debut), "Transmission" and "Love Will Tear Us Apart" before the full band returned to South America as part of Lollapalooza. The new single "Singularity" was introduced in Chile and by the time they summered in the US, it was joined by "Plastic". The shows were bigger and brighter, featuring backdrops of cityscapes and children's television favourites the Teletubbies, plus a giant disco ball. "They might be using the name New Order," Hooky, who now referred to them as "New Odour", grumbled to *Musical Instrument Professional*. "But they're not New Order."

Inspired by Hooky's literary success, Bernard's autobiography *Chapter and Verse* was published in September. "Bookstores won't know whether to file it under fantasy or tragedy," quipped Hooky. It lacked candour.

Earlier in the year, the compilation titled *Of Factory New York* featured a 1989 live version of "Your Silent Face" and its proceeds went to Michael Shamberg. He would die on 1 November, aged sixty-two. "A lovely man, a true revolutionary," remembered Hooky.

Finally, it was time to make a new album, but first they needed a deal. The new songs were taking shape. Bernard was writing the way he'd come to love, on his own at his home studio, usually in the winter, starting at 6 p.m. and working through until 2 a.m. "I sit in the dark with a bottle of wine and dream," he said. Despite his claim that "at the end of the '90s, I'd reached a point where I'd said everything I wanted about making an electronic record," Bernard had rediscovered electro, not least since the technology had advanced to the point where it was quick and simple to use.

"Over the past three years," added Tom Chapman, "it's been amazing to see how well the dance stuff goes down live. That got us in the mood: we just wanted to write some more dance stuff."

They played the eight songs they'd been working on to Daniel Miller, the hands-on boss of the Mute label, to whom Depeche Mode

Iggy Pop with Barney at the 27 Annual Tibet House Benefit concert at Carnegie Hall, New York, 11 March, 2014. Pop sang "Californian Grass", "Transmission" and "Love Will Tear Us Apart".

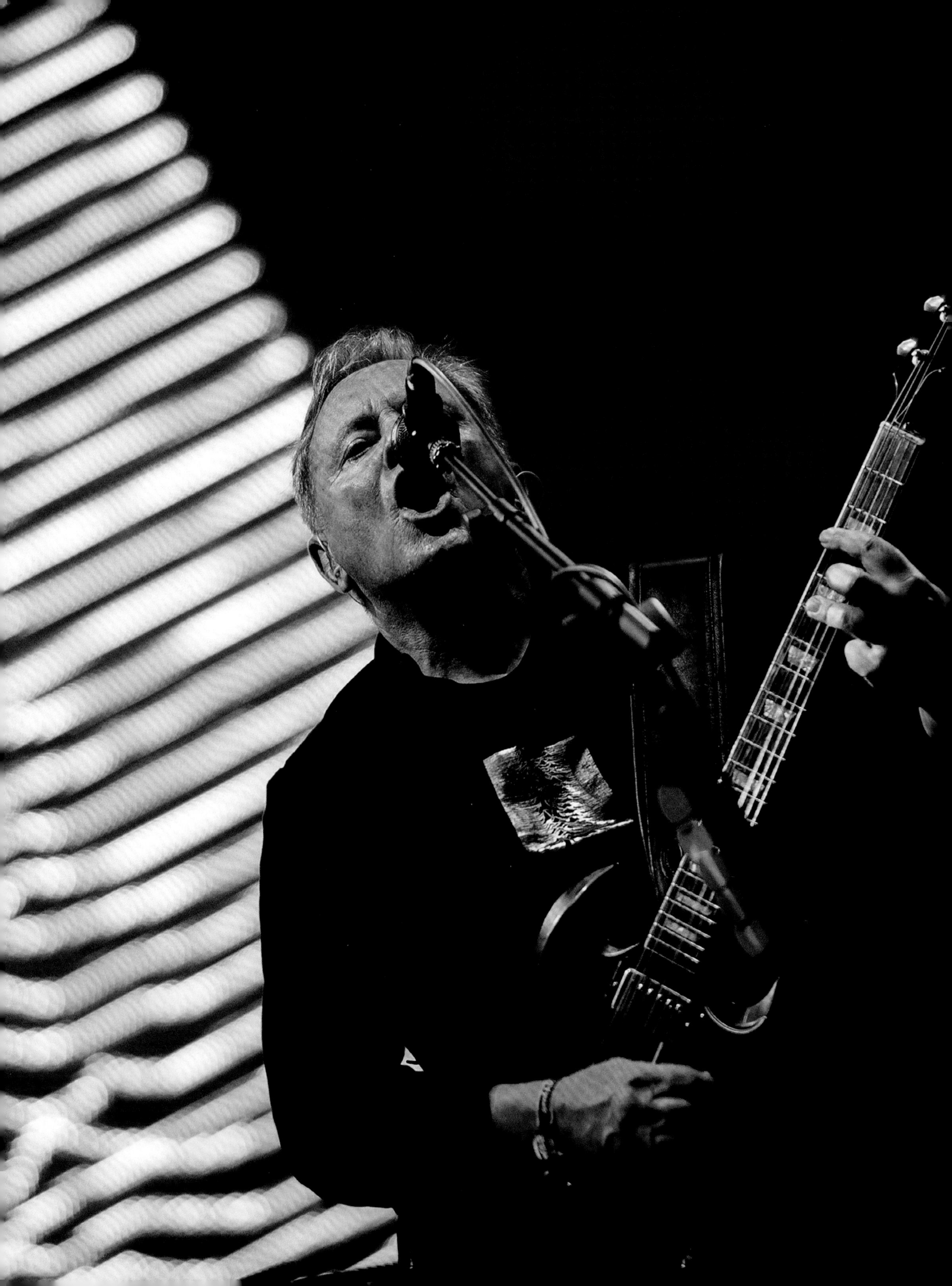

were still signed after almost four decades. In September, Miller bit: "I had no doubt Mute would be the right home for New Order. We've already had a number of creative conversations," he gushed. Bernard explained, "The DNA of the band had changed and therefore we felt the DNA of the label should have a certain synergy with that."

The original idea was for the tenth album to be a collection of EPs released during 2015, a very Factory notion. Common sense prevailed in a way that it rarely had at Factory. They knuckled down at the luxurious 80 Hertz in Manchester – the studio had showers! – and set about recapturing the magic from the period when they had no option but to record in Manchester.

Bernard renewing his electro vows was a direction electro-master Daniel Miller was delighted to facilitate. The new boss wasn't the same as the old boss. A regular visitor to Stephen and Gillian's studio and 80 Hertz, Miller would help record and mix and would be credited as executive producer.

Three songwriting teams emerged as they recorded over the winters of 2013 and '14: Bernard, who wrote all the lyrics; Gillian and Stephen, although even she fled when the drums were being recorded; Phil Cunningham and Tom Chapman. "There was an imaginary hat on the table and if someone had an idea, they'd throw it in," claimed Bernard. He wanted guests and, having enjoyed his work with Elbow and James, Bernard invited Manchester conductor and composer Joe Duddell in, with a sixteen-piece string section, the Manchester Camerata.

"It was Bernard's vision to introduce live strings. They complement the ethos of this album: electronics and guitars in balance. The brief was loose and the songs were at an early stage," explained Duddell, whose charges were featured on "Restless", "Tutti Frutti", "People On The High Line", "Nothing But A Fool" and "Superheated". "I tried to fit strings into the classic New Order sound, but I also had scope to introduce things."

Titled with a vaguely Kraftwerkian bent and with Stephen suggesting the running order, the tenth New Order album, *Music Complete*, was released in September 2015. Mostly self-produced, it was their first recorded work without Hooky. Gillian was back for good and Peter Saville designed the sleeve. "It just seemed like the time was right to return to synthesisers and electronics," Bernard told *Rolling Stone* before disingenuously adding, "We can now do what we've always wanted." Imaginary hats notwithstanding, without Hooky, there was no longer any suggestion that they were a collective. As Stephen told *Uncut*, "Democracy never works in pop bands."

The opening few seconds of "Restless" was New Order twinkling like they'd rarely twinkled before. The rest of the song never quite recaptured that lambent beginning, but the chorus was solid, Tom Chapman's bass was remarkably Hooky-esque and, unusually, Bernard was writing about himself. "It's a little diary of a day and what's going on in the world

Barney, Lollapalooza Brazil, Autodromo de Interlagos, Sao Paulo, 6 April, 2014.

"DEMOCRACY NEVER WORKS IN POP BANDS."
STEPHEN

around me. Part of it is about how materialistic we've become. I'm as guilty as anyone." It didn't chart as a single but, as a calling card for *Music Complete*, it worked a treat. "Tom really came into his own on *Music Complete*," enthused Bernard. "Not that the other bass in our history wasn't great. It was…"

Before it explodes into all-out electro, for precisely forty-seven seconds "Singularity" resurrected Joy Division and it's New Order's funniest musical joke. Co-produced at Stephen and Gillian's studio (and co-written) by Chemical Brother Tom Rowlands, the song originally titled "Drop Guitar" has something of the Chemicals' cacophony, but when Bernard sings "For all lost souls/ Who can't come home/ Friends, not here/ We share our tears" it's beautifully elegiac too. Unlike with "Restless", Bernard was insistent that his lyrics not be taken literally. "You've got to watch it with my lyrics. You can't assume they're autobiographical. Because I'm a private person. I scout around for things to write about instead of myself." The single was another flop.

Speaking of flop singles, "Plastic" made surprisingly few inroads. Already played live, it was proudly electro, but it soared like they hadn't soared in years, aided immeasurably by backing vocals from Dawn Zee, Elly "La Roux" Jackson and Denise Johnson, once of Manchester's A Fifth Of Heaven, but more recently an Electronic collaborator. It was as strong as anything in their canon.

Yet another flop single, "Tutti Frutti" featured Jackson on co-vocals. "She's got a chest voice and a head voice," Bernard told a baffled *NME*. "I wanted her to sing from the chest voice." Her "chest voice" blended seamlessly with Bernard's nasal tones on the chorus. However, plodding where it could have sprinted, "Tutti Frutti" sounded as if they were still marooned in the "Confusion" period and, for all Bernard's

Barney, Phil Cunningham, Gillian and Stephen with Mute Records label founder Daniel Miller at The Groucho Club, London, 2 September, 2014. "The right home for New Order," said Barney.

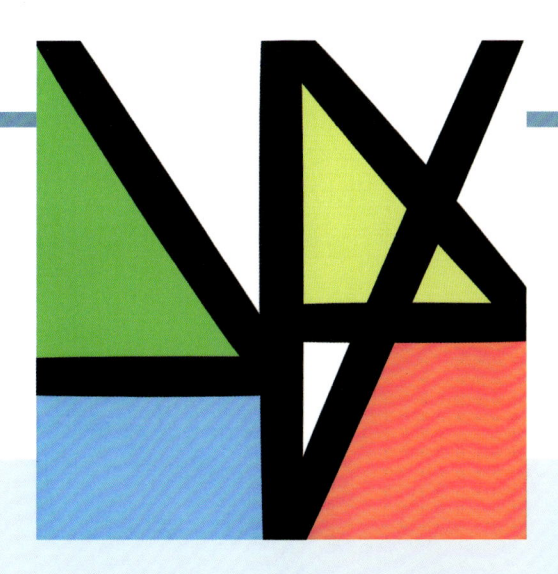

MUSIC COMPLETE

TRACK LISTING

Restless
Singularity
Plastic
Tutti Frutti
People On The High Line
Stray Dog

Academic
Nothing But A Fool
Unlearn This Hatred
The Game
Superheated

Released 25 September 2015
Label Mute – CDSTUMM390
Recorded at 80 Hertz Studios, Manchester, England
Produced by New Order, Stuart Price, Tom Rowlands
Personnel
Bernard Sumner: vocals, guitar, keyboards, synthesizers
Stephen Morris: drums and percussion, keyboards, synthesizers, drum programming
Gillian Gilbert: keyboards, synthesizers
Phil Cunningham: guitars, keyboards, synthesizers, electronic percussion
Tom Chapman: bass, backing vocals, synthesizers
Additional Iggy Pop: vocals (track 6); Brandon Flowers: vocals, mixing (track 11); La Roux: vocals (tracks 4, 5), backing vocals (track 3); Dawn Zee: backing vocals (tracks 3, 8); Denise Johnson: backing vocals (tracks 3, 8); Giacomo Cavagna: Italian spoken vocal (track 4)
Cover Art Peter Saville: art direction; Paul Hetherington: design
Notes
Gillian Gilbert returned to the band after a decade's hiatus, and bassist Tom Chapman replaced founding member Peter Hook who quit over creative and personal differences. The cover art was designed by long-time collaborator Peter Saville and comprises a montage of lines with four colour schemes: red, yellow, green, and blue. The placement of the colours varies depending on the format of release.

increasing powers as a vocalist, crooning the verses was never going to be viable. "I'd had a few glasses of wine," he admitted. Stephen added, "It's not about ice-cream. When we started, we used to listen to a lot of Italian electro records. So, we decided to get a bit of Italian playfulness in it."

Jackson returned on "People On The High Line", the keyboard-dominated fifth and final flop single. It's full of life and the parts where Tom Chapman channels Chic's Bernard Edwards and the demented instrumental break take it beyond adequate.

Iggy Pop had sung with most of the band at 2014's Tibet benefit and so New Order inviting the singer Ian adored so much to guest on "Stray Dog" completes a circle. Pop recorded his vocals in Miami after Bernard sent him a demo. He does a sterling spoken-word turn on Bernard's poem, which mentions Grimpen Mire, the boggy swamp in The Hound Of The Baskervilles. The electro backing suggests Swiss mavericks Yello grappling with Joy Division. It's an interlude albeit, at six minutes, a lengthy one.

Primarily a Phil Cunningham idea, the guitar-propelled "Academic" was "Plastic" without the inspiration, but the chorus was manly and Bernard duets with himself while singing about the sea once more.

The longest track, "Nothing But A Fool" is the most jerry-built. Joy Division-style guitars, drifting verses and a giant, super-tight chorus. The disparate elements blend with surprising sure-footedness, Dawn Zee and Denise Johnson are superlative and Joe Duddell's finest moment – the lengthy instrumental coda – is truly life-affirming.

"Unlearn This Hatred" was originally submitted by Bernard in raw demo form to a German band he refuses to name. It was probably Kraftwerk. They rejected it and it became Tom Rowlands' second co-write and co-production. It's an awkward affair, which falls between the stools of being an all-action Balearic bouncer, a slab of retro electro and a haunting advice song. For once, they failed to

Elly "La Roux" Jackson with New Order, Bill Graham Civic Auditorium, San Francisco, 11 July, 2014.

sew their influences together. Unusually for New Order, the vocal was recorded first and the music was then built around it.

Stephen and Gillian saw their baby, "The Game", as almost folky. It begins woozily and slips into New Order by numbers. It was as if everyone had run out of songs and ideas. Bernard's guitar solo at the end almost blows some life into it, but it's too little too late.

Brandon Flowers had always adored Joy Division and New Order. He even named his band The Killers after the fictitious act in the "Crystal" video. After meeting Bernard in the urinal at the *NME* Awards ("He started singing 'Somebody Told Me' in my ear; it was surreal"), he'd been a very occasional guest at New Order shows and Bernard had sung "Bizarre Love Triangle" with The Killers. So when Bernard and Stuart Price had a song they couldn't quite finish called "Superheated", Bernard invited Flowers to write the chorus and do most of the singing for the last track on the album and the last track to be recorded.

The song itself sounded like what it was, part New Order, part The Killers and it brought out the best in both parties. Flowers mostly recorded his vocals in his Manchester Arena dressing room after a show during which Bernard had guested on their version of "Crystal". He and Bernard sang like lovers, while the backing keyboards and the Manchester Camerata jostled for position in a most seductive manner. Again, New Order were pushing boundaries.

Music Complete wasn't an unmitigated success, but it would make number two in the UK and thirty-four in the US. To the usually restrained *Allmusic*, it was a "watered-down and uninspired album by a band that lost the plot long ago and now only capture an occasional glimmer of what made it so great in the first place," which seemed a little on the strong side. Bernard was naturally more effusive: "It's very unusual for bands to stay successful and make an album that doesn't sound tired this deep in your career." *The New Yorker* understood, albeit expressing it clunkily: "It contains a handful of songs to add to other treasures in the band's catalog, along with many that are forgettable by the group's own standards."

Just as the guitar albums had been, *Music Complete* was made to be played live. New Order were soon out there, playing most of the

Setlist, plectrums, notebook and pencil, Sydney Opera House, 2 June, 2016.

"IT'S VERY UNUSUAL FOR BANDS TO STAY SUCCESSFUL AND MAKE AN ALBUM THAT DOESN'T SOUND TIRED THIS DEEP IN YOUR CAREER."

BERNARD

Right: *Moby and Hooky at Book Soup & Spaceland Present An Evening Of Conversation With Co-founder Of Joy Division & New Order, Peter Hook, Regent Theatre, Los Angeles, 3 February, 2017.*

Below: *Barney, Radio City Music Hall, New York, 10 March, 2016.*

tracks and, startlingly, "Lonesome Tonight". Joy Division material was mostly relegated to "Atmosphere" and "Love Will Tear Us Apart" in knockabout encores, although they did use projections of Ian as a backdrop. Elly Jackson joined them at two Brixton nights where Bernard dedicated "Love Will Tear Us Apart" to victims of the recent terrorist attack at the Bataclan, the Paris venue they knew well. Half-French Tom Chapman wore a France football shirt.

Getting more game by the month, they even briefly appeared at Brian & Robin's Christmas Compendium Of Reason, a fun night at the Eventim Apollo (the venue formerly known as Hammersmith Odeon) hosted by comedian Robin Ince and popular scientist Professor Brian Cox, once a member of "Things Can Only Get Better" hitmakers D:Ream. The professor played keyboards on "Your Silent Face" and "Temptation".

The official line was that the days of tour excess were over. "The most I get up to on tour is too many glasses of wine," suggested Bernard. "You've only got your capacity to be off your head so many times and I've used up my allocation," admitted Stephen.

Meanwhile, Hooky decided to sue New Order for unpaid royalties, merchandising and performance fees worth circa $3.5 million. He also wanted to formalise future income.

New Order released a statement. "Peter still receives his full share of all back catalogue royalties. This dispute relates only to the share of income he takes from our work without him since 2011."

Bernard was more forthcoming in a *Salon* interview. "We pay Peter Hook a license fee for all our activities. We pay him a percentage of everything we do. It's just not enough for him. He wants more money. But he doesn't pay us anything when he tours the albums. He thinks that's OK, but we should pay a lot more than what we pay him. Let's be kind and say it's a bit unfair."

The case would rumble on for two years. Before a Light show in Porto Antico, Genoa, in December 12 which ended in a friendly stage invasion, Hooky visited the *Closer* tombs for the first time. "I'm feeling very honoured to be here

Left: *Barney, Radio City Music Hall, New York, 10 March, 2016.*

Right: *Hooky's Joy Division Orchestrated, Royal Albert Hall, London, 5 July, 2019.*

and also very humbled, Ian would have loved to see this," he sighed.

Mute were delighted by *Music Complete*'s success. But they wanted more bang for their buck. With remixes of all the flop singles already abounding, they decided to go the whole hog and chance their arm on a remix album, with the band's full input.

And so, *Complete Music* was first issued as a vinyl box set. On disc it initially came with a copy of *Music Complete*. Properly released in May 2016, with the Peter Saville artwork a minor variation on his *Music Complete* cover, it was a remodelling of all eleven tracks. "I almost prefer it to the original," smiled Bernard.

The albums belong together, inevitably much more than the *Sirens* albums. For all that it might have been better remaining as a free coda to *Music Complete*, there is plenty to savour on *Complete Music*, mostly the time and space the new versions bring. "Plastic" spends two teasing minutes threatening to break into "I Feel Love" before retreating; "Superheated" almost morphs into "Your Silent Face" and the chorus of "Academic" finds added oomph from nowhere. As ever with these projects, not everything

blossomed. "People On The High Line" is shorn of its joie de vivre; the backing vocals on "Nothing But A Fool" are too timid and "Stray Dog" deploys Iggy Pop much too soon and then has nowhere to go.

Its rather confused release meant it didn't chart properly, unless number thirty-five in the US Independent Chart counts.

A slightly revamped version of the *Singles* compilation appeared in September, but in October 2016, Hooky's sledgehammer second memoir *Substance: Inside New Order*, spared nobody, least of all himself. The claims that Caroline Aherne had physically abused him during their marriage were all the more poignant since she had died of cancer in July.

In May 2017, the live album *NOMC15* featured the Brixton show of 2015, but in September the court case with Hooky ended with a "full and final" settlement. The details were legally confidential, but resolution meant that the case wouldn't go to court and nobody would go bankrupt.

The year also saw *New Order Presents Be Music*, a beguiling three CD compilation of productions from the band from 1982–85 (and

226 Decades: Joy Division + New Order

Everybody's Happy Nowadays 227

228 Decades: Joy Division + New Order

some of New Order's "Video 586"). Taking in everything from Marcel King to Thick Pigeon, it was a treasure trove of innovation and wonder.

In May 2019, Stephen's first memoir, *Record, Play Pause: Confessions Of A Post-Punk Percussionist Volume 1* filled in some of the gaps in the very early years. He too had taken to DJing.

The Light was still shining and gigging with manic intensity across the globe, but Monaco returned with the anthemic single "Higher, Higher, Higher Love", which Hooky debuted at an orchestrated (by the Manchester Camerata no less) show at the Royal Albert Hall in July.

A fortieth anniversary version of *Unknown Pleasures* reached number five in the British charts and an extravagant *Movement* box set tidied up that era. There was even a New Order album of sorts: $\Sigma(No,12k,Lg,17Mif)$, which stood for "New Order, 12 Keyboards, Liam Gillick, 2017 Manchester International Festival".

It was recorded during their five-night residence on the site of the old Granada Studios where Joy Division had made their television debut. The set was a connoisseurs' selection, chosen after three days spent re-evaluating the entire catalogue. "I don't think Bernard had listened to *Movement* since it had been recorded," chuckled Phil Cunningham. "He looked physically uncomfortable listening to it again." "Ultraviolence" was played for the first time in years, as was "Decades", while "Times Change" was now an instrumental sans Bernard's rap. The beautifully staged set was a collaboration with conceptual visual artist Liam Gillick, while Joe Duddell arranged both the strings and the orchestra of student synthesiser players who performed in individual small cells with venetian blinds at the back of the stage. "We've pulled the molecular structure of those songs apart," said Bernard. It was even a mini hit, reaching thirty-five in the UK, but it couldn't quite escape the notion that New Order were old dogs seeking new tricks.

"Everyone in the band gets on now," claimed Bernard. "We tour in a measured way. We don't do too many gigs, but we do really cool ones. It

Phil Cunningham and Barney, Victorious Festival, Southsea Common, Portsmouth, 25 August, 2019.

Everybody's Happy Nowadays 229

works now, it didn't work before. These last few years have been fantastic. Please let nothing else go wrong, please. We can enjoy it now. Let it be. We've had enough shit."

2020 promised to be a better year. Hooky began it by co-writing and playing a signature bassline on "Aries", alongside Georgia, daughter of Leftfield's Neil Barnes. It was a track by Gorillaz, Damon Albarn of Blur's phenomenally successful spin-off group. Hooky had guested with Albarn's Africa Express collaboration live in 2012.

The fires of antagonism with his old group still burned beneath the platitudes. "Damon got in touch to say he'd like to do something. I was absolutely terrified," Hooky recalls. "I'm not very good on occasions like that. He's a fan of bass playing and I'm not the greatest at recognising or appreciating people. When they heard 'Aries', everybody phoned and said, 'Bloody hell, that's what New Order should sound like'. Them deciding to come back without telling me seemed very, very underhand. I've always been a boxer on the ropes: occasionally you land a good punch. 'Aries,' thanks to Damon, was one of those. I was touched that Gorillaz fans started a petition to make me a full member. It was a wonderful compliment. You never know... New

Barney and Stephen, The Fillmore Miami Beach, Jackie Gleason Theater, 15 January, 2020.

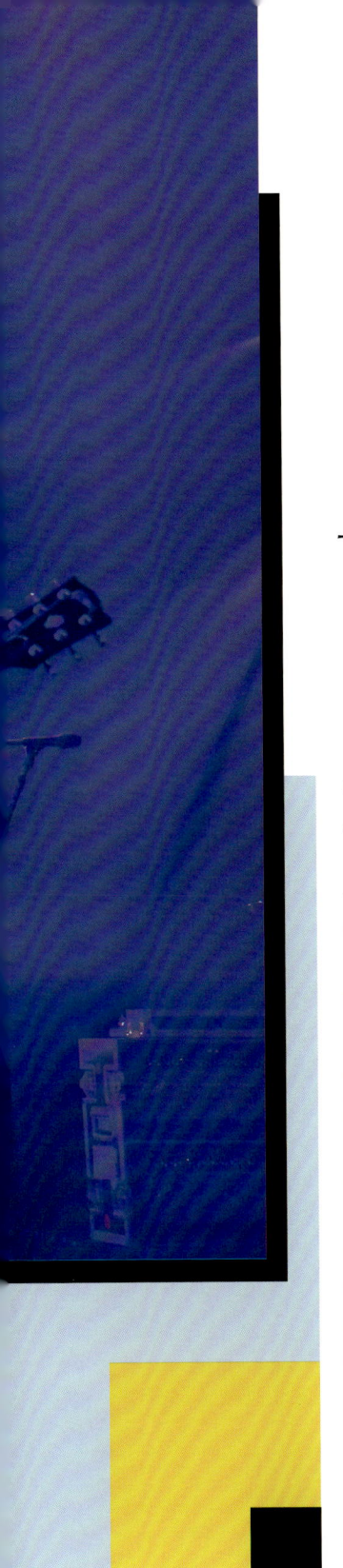

> "THE DAYS OF *POWER, CORRUPTION & LIES* WERE REALLY HEADY. YOU FELT LIKE YOU WERE CHANGING THE WORLD AND JOY DIVISION AND NEW ORDER DID THAT CULTURALLY AND MUSICALLY."
>
> **HOOKY**

Order after me sounded like Bad Lieutenant crossed with Electronic. But life goes on."

By March, New Order were in Australia – they played "Disorder" in Sydney, where Bernard sang a "Krafty" verse in Japanese – and a co-headlining US tour with Pet Shop Boys loomed. The Light were celebrating their tenth anniversary and *Closer*'s fortieth with gigs comprising a New Order opening set and both Joy Division albums in full. Then Covid-19 struck, much to Bernard's dismay, not least when he was prevented from visiting his boat, moored in Wales, where pandemic regulations were stricter than in England. "I've got a brand new boat waiting for me in Wales. I can't go to it because the fucking Welsh won't let me. It's doing my fucking nut in."

Dates were rescheduled, but Peter Hook & The Light ended up playing the tenth Salford Music Festival virtually, in split screen form, from their individual homes. A shorts-wearing Hooky emerged from a portaloo to play four Joy Division songs (just the piano and bass on "Love Will Tear Us Apart") and three from New Order. It was a triumph. His lockdown was seemingly less stressful than Bernard's.

"I've been sitting in the garden, playing with the dogs. Not very fruitfully, but I've enjoyed it. I suppose the weird thing about being an old man is that we return to a solitary existence. It actually fulfils me in that respect."

Meanwhile, shortly before Stephen's second memoir, *Fast Forward*, was published, *Closer* was given a fortieth anniversary reissue, Bernard co-designed a clothing range with Adidas, and New Order had been busy too. October would see *Power, Corruption & Lies* reissued with a disc of rarities and two live DVDs, plus, separately, its concomitant singles. The reissue gave Hooky much to mull. "The days of *Power, Corruption & Lies* were really heady. You felt like you were changing the world and Joy Division and New Order did that culturally and musically. It's heart-warming to realise what you've achieved together. Maybe someone should sit us all down in a room, play this album and go, 'Why the fuck are you arguing like this when you did this?' It was a wonderful achievement and it makes me feel immensely proud. I always wonder what the third Joy Division album would have been like."

The foursome were reunited, in a sense, on *Transmissions: The Definitive Story* which told the whole saga in podcast form. Even Bernard had long-acknowledged that looking back was as important as looking forwards and when Gillian declared "We did everything how we wanted it to sound," she encapsulated the mood in the

Everybody's Happy Nowadays 231

> "EVERYONE IN THE BAND GETS ON NOW. IT WORKS NOW, IT DIDN'T WORK BEFORE."
>
> BERNARD

camp as they lolloped towards their half-century.

After the United Kingdom locked down, on March 23, the band met just once in 2020. "We had to down tools," explained Bernard, who worked from home, producing and engineering a new track. "I emailed the others to ask what they thought; they didn't say anything."

On September 8, that new track, "Be A Rebel" appeared. Upbeat and optimistic, it was a message of encouragement to his youngest son Finley. "Being so positive is unusual for me, a fluke," he told Minnesota radio station, The Current. "It says be an individual, try something different from everyone else."

Two months later, Bernard himself was struck down with two bouts of Covid-19. He lost his sense of smell and weeks later, his voice remained as grizzled as Leonard Cohen's, but, as he noted "I'm one of the lucky ones".

"Be A Rebel" had been planned to herald the re-scheduled tour with the Pet Shop Boys, which would be postponed again, until 2021. As Bernard noted in a message to the fanbase, "In tough times we wanted to reach out with a new song. We can't play live for a while, but music is still something we can share. We hope you enjoy it… until we meet again." It began with a harpsichord and moved into sublime, dreamy territory, like a more up-tempo "Thieves Like Us". It was, after all these years, classic New Order.

Barney and backdrop, Tempodrom, Berlin, 7 October, 2019.

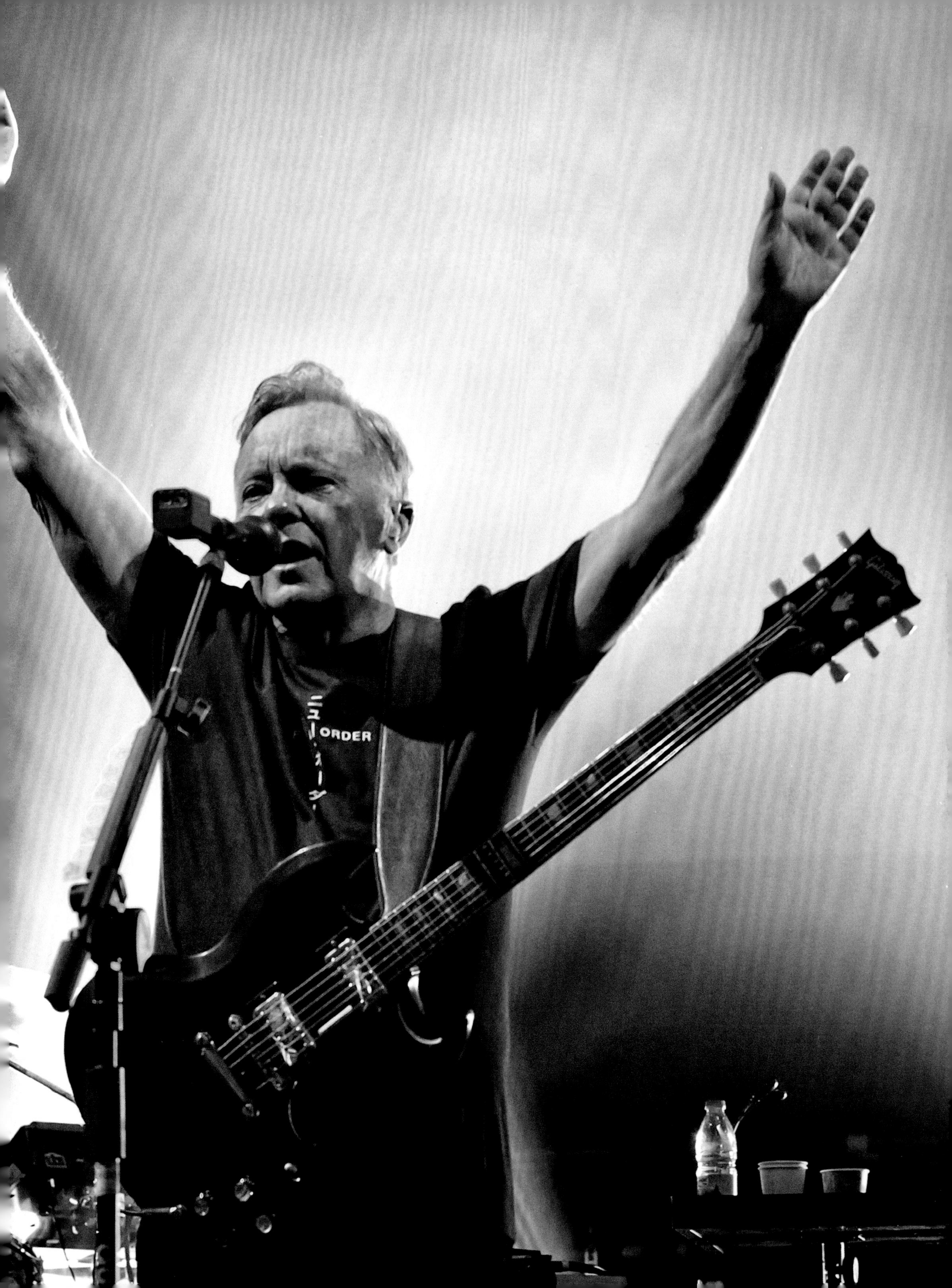
ORDER

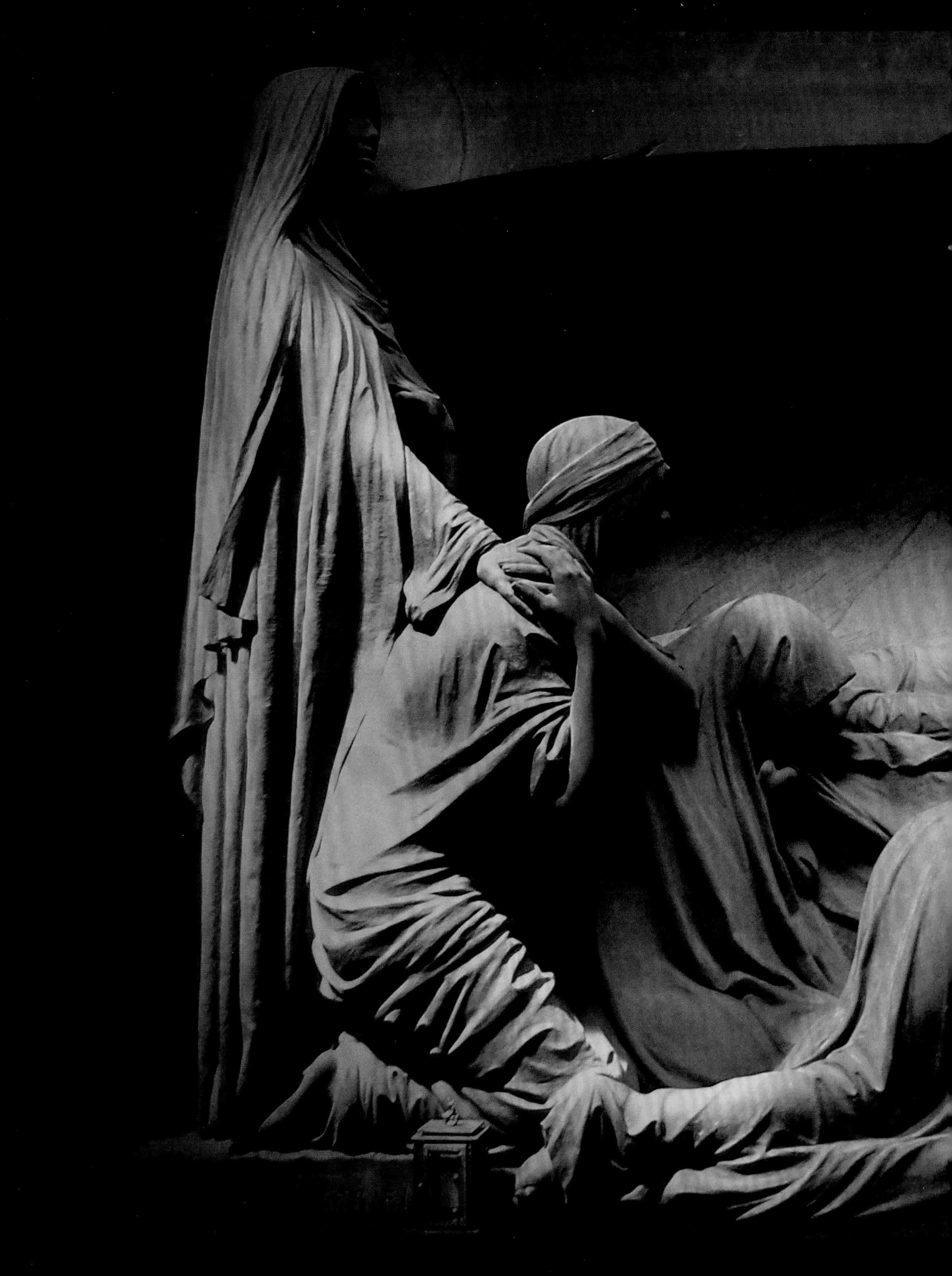

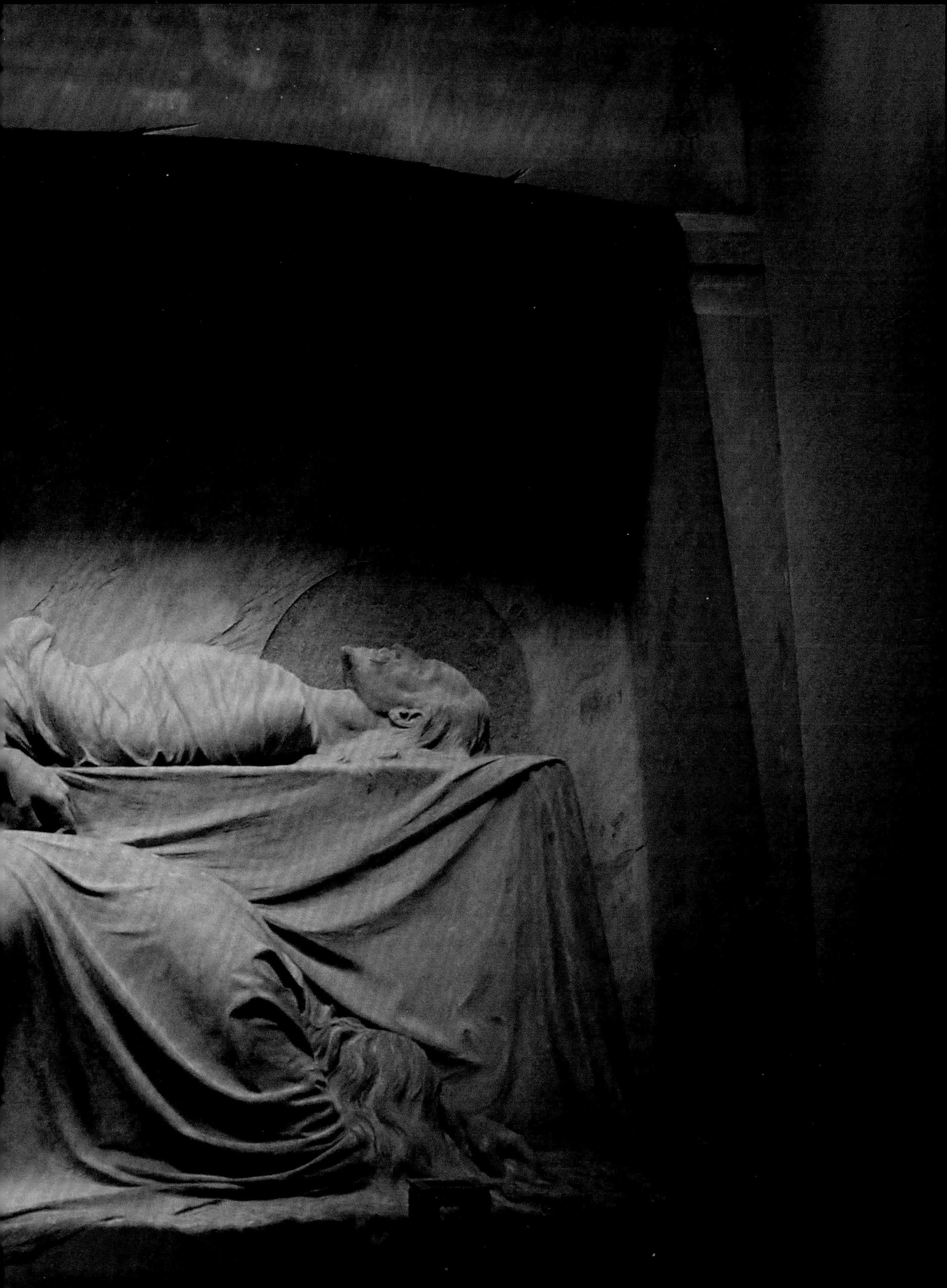

AN AFTERWORD

In a sense, this has been less the story of two bands, more a tale of two men: Bernard Sumner and Peter Hook. Almost everything Joy Division and New Order achieved stemmed from their complicated relationship – Cain and Abel without a father figure. They recruited Ian Curtis and Stephen Morris. They agreed Rob Gretton was the right manager and they sanctioned signing to Factory. Martin Hannett wasn't their idea, but their initial roles as passive actors allowed him to weave the spell that would cast Joy Division into immortality. Later, they would accept Gillian Gilbert; they would sign up for the Haçienda farrago and they would oversee the change from being Joy Division copyists swathed in gloom to 24 Hour Party People. They would let the sun in, both metaphorically and, when they embarked on their Ibiza jolly, literally. And, lest we forget, while hindsight has apportioned the blame for that Ibiza sojourn to Hooky, none embraced the madness with more gusto than Bernard.

Now they're squabbling like betrayed lovers, and it's hard not to see the way in which each of them flies the Joy Division/New Order flags as semaphoring the other. Whether it's Hooky doing what Bernard would never do and maintaining Joy Division and New Order's past in a live setting or Bernard seeking new ways to both maintain the brand and push forwards – they're both doing the right thing of course.

One thing they do agree upon is that their relationship was never simple. Together, they

236 Decades: Joy Division + New Order

This is who they were. Joy Division at Bowdon Vale Youth Club, 14 March, 1979.

were the annoying lads at the back of the class and they socialised outside of school. They discovered music together – surely nothing other than love for Hooky would have induced Bernard to see Deep Purple.

Having discovered music, they made it together. They started a band and they gave Ian licence to fly. When Ian died, each could have stepped away from the other. They both chose not to without a second thought.

In New Order, Bernard and Hooky agreed to bury Joy Division. They brought New Order to global popularity together. And yes, while the battle for musical supremacy would lead to the death of New Order's first incarnation, and that divorce was bitter, when Hooky emerged from rehab, with whom did he spend his first sober New Year's Eve DJing alongside? He gravitated back to Bernard.

It can appear as if they were a pair of master planners, architects of their own rise from Salford's back streets to arenas in every continent. As we now know, it wasn't like that at all. Ian was why Joy Division was great. For all the pain it caused and for all the pain Ian was in, his death was, perversely but unquestionably, a blessing for Joy Division's legacy. This most abrupt of full stops left a legacy of just two albums, both as close to perfection as popular music can come, and a handful of extraordinary non-album tracks. The live albums and that misguided false start with RCA needn't trouble us. Instead, let's celebrate the purity of the vision: the absence of remixes (except for Permanent's "Love Will Tear Us Apart"); of so-called re-imaginings and of mysteriously exhumed unfinished tracks. The unbending will of the remaining trio in refusing to carry on as Joy Division created New Order.

But the strangest and the most magical aspect of Joy Division was that Ian worked under the band's own radar. It continues to astonish that three members of a band simply couldn't be bothered to read the fourth member's lyrics – the very words they were playing along to. But it's true and it meant that Ian operated undetected, without input from the others. But their wilful ignorance also meant that, despite Bernard and Ian's late-night walks through graveyards as the awful end loomed, they were genuinely shocked when their comrade took his own life.

Bernard and Hooky didn't even notice how great their band was. Both expressed substantial reservations vis-à-vis the finished versions of *Unknown Pleasures* and *Closer*, albums which they had both played such a major part in creating. They both hated – for almost identical reasons – how Martin Hannett fashioned their songs into something different. For all that, it's trite and wrong to say Joy Division's perfection was *in spite* of two of its members. Joy Division was a succession of accidents entwined with genius.

What would have happened had Ian lived? The prevailing wisdom is that he was too – that word, for the very last time – fragile for rock 'n' roll. Maybe he'd have become a full-time writer or, as Bernard suggested, opened that bookshop in Bournemouth he briefly fantasised about while making *Closer*, possibly alone, possibly with Debbie and Natalie or, slightly more likely, with Annik. But, realistically, Ian was too driven and too eager for mainstream success to be another Nick Drake. Moreover, his problems – his awful illness, his complicated love-life (has there been a less competent adulterer than Ian Curtis?) – were not directly caused by being in Joy Division, even if the rock 'n' roll lifestyle was far from good for him.

Whether he'd have stayed working with Bernard, Hooky and Stephen is more open to question. Certainly, Ian would have pushed Joy Division to create more albums and achieve greater success and international acclaim. "Ceremony" and "In A Lonely Place" were tantalising, brilliant glimpses of the next stage of Joy Division and the development of Ian's writing. He would surely have taken a solo route at some point, perhaps at the moment Bernard became a dance maven, although Ian had been the one to introduce him to Kraftwerk. Surely, too, Ian would have wanted to be part of the orchestrations both Bernard and Hooky have embraced of late.

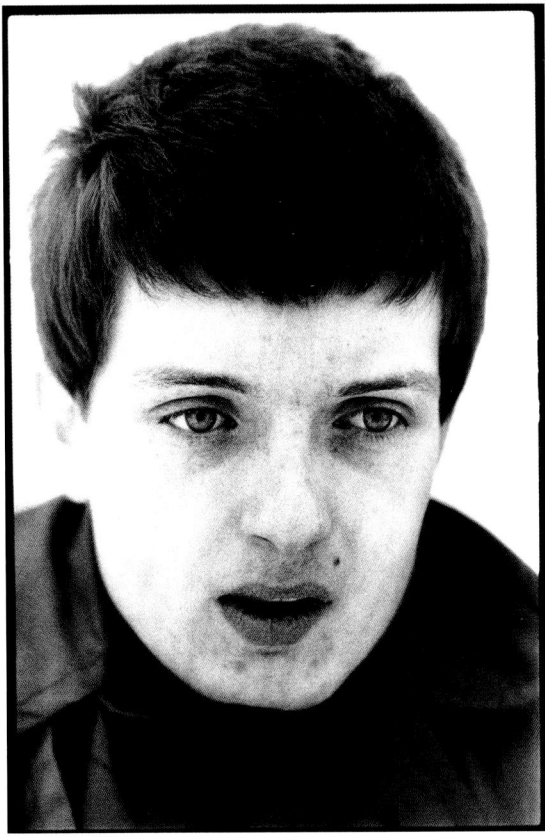

Ian simply could not have continued to write lyrics with the death-wish intensity of *Closer* without slipping into self-parody, but lightening up wouldn't need to mean dumbing down. Music was no longer a pursuit solely for the young when Ian was alive. Since his passing, it's even less so. Leonard Cohen, Roger Waters, Neil Young. Bob Dylan, Nick Cave, Neil Diamond, amongst so many others, have pointed the way to different futures for a man who would now be in his seventh decade. Imagine being able to hear Ian now…

We know where Bernard and Hooky went without him and they can overwhelmingly be proud of themselves. But with Ian alongside them, who knows what they could have achieved?

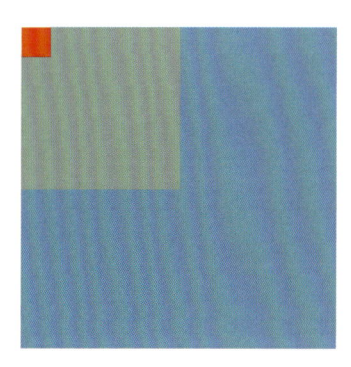

ACKNOWLEDGEMENTS

Thank you to New Order, who were very kind to (and very patient with) a very young writer a very long time ago. Thank you to Jonathan Green and Simon Majumdar for coming to see Joy Division with me on a cold Sunday night. Thank you to the anonymous doorman at Romeo & Juliet's, Sheffield, who let me see New Order when I was closer to primary school age than the legal one for attending nightclubs. Thank you to Rob Nichols for playing a lockdown blinder in the most difficult of times, for deft editing and for even more kindness and patience. This is for Michelle, Jessica and Oscar: everything's for them, really.

SOURCES

Magazines & Newspapers
Barmcake, Billboard, Classic Rock, Due South, Financial Times, GQ, The Guardian, Macclesfield Express, Manchester Evening News, Melody Maker, Mojo, NME, New Yorker, Pitchfork, Q, Record Collector, Record Mirror, Smash Hits, Sound On Sound, Sounds, The Times, Trouser Press, Uncut, Wessex News

TV, Radio & Websites
www.allmusic.con; www.joydivisioncentral.com; www.neworder.com; www.neworderonline.com; www.newordertracks.wordpress; www.pitchfork.com; www.salon.com;
Discovering New Order (3DD Productions); *New Order: Decades* (Sky Arts); *The New Order Story* (ITV) *Transmissions: The Definitive Story Of Joy Division & New Order* (Apple podcasts)

Books
Aizlewood, John, *Playing At Home*, Orion, 1998
Boll, Heinrich, *Group Portrait With Lady*, Penguin, 1988
Curtis, Deborah, *Touching From A Distance: Ian Curtis & Joy Division*, Faber 1995
Hook, Peter, *Unknown Pleasures: Inside Joy Division*, Simon & Schuster, 2012
Hook, Peter, *Substance: Inside New Order*, Simon & Schuster, 2016
Kynaston, David, *Smoke In The Valley: Austerity Britain 1948-51*, Bloomsbury, 2007
Middles, Mick, *Factory: The Story Of the Record Label*, Virgin, 2009/2016
Patterson, Sylvia, *I'm Not With The Band*, Sphere 2016
Ryder, Shaun, *Twisting My Melon: The Autobiography*, Transworld 2011
Sumner, Bernard, *Chapter & Verse (New Order, Joy Division & Me)*, Transworld, 2014

JOY DIVISION + NEW ORDER PICTURE CREDITS

Courtesy of Alamy AF Archive: 191; Andrew Turner: 89, 90; Charlie Raven: 228; David Pearson: 227; Everett Collection, Inc.: 132; Fabrizio Robba: 80; John Woods: 234; M&N: 27; PA Images: 190; Phil Portus: 14; Pictorial Press Ltd: 16, 18t, 100, 105, 196; SJBooks: 25; Steve Speller: 133; TCD/Prod.DB: 202; Trinity Mirror/Mirrorpix: 24, 165; Weinstein Company/Courtesy Everett Collection: 204; WENN Rights Ltd: 207
Courtesy of Avalon Andy Sturmey: 209
Courtesy of BBC BBC Archive: 108
Courtesy of Getty Araya Diaz: 225; Bob Berg: 10, 146, 157; Brian Cooke/Redferns: 103; Brian Rasic: 169, 174, 176, 180; Buda Mendes: 11, 218; Chris Mills/Redferns: 4, 9, 46, 58, 66, 71, 76, 82; David Corio/Michael Ochs Archives: 84, 87; David Corio/Redferns: 48, 96; David Tonge: 172; David Warner Ellis/Redferns: 23; Ebet Roberts: 85, 86, 94, 145; Echoes/Redferns: 102; Fin Costello/Redferns: 22; Frank Hoensch/Redferns: 233; Frazer Harrison: 226; Gems/Redferns: 41; George Pimentel/WireImage: 212; Gie Knaeps: 119, 120, 127, 128; Gijsbert Hanekroot/Redferns: 107; Gus Stewart/Redferns: 31; Howard Barlow/Redferns: 178; Ian Dickson/Redferns: 43; Jan Housewerth/The Boston Globe: 135; Jason Koerner: 230; Jim Dyson: 177, 219; Jo Hale: 201; John Atashian: 156; Kerstin Rodgers/Redferns: 92, 114; Kevin Cummins: 20, 29, 30, 34, 36, 37, 40, 42, 44, 49, 53, 55, 56, 99, 113, 117, 123, 124, 129, 130, 143, 152, 160, 164, 166, 183, 208, 223, 239t; Lex van Rossen/MAI/Redferns: 61; Lisa Haun/Michael Ochs Archives: 110, 238l, 238r, 239b; Martin O'Neill/Redferns: 32, 51, 57, 237; Martyn Goodacre: 158, 161, 163, 184; Matthew Lewis: 206; Michael Ochs Archives: 26; Michael Putland: 118; Mick Hutson/Redferns: 193; Myung J. Chun/Los Angeles Times: 198; Neilson Barnard: 217; Nicky Digital/Corbis: 224; Paul Natkin: 138; Paul Welsh/Redferns: 18b; Peter J Walsh/PYMCA/Avalon/Universal Images Group: 141, 171; Philip Wayne Lock/Fairfax Media: 106; Photoshot: 170; RDImages/Epics: 12; Richard Corkery/NY Daily News Archive: 192; Rob Verhorst/Redferns: 39, 62, 65, 69, 72, 75, 78; Shirlaine Forrest/WireImage: 205; snapshot-photography/ullstein bild: 213; Steve Rapport: 134, 151; Sunday Mirror/Mirrorpix: 7, 15; Suzanne Kreiter/The Boston Globe: 137; Tim Hall/Redferns: 149, 155, 187; Tim Mosenfelder: 188, 222; Tony Woolliscroft/WireImage: 210, 214; Vinnie Zuffante/Michael Ochs Archives: 162; Virginia Turbett/Redferns: 28; WATFORD/Mirrorpix: 17; Wendy Redfern/Redferns: 195